MALIGN MASTERS

GENTILE HEIDEGGER LUKÁCS WITTGENSTEIN

Also by Harry Redner

IN THE BEGINNING WAS THE DEED

THE ENDS OF PHILOSOPHY

THE ENDS OF SCIENCE

A NEW SCIENCE OF REPRESENTATION

ANATOMY OF THE WORLD (*with Jillian Redner*)

AN HERETICAL HEIR OF THE ENLIGHTENMENT (*editor*)

Malign Masters
Gentile Heidegger Lukács Wittgenstein

Philosophy and Politics in the Twentieth Century

Harry Redner

First published in Great Britain 1997 by
MACMILLAN PRESS LTD
Houndmills, Basingstoke, Hampshire RG21 6XS and London
Companies and representatives throughout the world

A catalogue record for this book is available from the British Library.

ISBN 0–333–69192–X

First published in the United States of America 1997 by
ST. MARTIN'S PRESS, INC.,
Scholarly and Reference Division,
175 Fifth Avenue, New York, N.Y. 10010

ISBN 0–312–17324–5

Library of Congress Cataloging-in-Publication Data
Redner, Harry.
Malign masters : Gentile, Heidegger, Lukács, Wittgenstein : philosophy and politics in the twentieth century / Harry Redner.
p. cm.
Includes bibliographical references and index.
ISBN 0–312–17324–5 (cloth)
1. Gentile, Giovanni, 1875–1944. 2. Heidegger, Martin, 1889–1976. 3. Lukács, György, 1885–1971. 4. Wittgenstein, Ludwig, 1889–1951. I. Title.
B3624.G5R43 1997
190'.9'04—dc21 96–37665
CIP

---

10 9 8 7 6 5 4 3 2 1
06 05 04 03 02 01 00 99 98 97

Printed in Great Britain by
The Ipswich Book Company Ltd
Ipswich, Suffolk

To my mother, who survived the worst of totalitarian terror

Contents

After such knowledge, what forgiveness? Think now
History has many cunning passages, contrived corridors
And issues, deceives with whispering ambitions,
Guides us by vanities. Think now . . .

T.S. Eliot

Foreword

'Since brevity is the soul of wit, I will be brief,' promises prolix Polonius. In this book I, too, promise to be brief. But brevity has its drawbacks – the Poloniuses of philosophy will no doubt demand the lengthy expositions and demonstrations of every point that I have deliberately avoided. To them I can only reply, turn to some of my other, much longer works if you want 'more matter with less art'. In particular, I can recommend my recently published *A New Science of Representation*, which establishes the overall background, both philosophical and historical, against which this work must be seen. There they will also find some of the punctilious presentations of arguments that can only be briefly adumbrated here. At the very least, that should convince anyone that I can be as turgid and tedious as the best of them.

If what I have lost through brevity I have gained in wit, then so be it. Anyway, it has not been possible to provide complete accounts of four such copious writers as the malign masters whose extant *Nachlass*, most of it now in print, runs to tens of thousands of pages each. Anyone who believes that this work should be more aptly entitled *Maligned Masters* will easily be able to show that there are all sorts of things in these writings I have missed, that there are hidden virtues in these authors I have overlooked, and that there are many indispensable commentators I have not read. I make no claims to omniscience regarding any of this. I simply stand by the weight of my criticisms. Let those who disagree try to provide the counterweight to balance these.

However, I should warn them in advance of any such attempts that I have not yet finished with this chapter in the history of philosophy. I intend to publish at least one more book, perhaps entitled *Benign Masters*, for I, too, have my list of champions to set against those whom nearly everyone else admires. Anyone too disheartened by the mainly negative proscriptions in this book might take heart from the more positive prescriptions to come in the next.

What I wish to achieve with this 'negative' book is simply to spare others, especially the young, all the painful effort I expended trying to make profound sense of the temptingly fascinating works of the malign masters. I wasted many of what should have been my best years on such futile endeavours. However, if my experience, as condensed in this book, saves some others from embarking on a similar quest, then perhaps my blighted years might not have been so wasted after all. Though I hope this book will be of use, I make no special claims on its behalf, nor do I wish to use it to preach to others. I see myself merely in the role of the boy in Hans Andersen's fairy tale who exclaimed that the emperor has no clothes. Those who are in the emperor's entourage – the prudent Poloniuses of philosophy, for whom a cloud can look as much like a weasel as a whale – will no doubt continue to see him resplendently attired. I can only reiterate that there is more in heaven and earth than is dreamt of in their philosophies.

Introduction

'A modern philosopher who has never experienced the feeling of being a charlatan is such a shallow mind that his work is probably not worth reading.'[1] So states Leszek Kolakowski at the very start of a work on modern philosophy. His acerbic comment is no doubt true, but it somewhat misses the real point, for it implies what can no longer be taken for granted: that there still is a clear differentiation to be drawn between those philosophers who are worth reading, the geniuses presumably, and those who are mere charlatans. In effect, he maintains that any modern philosopher who has never doubted himself sufficiently to entertain the possibility of being a charlatan is most probably in fact a charlatan. But most of the widely read and acclaimed modern philosophers were not given to such self-doubts. Despite this, one cannot castigate them as simply charlatans either.

Genius or charlatan – the two opposed extremes of romantic valuation, deriving from the aesthetic sphere and most frequently applied to artists – do not fit well those unusual thinkers who are the most famous twentieth-century philosophers. Other more precise terms are required to register their undoubted achievements and failings. I have coined the expression 'malign masters' for this purpose, for that registers both that these philosophers are indeed masters, but also that they themselves and their influence are malign and even at times malignant. This avoids the exclusive alternatives of genius or charlatan or the resort to such clichés as 'evil genius'.

In this work I focus on just four such malign masters. Though these are not the only ones who can be discussed in these terms, there are other candidates as well, as we shall see, they are the four most representative of twentieth-century philosophy since the First World War and so, arguably, the four most important ones. Gentile, Lukács, Heidegger and Wittgenstein: I have listed them in an approximate order of temporal precedent, with Gentile the oldest and the one already established even before the war first; Lukács second, with his early publications appearing just before the war; Heidegger third, with only one minor publication during the war; and Wittgenstein last, with his first work appearing after the end of the war. As I shall show presently, all of them are thinkers whose work was strongly influenced by the war and the revolutionary upheavals that followed it. Each of them was himself a philosophical revolutionary who broke away from the prior, more rational, forms of thought on which he was raised and inaugurated a new oppositional departure that has become by now a vast movement, one which is much more than a mere school of philosophy. Hence, they are masters of contemporary thought in every sense of the word: they wrote masterworks, they exercised undisputed mastery over many disciples and even more numerous followers, and their texts are still read *ex cathedra* as magisterial writ from nearly all the Chairs of Philosophy.

Lest it appear otherwise, I wish to stress right from the outset of this critical endeavour that it is not my intention to belittle or malign the mastery of these masters. They are undeniably masters; but, as I shall try to show, masters of a very peculiar kind, hardly at all commensurate with the great thinkers who preceded them, or even their own teachers. And just as the great dictators of their time, whom they followed, cannot be compared to the great statesmen of the past – for their achievements and failures, though far more momentous, were of a completely different order – so, too, the works of the malign masters cannot be placed besides those of the great philosophers. In speaking of Mahler, Wittgenstein said that 'it took a set of very rare talents to produce this bad music.'[2] One might, with considerably more justice, turn the remark back on him and say that it also took a very rare set of talents to produce his kind of 'bad philosophy'. One might with equal justice address his remark to all the malign masters, except that their philosophies cannot be called 'bad' in any ordinary sense. Certainly there are many ways in which they can be considered inferior in comparison to the great philosophers of the past, but that does not make their philosophies akin to the bad philosophies of the past. One needs a new concept of 'badness' to describe their work, for ordinary bad philosophy could not possibly have had the extraordinary impact that their philosophies had in the twentieth century. I have resorted to the term 'malign' to express something of this paradox.

The fact that they were malign becomes evident when it is recalled how all of them related closely to the totalitarian movements of their time and place, and in most cases also to the totalitarian leaders, the great dictators themselves. Thus Gentile, the earliest of the malign masters to come to prominence, proclaimed himself the 'philosopher of Fascism', whose political theory he expressed with his own neologism 'totalitarian'. He was personally close to Mussolini, whom he hyperbolically personified as *l'Uomo*, the Man, and considered the chosen agent of Providence to lead the Italian nation. He remained devoted to him right down to his untimely end.

Heidegger was no less devoted to Hitler, whose moustache he aped, at least until the end of the war. What he thought of Hitler after the war is not known. But since before the war he had held Hitler to be the incarnation of Destiny sent to save Germany and the West from the clutches of nihilism, and since after the war he still continued to believe in the 'inner truth and greatness of National Socialism',[3] the movement Hitler had founded, it is doubtful whether he ever turned his back on him. In 1943, just after the battle of Stalingrad, he declared in a lecture on Heraklitus, 'the Germans and they alone can save the West'.[4] John van Buren, who quotes this, goes on to state that 'he maintained some version of this view right up until his 1966 interview in *Der Spiegel*.[5] Thus, despite his carefully staged pretence at rehabilitation, Heidegger never admitted that he had been mistaken in supporting Hitler. He continued to believe that in defeating Hitler and his Germany, the West had lost its last chance of redemption and had fallen irremediably into the dark night of nihilism from which 'only a god could save it'.[6]

Lukács also always believed in his chosen leader, Stalin, right from the start of the murderous battle for succession after Lenin's death till after Stalin's own demise. When the Party itself reversed its line on Stalin with Krushchev's revelations at the Twentieth Party Congress, Lukács went along, but he did not altogether give up his belief in Stalin. Since he continued to hold that even the worst of socialism was better than the best of capitalism, it is unlikely that he would ever have abandoned his faith in what Stalin had achieved. Throughout Stalin's own time he served ably as an official apologist of his regime; perhaps the one most respected internationally, and so given the most credence when he spoke freely the required lies on its behalf. For though it cannot be held against him that he made the right verbal obeisances, yet it cannot be pretended that he was compelled to utter all the things he said. There is now considerable evidence that he actually came to believe his own lies in an intricate act of double-think of which he was one of the earliest exponents.

Wittgenstein seems clearly the odd man out in this line-up of totalitarian stalwarts, for his seems by comparison a mere flirtation with totalitarianism rather than the full engagement and consummated marriage of the others. Yet there was considerable infatuation there with both extremes of the political polarity. His background predisposed him to the conservative and even reactionary causes of old Vienna, so much so that a communist friend in Cambridge, Fania Pascal, saw him as an 'old time conservative of the late Austro-Hungarian empire'.[7] But actually his cultural views were more revolutionary conservative: he espoused the cultural pessimism of Spengler; he tended to an anti-intellectual authoritarianism in religion and politics; and he was anti-Semitic, if not quite with the virulence of the Nazis, yet far more so than his mentor in these matters, the self-hating Jew, Otto Weininger.

But at the very time when Fania Pascal made this assessment of him, she was teaching him Russian so that he and his friend might emigrate to the Soviet Union to which he was sympathetically drawn for all the right fellow-travelling reasons. He declared numerous times in the 1930s to disciples and friends in private, 'I am a communist at heart'; he always evinced considerable understanding for what Stalin 'had to do' even after his visit to Russia in 1935 at the height of the purges; and he continued to entertain plans to settle there at least until the *Anschluss* in 1938. Keynes, in his letter of recommendation of 1935 to the Soviet ambassador Maisky, puts it mildly when he states, 'he is not a member of the Communist Party, but has strong sympathies with the way of life which he believes the new regime in Russia stands for.'[8] His communist friends of 'Red Cambridge', with whom he extensively associated, considered him a strong supporter if not an outright Stalinist.

It seems, therefore, that Wittgenstein was somewhat divided in his political loyalties, following, as it were, a Rightist line in his native Vienna and the opposite Leftist one in Cambridge – a queer tale of two cities. It is unclear whether this was because of sheer political ineptitude and naiveté or some paranoid policy of double-think. His one-time student, Findlay, maintains that his difficult personality 'is technically describable as "schizoid": there was something queer, detached, surreal, incompletely human about it.'[9] On the other hand, it is possible that he was much more consistent about it and subscribed to that paradoxical politics of extreme Right and Left known in the 1920s as National Bolshevism, such as then espoused by the proto-Nazis Niekisch and Jünger. Or, as seems most likely, he arrived at some peculiar variant of his own combining all of these factors. His highly secretive personality makes it difficult now to elicit what was going on in his mind about all this.

Unlike the other malign masters, Wittgenstein was a recluse, who did not seek to establish direct contact with any of the great dictators or to play any significant political part. The others did so, for in their heart of hearts they did not consider themselves as mere followers of their chosen leaders, they saw themselves as their rivals as well, vying with them for the intellectual expression of the historic meaning of their common totalitarian causes. This is well stated by Lucien Goldmann, a follower of Lukács, in the course of an extended comparison between him and his main philosophical-political rival, Heidegger: 'in a historical perspective, Heidegger situates himself at the same level as Hitler, Lukács at the same level as Stalin and, since they expressed the same totality on the level of consciousness, it goes without saying that they understood the nature of the political fact better than the political leaders themselves.'[10] As I shall show later, it was this expression of totality in their philosophy that led them almost inexorably to an expression of totalitarianism in their politics.

But the step from totality to totalitarianism is by no means simple or obvious, and, *a fortiori* logically considered, not necessarily inevitable even though all of the malign masters did in fact pass through that sequence.

Gentile was the first to do so, for he thought he understood Fascism better than Mussolini since he was able to ground it in his philosophy of totality. At one point he even 'ghosted' Mussolini's article giving the official definition of Fascism for the *Enciclopedia Italiana*, which he edited. He was irked that in the world of practical politics he counted for so little. All the more so as he did not consider his Actual Idealism as merely one philosophy among others, albeit the true and correct one, but as more than just a philosophy, as the ultimate expression of the religious spirit of mankind. It was beyond argument or debate because it had history on its side:

> With the advent of Idealism, philosophy left the classroom and the library, just as it had done during the glorious period of the Risorgimento, and entered the universal movement of the Spirit on the magisterial road of History. And it really proceeds on this way with a force that no polemic can stop.[11]

What remains unstated, but is necessarily implied, is that the purveyor of this irresistible intellectual force is none other than Gentile himself.

There is more than a touch of a similar religious megalomania in the ambitions of the other malign masters as well. According to one of his close disciples, Ferenc Feher, Lukács 'had the intellectual ambition to become the new Augustine of an *ecclesia universalis et militans*'.[12] Heidegger, too, had analogous spiritual aspirations in relation to Nazism, which he saw as the only movement capable of saving the world from the deadly fate of nihilistic technology. He saw himself as leading this movement towards what his disciple Hans-Georg Gadamer describes as 'the great renewal from the spiritual and moral strength of the people that he dreamed of and that he longed for as the preparation for a new religion of human kind'.[13] Not unexpectedly, 'later, when he continued to dream his dream of a "national religion" despite all realities, he was naturally very disappointed in the course of events.'[14] Above all, presumably, because Hitler lost the war. By contrast with the others, Wittgenstein did not have such immediate political and religious ambitions for his work in his own time and place, but he did have apocalyptic hopes for it in the future. According to his official biographer, Brian McGuiness, he believed that he was 'writing for a future race, for a people who would think in a totally different way, here his kinship to Nietzsche is very evident.'[15] Not only is there a kinship to Nietzsche evident in this respect, but even more so to the other malign masters who were his contemporaries and who had similar hopes for the future.

Such ambitions were not altogether vainglorious dreams in the political and cultural turmoil of Europe after the First World War, the period during which the malign masters came to maturity. In fact, three of them briefly attained extraordinary worldly power, which made it seem as if philosophers could be kings at least for a day. Lukács became a Commissar of Culture in Bela Kun's dictatorship and so controlled Hungary's whole artistic and academic establishment for a few score of days in 1919. A few years later Gentile became Minister of Education in Italy for somewhat longer and carried out 'the most fascist of all the reforms', according to Mussolini himself. Heidegger did not attain any such high position in Hitler's regime, but perhaps inspired by Gentile, as Croce seems to suggest, he strove for an even more exalted role.[16] He threw himself with great ardour into the academic and political machinations that followed the Nazi attainment of power and the institutionalization of the anti-liberal and anti-Semitic policy of *Gleichschaltung*, which Heidegger celebrated and faithfully carried out as Rektor of Freiburg.

Despite their great abilities and devotion to their cause, invariably the moment of power and glory for each of the malign masters was fitful and brief. They very quickly outlived their usefulness to their masters and political superiors in their respective parties. In exile, after the failure of the revolution in Hungary, Lukács soon came to policy blows with Kun, the party leader favoured by Stalin. Stalin looked on Lukács as no more than a minor, serviceable, intellectual underling. Gentile was thought of much better by Mussolini, but nevertheless he was soon kicked upstairs to an honorific, but powerless, post as a Fascist senior dignitary. Heidegger withdrew into his academic retreat of his own volition for complex reasons which are still not altogether clear, but might, as Farias suggests, have something to do with Röhm's assassination and its consequences. Wittgenstein never emerged from his semi-monastic isolation in academia, for he was the only one without clear political ambitions.

All this, as I shall show, had a great influence not only on the careers of the malign masters, but also on their works as well, for these, too, are to a considerable degree a function of their time. The malign masters were of the same post-1914 generation as the great dictators, men who emerged out of the trenches of war and of the subsequent demonstrations and marches of revolution and entered the totalitarian movements that mobilized for total war. The character of their works reflects this extreme experience of their generation. Karl Löwith was perhaps the first to show how the very terms of Heidegger's early philosophy 'reflect the disastrous intellectual mind-set of the German generation following World War I': 'at the base, all these terms and concepts are expressions of the bitter and hard Resolve that affirms itself in the face of nothingness, proud of its contempt of happiness, reason and compassion.'[17] Something similar holds for the early works of the other malign masters, as I shall go on to show.

Like the great dictators, who founded their causes and found themselves during the course of war and revolution, the malign masters also experienced their 'baptism of fire'. Directly or indirectly they were subject to the violence of the time. Wittgenstein served on the front with great bravery; Heidegger tried to make out that he did so as well, but his was the postal service behind the lines; Lukács also avoided the fighting in the post office, but he tried to make up for it during the subsequent revolution; Gentile was too old for combat, yet excelled himself as a war propagandist. As a result of these experiences, all of them underwent, more or less simultaneously, a process of quasi-religious conversion. Wittgenstein was the first to 'convert' in 1916 when he discovered primitive Christianity through the writings of Tolstoy and turned to a form of doctrineless ineffable mysticism. Gentile 'converted' to the religion of the Nation under the impact of the defeat at Caporetto in October 1917, which he said made Italians aware for the first time of the ethical and religious character of the state. This was the prelude of his later adhesion to Fascism of which he also spoke in religious terms, insisting that 'like every faith, Fascism, too, has a religious character'.[18]

A recent biographer of the young Heidegger, John van Buren, notes that 'the details of Heidegger's theological and philosophical *conversion* in the wartime years of 1917–18 are becoming more known to us today, but they are to a great extent still shrouded in darkness.'[19] What is clear is that Heidegger had undergone a crisis of faith which made him abandon his native Catholicism and convert to a species of private Protestantism. Thomas Sheehan states that 'in a letter to Professor Rudolf Otto . . . Husserl would recall – as if describing the conversion of a modern St. Augustine – the hard times Heidegger had gone through and the "difficult inner struggles" that had led him to "radical changes in [his] basic religious convictions". But the outcome, Husserl wrote, had been happy: Heidegger had "migrated over to the ground of Protestantism".'[20] Later, in 1931, Husserl became less sanguine about this 'happy' outcome and said that 'the war and the ensuing difficulties drive men into mysticism'.[21] The war had a similar effect on Lukács, who converted to Bolshevism, a creed he had thus far rejected, apparently in the course of a single week; as Anna Lesznai, one of his close friends saw it, 'between one Sunday and the next . . .

Saul had become Paul.'[22] This illumination on the road to Moscow gave him relief from his unhappy previous years of unsatisfied yearning and an aim and goal for his pent-up, but as yet indeterminate, eschatological despairs and hopes.

The religious beliefs that each of the malign masters cultivated might be called a private theology, one which more or less approximates to a past Christian heresy. As Hans Jonas and Karl Löwith have noted, Heidegger's philosophical theology is a modern, secularized version of ancient Gnosticism, and Jaspers wrote in the same vein of 'die Verwandlung von Existenz philosophie in Ontologie und Gnosis'.[23] Lukács' 'heresy' is a politicized version of chiliastic Messianism in the guise of Marxism, itself an apocalyptic creed of secularized theology. His close friend Ernst Bloch was well aware of the religious provenance of their common politics and tried in his book of 1921, *Thomas Münzer: Theologian of Revolution*, to outline the heretical precedents of their revolutionary chiliastic thought:

> The Brothers of the Valley, the Cathari, the Waldensians, the Albigensians, Joachim of Floris, Francis and his disciples, the Brothers of Good Will, of Communal Life, of the Free Spirit, Meister Eckhart, the Hussites, Müntzer and the Baptists, Sebastian Franck, the Englightenment philosophers, Rousseau's and Kant's humanist mysticism, Weitling, Baader, Tolstoy . . .[24]

Wittgenstein's peculiar brand of heresy takes off from that of Tolstoy and looks back to some of these earlier more quietist heresiarchs. It returns to the simplicities of Gospel Christianity, to a belief that faith is of the heart and not of the head, that humble people and children are nearer to God and the truth of life than philosophers and divines. Gentile expounded a heretical variant of Catholicism bereft of Christ and Church and consecrated instead to Nation and State. He held that his philosophy, Actual Idealism, was a religion or what he called, following Vico, a '*filosofia teologizzante*'.

The malign masters were fully aware of the religious provenance of their thought and were occasionally prepared to admit this in their private writings and *obiter dicta* more so than in their published works. Thus in a letter of 19 August 1921, to his disciple Karl Löwith, Heidegger writes 'I work concertedly and factically out of my "I am", out of my intellectual and wholly factical origin, milieu, life-context, and whatever is available to me from these as a vital experience in which I live . . . To this facticity of mine belongs what I would in brief call the fact that I am a "Christian theologian".'[25] Wittgenstein declared late in life to his disciple Drury, 'I cannot help seeing every problem from a religious point of view.'[26] Gentile more publicly proclaimed himself to be a Catholic and his philosophy

Christian, despite his equally open hostility to the Church. Lukács, though converted to Lutheranism early in his life, was later strongly drawn to Catholicism, which he praised in extravagant terms, together with his friend Bloch. He turned to communism because he saw it as the modern successor to Catholicism, writing in his book of 1911 that 'the system of socialism and its view of the world, Marxism, form a synthetic unity – perhaps the most unrelenting and rigorous synthesis since medieval Catholicism.'[27] And in a letter of 1913 he writes that 'the last culturally active force in Germany, naturalist-materialist socialism, owes its efficacy to hidden religious elements.'[28] Little wonder that Thomas Mann cast him in the role of Naphta, a Jesuit of Jewish origin espousing communistic revolutionary ideas under the cloak of the Church.

I note it here merely as an interesting fact, which might not be mere coincidence, that almost without exception the malign masters and the totalitarian dictators were drawn from or drawn to a perverted form of Catholicism. The only exception is Stalin, who, nevertheless, began as a seminarian in the Orthodox Church of Georgia which has some similar features. These features reflect themselves in numerous ways in the thought of the philosophers and in the organizational and symbolic practices of the politicians. This is something to which historians have not given much attention. I shall not be taking it up again for to give it the full historical treatment it deserves is beyond the scope of this book.

The malign masters were not the only ones to develop a theologizing philosophy in this period, many others did so as well, and not necessarily so as a derivative from Catholicism. Protestantism, Russian Orthodoxy and Judaism also provided the bases for such philosophies which are now collectively known as Existentialism. Karl Löwith mentions many such thinkers and draws a close parallel between Heidegger and the Jewish existentialist thinker and friend of Martin Buber, Franz Rosenzweig, ironically so in the light of Heidegger's well-known hostility to Jewish philosophers. Rosenzweig, who also philosophized out of his war experiences, argued for the interpenetration of theology and philosophy, as Löwith notes:

> Philosophy, says Rosenzweig, today demands that theologians philosophize. Philosophy and theology depend on each other and together produce a new type of theological philosopher. Theological problems need to be translated into the human and the human problems pushed forward into theological ones – a characterization of the 'new thinking'which can be applied to Heidegger as well as Rosenzweig, although Heidegger's attitude towards Christianity is that of estrangement, while Rosenzweig's attitude towards Judaism is that of return.[29]

Löwith makes it clear that many others thought along these lines, 'the same spirit of the age produced the first writings of E. Rosenstock, M. Buber, H. and R. Ehrenburg, C. von Weizsäcker, and F. Ebener [and] the beginning of "dialectical theology" also belongs to this historical period that followed the First World War.'[30] One could easily add to this list numerous names from many other countries right across Europe.

But if this was a common tendency characteristic of a whole generation, so to speak expressive of the 'spirit of the age', why was it that the malign masters were the ones to capture it so decisively, that they are the ones who came to dominate later philosophy? In other words, what distinguished the malign masters from the many others who also developed a *filosofia teologizzante* at this time? A simplistic answer would be to say that they were the most able, the geniuses, while the others were somehow inferior. But this answer will not do since each of the malign masters had one or more colleagues who were not always markedly inferior as thinkers, yet who did not attain anywhere near the same level of fame and influence. Is Jaspers so much worse than Heidegger, or Bloch less able than Lukács, is Moore or Schlick no match for Wittgenstein? On the other hand, to say that the malign masters were more cunning in being able to present the religious 'message' that the age demanded in a suitably disguised way acceptable to non-believers who would not resort to the official Churches and creeds, would only be to portray them as superior charlatans. But as I have previously stressed, they were neither geniuses nor charlatans in any obvious sense. It is true that they were thinkers of great opportunistic astuteness, who knew how to mystify and conceal their thought so as to give it the aura of inaccessibility and great profundity and this is undoubtedly a factor in their success, but it cannot be the whole explanation.

At least some part of the explanation must be sought in their unusual personalities and the effect this had on others, particularly younger students and followers, at a time when 'personality' became such a crucial factor in determining who people followed and what they accepted and believed in intellectual no less than in artistic and political matters. There is no doubting the charismatic effect that the malign masters had on their pupils and friends; even their mentors were from the start unusually impressed. Husserl, writing a reference for Heidegger to Natorp at Marburg, does not overlook to mention his *Privatdozent*'s 'original personality' (*originelle Persönlichkeit*). Hannah Arendt, once a young student and mistress of Heidegger, ascribes much of his success to this personality factor: 'indeed it is open to question whether the unusual success of this book [*Sein und Zeit*] – not just the immediate impact it had inside and outside the academic world but also its extraordinary lasting influence, with which few of this century's publications can compare – would have been possible if it had not been preceded by the teacher's reputation among the students . . .'[31] Findlay, who had met many philosophers in his long life, wrote towards the end of it that 'Wittgenstein had a much greater intellectual charisma than any other philosopher I have ever encountered.'[32] Apart from a few, such as Findlay himself, most of his pupils became disciples with a life-long devotion to him and his work. Gentile's students were no less devoted to him, at least for a time, for some broke with him when he became a Fascist and most when Fascism collapsed; only a rare few persisted in undiminished loyalty. However, in his heyday in the 1920s, his English translator, the philosopher H. Wildon Carr, wrote that 'Gentile has been famous in his country on account of his historical and philosophical writings and even more by the number and fervour of the disciples he has attracted.'[33] Lukács did no university teaching until late in life, when his influence on students was also profound; but even much earlier, at the very start of his intellectual career, his friends in the so-called Sunday Circle in Budapest already treated him as an established master and an acknowledged genius.

How and why the malign masters managed to impress their students, friends and mentors is well conveyed by Hans Jonas, one of Heidegger's students in Freiburg during the late 1920s, where he came to study with Husserl, who seemed far less impressive to him:

> Edmund Husserl and Martin Heidegger: of the two Heidegger was the much more exciting . . . Firstly, because he was much more difficult to understand. This was strangely attractive for a young and ardent philosophy student who was still in the apprenticeship stage: a strange attraction, a totally compelling assumption that there must be something hidden behind it that was worth being understood, that something was going on there, that work was being done on something new . . . Here one is coming close to the centre of philosophical thinking. It is still a mystery, but something is going on here in which (how should I say it) the last (ultimate) concerns of thinking in general, of philosophy, are dealt with.[34]

One could almost certainly unearth analogous testimonials to the teaching abilities, their extraordinary capacity to excite and mystify at the same time, of the other malign masters as well. And it must not be supposed that they were thus able to work only on young, unschooled and impressionable minds. For time and again one also finds older intellectuals and even seasoned philosophers succumbing to the very same mesmeric influence of the cult of the 'new' preached with utter self-certitude that admits of no doubt. It is instructive in this respect to read Friedrich Waismann's account of Wittgenstein's monologues – for they cannot be called 'conversations' – before the distinguished philosophers who were members of the Vienna Circle, men such as Schlick, Carnap, Feigl, Hahn and others. They listened respectfully while Wittgenstein expostulated views that could only have been abhorrent to most of them, especially views on ethics, religion and other philosophers, such as Heidegger, for whose ideas Wittgenstein at this time had considerable sympathy, but the others did not.[35] Later some of them woke up from the hypnotic spell; others, such as Schlick, never did and Waismann not completely. What was it that made such people so susceptible to the malign masters?

In the volatile climate following The First World War, when the old truths and the older masters who maintained them seemed utterly discredited, together with the old 'bourgeois' culture that nourished them, when cults of youth proliferated and anyone with a daring, bold, paradoxical or perverse idea was given a ready hearing – at such a time of turmoil, both inside and outside the universities, 'personality' or charismatic appeal was a crucial determinant of success and fame in all spheres of society. In the universities teachers who were preachers came to the fore. In the streets, on the lower levels of mass politics, the great demagogues were beginning to exercise a charismatic sway over the assembled crowds. There are clear parallels between what was happening inside and outside the lecture rooms. The vacuum created by the discrediting of the older generation and its culture sucked in self-appointed saviours, prophets and leaders. At a time of distress – in all respects, political, moral, artistic and intellectual, not to speak of social and economic – new creeds, ideologies, artistic movements and, for a more restricted audience, new philosophies were eagerly embraced. In his autobiographical recollections Löwith presents very graphically the kinds of pressures that made him 'choose' Heidegger as his master:

> In those decisive years after the collapse of 1918, my friendship with P. Gotheim confronted me with the choice of either joining the circle around Stephan George and Gundolf, or of becoming the lone follower of Heidegger who – albeit in a completely different fashion – exercised a no less dictatorial power over young minds, although none of his listeners understood what he was really driving at. During periods of dissolution there are different types of 'Führer' who resemble each other only in so far as they radically reject what exists and are determined to point a way to 'the one thing that matters.' I decided for Heidegger and

> this positive decision also forms the foundations of the critique that I published thirty-five years later, under the title *Heidegger: Denker in dürftiger Zeit* (1953), to break the spell of a sterile imitation on the part of his spellbound followers, and to make them conscious of the questionability of Heidegger's existential-historical thought.[36]

Unfortunately, by the time he came to publish his critique it was already far too late, Heidegger, just as the other malign masters, had already achieved an unbreakable hold over far too many followers for a few defections to make any difference.

Under these unusual circumstances, the malign masters exercised a most paradoxical cultural influence, for they can be counted as among the first modernist anti-Modernists. This oxymoronic expression is meant to convey the modernist up-to-date standpoint from which the malign masters attacked the very Modernism out of which they themselves arose. Max Weber refers to this kind of paradoxical development – which he had already observed prior to 1918 before any of the malign masters had come to the fore on the philosophical scene – as a 'modern intellectualist form of romantic irrationalism', an expression which is also implicitly oxymoronic.[37] He ascribes this trend to a search for pseudo-religious 'experience' characteristic of the new generation of what he calls 'German youth'. This is the same generation to which the malign masters appealed almost immediately after 1918 with works that embodied, in various different ways, just such a 'modern intellectualist form of romantic irrationalism'. With their 'irrationalist' anti-scientific and anti-liberal drift, and their pseudo-religious intimations, these works exemplify the tendencies against which Weber pronounced his strictures before they were even written, delivering a *critique avant la lettre*, as it were.

The 'youth' Weber addressed took no heed of his warnings, either in philosophy or politics. His declaration that 'the prophet for whom so many of our younger generation yearn simply does not exist' was not credited.[38] Neither did they accept his view that 'if there is no such man, or if his message is no longer believed in, then you will certainly not compel him to appear on this earth by having thousands of professors, as privileged hirelings of the state, attempt as petty prophets in their lecture-rooms to take over his role.'[39] Out of the thousands of professors who tried but failed, nevertheless, a few did succeed in getting themselves accepted as 'ersatz armchair prophets', or literally as university chair sages.

The ones who succeeded best were those who preached a message of destruction, of doing away with the old order in philosophy and bringing it to some kind of an end. This is the apocalyptic message which can easily be located in the works of the malign masters. That they were fully aware of what they were preaching and what its consequences might entail is not so evident from these works themselves as from the pronouncements and other statements which each of the malign masters made at the time. Thus Heidegger, in a letter to Karl Löwith of the early 1920s, states openly that philosophical and cultural destruction is his aim and he is utterly unconcerned about the consequences:

> Instead of abandoning oneself to the general need to become cultivated, as if one had received the order to 'see culture', it is necessary – through a radical reduction and distintegration, through a destruction – to convince oneself firmly of the 'only thing' necessary, without paying attention to the ideal task and agitation of enterprising and intelligent men . . . My will at least is directed toward something else, and it is not much: living in a situation of *de facto* upheaval, I am pursuing what I feel to be 'necessary' without worrying whether the result will be a 'culture' or whether my quest will precipitate ruin.[40]

Writing at the start of his career before he had attained fame, in the intimacy of a letter to a disciple, Heidegger is here more forthright and honest than he was ever to be later in his published works. He was true to his word, he did manage through 'radical reduction and disintegration, through destruction', in some sense, to 'precipitate ruin'.

The other malign masters were also intent on destruction, though each of them understood this in his own peculiar way. That they succeeded in their endeavour, which is now beyond doubt, is largely due to the fact that during this critical time of turmoil each of them burst onto the philosophical scene with a highly provocative and unusual work, his first masterwork. In chronological order of appearance there came Gentile's *A General Theory of Spirit as Pure Act* (1916), Wittgenstein's *Tractatus Logico-Philosophicus* (1921), Lukács' *History and Class Consciousness* (1923), and Heidegger's *Being and Time* (1927). Gentile's book was the earliest, published during the course of the war (soon translated into English by Wildon Carr under the misleading title of *A Theory of Mind as Pure Act*). In most respects it was also the oldest and most philosophically traditional of all these works, just as Gentile himself was the oldest and most established of all these philosophers. It should be considered the introduction to his Idealist metaphysics, which was subsequently elaborated in his *Sistema di Logica,* published in two volumes in 1917 and 1923. Lukács, too, was no novice when his first major work appeared, for though not as yet academically established, he had published two important works on aesthetics before the war, *A Theory of the Novel* and *Soul and Form.* But it was his primary masterwork of 1923 which made his name and by which he will be remembered. He himself considered the others as mere preparatory works, and so I shall take it here. Wittgenstein and Heidegger were hardly heard of before they established their reputations with their primary masterworks; though Heidegger did publish his academic dissertation on Duns Scotus beforehand, and Wittgenstein dictated a dossier of notes on logic during his first period in Cambridge before the war, but this was known only to his friends.

With the possible exception of Gentile, it can readily be shown how each of the other malign masters infused his experience of war and revolution into his primary masterwork. This made for the extraordinary appeal and success of these works. Lukács' work, expounding a new kind of Hegelian Marxism, eventually became the point of departure for many other exponents of non-orthodox Marxism who together comprise the movement which later came to be known as Western Marxism. Wittgenstein's work helped to launch Logical Positivism, and continues to play a key role in the later Analytic Philosophy which is still current to this day. Heidegger's work had an analogous impact on the rising movement of Existentialist philosophy, and later on the so-called Continental school in general. Gentile's work was less influential outside Italy, though it did help sustain what was left of Idealist traditions all over the world. In Italy, however, its sway was exceptional for it merged into the rising tide of Fascism where it assumed a semi-official status. That it is now almost forgotten outside Italy has much to do with the collapse of Fascism after the Second World War and with Gentile's untimely death at the same time.

Characteristically, at about the same time during the late 1920s and early 1930s, each of the malign masters began to turn away from or to turn against his primary masterwork, to a lesser or greater extent, in a countermovement of thought to which Heidegger and his commentators have given the name *Kehre*. That each of the malign masters underwent his own turning or *Kehre* at about the same time is neither a mere historical coincidence nor a pre-established harmony in the history of pure Spirit. As I shall show, it relates closely to events in the outside political world, to the abrupt move into totalitarianism that then took place, also not merely coincidentally, in many of the major countries of Europe. I shall study the effects of this political process in the higher, abstruse and intellectual sphere of philosophy where it assumes the guise of an apparent 'logical' progression from totality to totalitarianism.

The involvement with totalitarianism proved to be a not altogether happy one for the malign masters. Each experienced his own disappointment and rejection. Each was forced to retreat into one or another kind of academic solitude. In such a condition of isolation each proceeded with writings which only appeared later, often posthumously, some time after the end of the Second World War. From among the numerous publications which have since appeared under the name of each master, I shall here restrict myself to one key work in each case, a secondary masterwork that complements the primary one. In this way I shall consider Gentile's *Genesis and Structure of Society* (1946), Lukács' *Destruction of Reason* (1952), Wittgenstein's *Philosophical Investigations* (1953) and Heidegger's *Nietzsche* (largely composed between 1935 and 1945, but published only in 1961). The difference between the secondary and the primary masterwork is that of a late to an early philosophy. Voluminous commentaries have appeared exploring this relation between the late and early philosophies of each of the malign masters separately. Nobody seems to have realized that there is a similar pattern at work in all of them and that analogous issues and problems arise. The pattern at its simplest is that of a primary masterwork, followed by a *Kehre*, followed by a secondary masterwork.

This pattern is least pronounced in the case of Gentile, who, as I have already stated, was much more like a traditional philosopher than the others. He seems to have persevered with the same philosophy of Actual Idealism from start to finish, and he never formally abjured his earlier work as the others did. Nevertheless, the pattern of an early and a late philosophy mediated by a turning is at least incipiently there in Gentile as well. Thus a sympathetic commentator, H.S. Harris, argues against the claim maintained by Mario Rossi, one of Gentile's friends, who wrote that 'no theoretical difference or inconsistency can be found between Gentile's first theoretical statement . . . and the *Genesi*, composed thirty years later'; Harris insists, to the contrary, that 'there is a "theoretical difference" of the first importance'.[41] And there is little doubt that the difference is largely due to his deepening involvement with Fascism, for his secondary masterwork, *Genesis and Structure of Society,* according to Harris, 'forms a sort of epitaph to his life as a Fascist'.[42] The *Kehre* which led from his primary to his secondary masterwork was in this case no abrupt turnabout, but a gradual turning, which faithfully followed the transformation of the Fascist regime from simple dictatorship into totalitarianism – at least in theory, for in practice, mercifully, Mussolini's rule was not all that terroristic. Much of that theory was due to Gentile himself, especially from 1928 onwards.

In that year also began Lukács' *Kehre*, forced on him by the precipitate lurch the Soviet Union took towards totalitarianism under the tightening iron grip of Stalin. For this was when he was made to renounce his more 'popular front'-inclined 'Blum Theses', so-called, and to denounce his primary masterwork, *History and Class Consciousness,* which was charged with the cardinal sin of 'idealist deviationism'. He did so in the ritual public confession of a 'self-criticism', an abject abnegation that he, as so many other communist intellectuals, had to endure as part of his *sacrificio intellectualis.* But he never went back on it, for even at the end of his life he still insisted that his criticism of *History and Class Consciousness* was at the time sincere and remained more or less correct; even though by this stage he tried to soft-pedal its supposed 'errors' in order to salvage what had become in the West an acknowledged masterpiece despite himself.

Heidegger's *Kehre* began at almost exactly the same time when he felt himself independent enough academically, having finally acquired Husserl's Chair at Freiburg, to reveal openly his conservative-revolutionary leanings and edge ever closer to Hitler and the Nazis. This culminated a few years later in his very public act of joining the Party after he became Rektor of his university in May 1933. In his philosophy he completely abandoned Husserl's phenomenology and became increasingly preoccupied with Nietzsche, who, it must not be forgotten, was considered the precursor and leading philosopher of Nazism by Hitler himself. At first Heidegger did not completely turn his back on *Being and Time*, but he subtly and surreptitiously adjusted its terms and categories to make them suit the new political realities of totalitarianism. The individualistic and subjectivistic Existentialist bent of the work was twisted in a collectivist and nationalist direction. As Richard Wolin, paraphrasing Löwith, puts it in brief, 'circa 1932 the ahistorical, individualistic conception of Dasein elaborated in it was given a collectivist twist: the existential "carrier" of the categories of authenticity, historicity, and destiny became the German Volk and its concrete, factical-historical situation.'[43] Much later, after the war, Heidegger tried to make out that this *Kehre* had nothing to do with politics or what was happening in the world, that it was a movement of pure thought following a logic of its own. In his introduction to Father Richardson's book, he states that such an idea 'was already at work in my thinking ten years prior to 1947', the period when in fact he first mentioned it.[44] He claims that a 'reversal' of Being and Time into Time and Being was already implicitly inherent in the primary masterwork: 'the question of *Being and Time* is decisively fulfilled in the thinking of the reversal.'[45] As devoted a disciple as Father Richardson accepts all this at face value and writes his lengthy book – where there is an exhaustive discussion of all Heidegger's works, including the notorious *Rektoratrede* – without as much as mentioning his Nazism or, for that matter, his known hostility to Catholicism during the Nazi period. However, Tom Rockmore believes that

Heidegger's declaration of a *Kehre*, made in the immediate post-war period, was an opportunistic move with strategic purpose in trying to get the ban against him lifted: 'the concept of the Turning seems a tacit, even graceful admission of an earlier complicity [with Nazism], combined with a suggestion of a fresh start.'[46] Hence, Heidegger's own statements about his *Kehre* must be treated with great suspicion.

If anyone's Turning might be thought to have nothing to do with politics, it is surely Wittgenstein's. Yet even in his case the political connections are not too far away to seek. One might date the beginning of his *Kehre* almost to the day, for it began when he heard Brouwer lecture in Vienna on Intuitionism in mathematics on 10 March 1928. As Herbert Feigl, who was present, later records it, after the lecture Wittgenstein and the others from the Vienna Circle went to a café where 'he became extremely voluble and began sketching ideas that were the beginnings of his later philosophy'.[47] But it was not merely pure mathematical philosophy that was at stake. One of the main motives behind Brouwer's lecture in Vienna was to deliver a blow in an ongoing battle against Hilbert and the Göttingen School of mathematical Formalists. He had previously given the same lecture in Berlin where it was considered an attempt at a 'mathematical Putsch'. Brouwer, a Dutch philogermanist, was closely allied in this increasingly more bitter academic-political campaign with Ludwig Bieberbach, who espoused ever more extreme Rightist views against what he came to call 'Jewish mathematics'. To this he opposed his own conception of 'Aryan mathematics' which, after Hitler's victory, he was able to impose on the German mathematical establishment, at least to the extent of founding a mathematical organization which enjoyed Party support. It is not known to what extent Wittgenstein was aware of these developments as he embarked at the same time on his own philosophy of mathematics, but he was certainly following a parallel anti-modernist course inspired by Brouwer and in similar ways also by Spengler, who treated mathematics relativistically as a series of culturally specific symbolic forms like art. Wittgenstein, too, stridently denounced Hilbert, Cantor and later Gödel as well, in pronouncements that few mathematicians, and not even his biographer Ray Monk, can now take seriously: 'his comments on Gödel's Proof appear at first sight, to one trained in mathematical logic, quite amazingly primitive.'[48] Here I merely wish to indicate that there is more to it than meets the politically unsophisticated eyes of philosophers of mathematics.

On the other side of the great political divide, which Wittgenstein unabashedly straddled, the political nature of the influences working on him at Cambridge during the period of his *Kehre* is much more openly apparent.

He himself acknowledges the decisive sway of his friend at Cambridge, the Italian economist Piero Sraffa, declaring, in the preface to his secondary masterwork, 'I am indebted to this stimulus for most of the consequential ideas in this book'; and explicitly mentioning that it was Sraffa's criticisms which freed him from the 'erroneous' theses of the *Tractatus*, namely, that brought about his *Kehre*.[49] Sraffa, as we now know, was a close friend of Antonio Gramsci and must have conveyed to Wittgenstein a basically Marxist orientation, which remained implicit in his new 'anthropological' approach to language encapsulated in the philosophically disastrous conception of the language-game, which displaced the equally simplistic picture-theory of language to be found in the *Tractatus*.[50] No doubt many others of his communist friends at Cambridge, such as Nicholas Bakhtin (the exiled brother of the now better known Russian literary critic) were pushing him in a similar direction. To what extent his over-sanguine view of the 'new life' in the Soviet Union under Stalin, which he wished personally to share, also contributed to his reconception of philosophy remains an open question. But a remark such as 'I am by no means sure that I should prefer a continuation of my work by others to a change in the way people live which would make such questions superfluous'[51] suggests, at least by implication, given the circumstances when it was made, that he might have had in mind such a change in the way of life as he believed was occurring in the Soviet Union. His view of communism as conveyed in Keynes' letter to Maisky, from which I previously quoted, backs this up.

It is clear even from these brief and summary accounts, which will be amplified and better substantiated later, that political realities of the time, that is, the apparent triumph of totalitarianism, played a leading role in the philosophical *Kehre* of every one of the malign masters. That is the main reason that they all underwent an analogous turning at about the same time. The whole pattern of their careers is similar for these kinds of reasons. This is not to say that their philosophies are alike, for this pattern is a purely structural one, and it does not reflect the content or style of their works, which *prima facie* look about as unlike as any heterogeneous worldviews brought together by the mere fortuitous chance of contemporaneity. Nevertheless, even in this diversity of content and style there are common themes and preoccupations to be found on closer analysis, as I shall show in the course of this work.

This book is divided into two major parts. In the first part I concentrate largely, though not exclusively, on the works of the malign masters, the texts themselves. In the second part I examine more closely the influences that brought these texts into being and that they in turn exerted on others

– the contexts and pretexts, so to speak, for these texts depended on prior texts, or literally pre-texts, and themselves gave rise to further texts. The multiple workings of these influences resulted in confluences that gave rise to unified schools and whole movements in philosophy. These confluences expanded in all directions like a field of intellectual force. This is the field encompassing most of what is now known as twentieth-century philosophy, the period in philosophy that is more or less coextensive with the era of totalitarianism from the First World War till the collapse of communism in the early 1990s. But, unlike totalitarianism, the philosophical field has not yet ceased to be active, the influences of the malign masters and the confluences these produce are far from exhausted; though there are incipient signs that they are waning, despite the waves of publications that periodically flood the field.

A study of influences and confluences falls under the heading of what might loosely be called the sociology of philosophy. This is, as yet, an undeveloped subject which philosophers have been loath to take up, despite the extensive proliferation of the allied discipline of the sociology of science. In my earlier book, *The Ends of Philosophy*, I attempted to provide some elementary methodological guidelines for this discipline, which I will not repeat here. However, I do reiterate my fundamental insight that the study of texts and the study of contexts are not two utterly distinct activities, that is to say, they cannot be separated into an 'internalist' and an 'externalist' approach. The one is not simply a matter of logical analysis and the other of social causation, for there is a social logic, or what I called a socio-logic, at work driving intellectual developments in given directions, moulding the context in which texts are produced and informing the content of those texts themselves. Texts do not arise by spontaneous generation in a cultural vacuum.

The starting point for each malign master, as for any thinker, was biographically contingent. Each was born in a different country, into a different social situation and began his intellectual career with the teachers he sought out or happened to have encountered. Perhaps coincidentally, it is possible to identify two such teachers in each case as the most important influences, one tends to be a younger man and the other an older one, as it were a father and grandfather figure. Thus Heidegger was influenced by Husserl and Rickert, Wittgenstein by Russell and Frege, Gentile by Croce and Jaja, and Lukács by Weber and Simmel. These teachers were themselves masters of the older generation of pre-1914 thinkers and intellectuals whose minds were formed and works mostly composed before the deluge of the First World War, and who were liberals and modernists in their general political and cultural orientation. They were exponents of what were then new ways of thought and new styles of doing philosophy. Their students, the malign masters, rebelled against them eventually in what might seem like a typical generational rebellion against tradition. But it was far from that, for what the teachers stood for was in no sense merely traditional. They were themselves innovative thinkers, who had already broken with any established traditions and undertaken the radical courses that are now dubbed modernist. Hence, in breaking with their teachers the malign masters were also going against the modernist trends in philosophy and culture in general in which they were themselves raised.

In order to get ahead of their fathers and grandfathers, the sons went behind their backs to the very traditions they had abandoned. Thus in philosophy they returned to the Idealist movement from which the former had liberated themselves and against which they had fought all their lives. In this way, the revolutionary impetus forward led backwards in a reactionary direction. This is clearly evident in the primary masterworks and is part of the secret of the extraordinary *éclat* that these works aroused in the postwar cultural turmoil amidst so many kinds of conservative revolutions and radical ones that quickly turned reactionary.

Part I
Early and Late Philosophies

1 The Primary Masterworks

Each one of the primary masterworks evinces a radically revolutionary conception of itself and proclaims its place at the apocalyptic culmination of the whole history of philosophy. *A General Theory of Spirit as Pure Act, Tractatus Logico-Philosophicus, History and Class Consciousness* and *Being and Time*: each one sees itself, in its own peculiar terms, as an 'end of philosophy'. Obviously these terms differ enormously and how each relates itself to the previous philosophical past also varies fundamentally. Yet in each one there is a firm insistence that this whole past, extending back to the origins of philosophy, is now at an end and something new and unprecedented – beyond philosophy or beyond metaphysics or beyond the Tradition or beyond whatever it is that is being surpassed – is about to be inaugurated. The future of thought is to be something utterly different from its past. In their sense of revolutionary overturning and apocalyptic fulfilment, of the end of the past and beginning of the future, the primary masterworks are clearly in tune with the nascent totalitarian movements which also called for an end to history in a Revolution that would be the start of a new time. After the Armageddon of History, the disasters of the First World War, the expectations of a new Revelation, whether in thought or in deed, were high. The malign masters were the ones who best met such expectations in philosophy with their primary masterworks.

Yet far from being totally new in their thought, the primary masterworks recover much of what is old and forgotten, themes that philosophy had abandoned centuries ago. Far from bringing metaphysics to an end, these works in fact revive old metaphysical speculations and procedures; far from putting an end to Tradition, these works are steeped in it; far from surpassing the present of modernity, in subtle ways they return to the past, even to very past theologies and mythologies that philosophy thought it had superseded. Their great achievement is to present the known old in the guise of the unknown new: hence, the more revolutionary they claim to be, the more reactionary they in fact are. And this is also a feature of the totalitarian ideologies of their time, especially the revolutionary conservative ones, in which projects for the near future are coupled with yearnings for the distant past.

In ideology it is possible to mix both past and future in a unified vision that has the character of myth, but in philosophy this produces glaring contradictions. What the primary masterworks claim for themselves and what they in fact consist of are directly in conflict with each other. If, as I shall presently show, these works are largely metaphysical presentations of theological, religious and at times even mythological themes derived from past contexts, how can this square with their own claims to be the last word in philosophy? Can they even surpass their own immediate philosophical predecessors, not to speak of the whole of the Tradition? If such contradictions can be demonstrated, as I shall try to do, then these works have a totally false consciousness of themselves. But this is part of their essential character, for if they were aware of themselves and owned up to what they were really about, they would not be the works they are, and certainly they could not have the appeal they exercise on their readers, the followers of the malign masters.

In these works there is a form of what can only be called double-think taking place, thought at a highly intellectualised level which seems to have nothing in common with the more ordinary manifestations of this process of self-deception. On the one hand, the claims these works make for themselves as ending philosophy, in the respective senses in which each makes it, must be granted and believed for the works to be accepted and to be intellectually efficacious. But, on the other hand, the real source of attraction of these works, in satisfying a hunger for metaphysical and quasi-religious answers to current problems, must also be indulged. Both sides of this contradiction must be entertained at the same time, in a kind of willing suspension of disbelief, before the subtle influence of these works can begin to be effective. And, of course, the one hand must not know what the other hand is doing. There can be no open admission that such diametrically opposed, and somewhat irrational, needs are being met. The skill with which they can do this is precisely a measure of the malign mastery of these authors in crafting their primary masterworks. Yet it is a skill that is in line with the cunning of the great demagogues in concocting their ideologies, which demand double-think on a much cruder and lower level. But let us not forget how easily the malign masters themselves swallowed these ideologies – after all, their own work had prepared them for it.

Wittgenstein's claim to be the last word in philosophy – indeed his insistence that this word is not a word at all, but the showing of an ineffable revelation – is well known to all readers of the *Tractatus*. For the moment, even disregarding this obvious difficulty that somehow has to be condoned, there is still the problem of what one is to make of his assertion – and what else could it be? – that metaphysics and the rest of traditional philosophy somehow vanishes thanks to the new logical notation that makes it possible to detect and eliminate all such 'meaningless' sentences. Thus the new logic not only wipes out all the metaphysics of the past, but acts as a fail-safe prophylactic for the future as well:

> The correct method in philosophy would really be the following: to say nothing except what can be said, i.e. propositions of natural science – i.e. something that has nothing to do with philosophy – and then, whenever someone else wanted to say something metaphysical, to demonstrate to him that he had failed to give a meaning to certain signs in his propositions.[1]

With remarks such as these before their eyes, it is little wonder that the Positivists, especially the members of the Vienna Circle, took it that Wittgenstein was of their party and cause.

It was a case of mistaken philosophical identity. They were to be sadly disappointed as this fact revealed itself in a series of misunderstandings which amounted to a kind of comedy of philosophical errors. For how could Wittgenstein be *against* metaphysics when his *Tractatus* is itself a work *of* metaphysics, full of metaphysical assertions, most of which are not even new, but can be traced back to their traditional sources, as I shall proceed to do in what follows? At the same time as stating them, Wittgenstein takes them all back, for according to his doctrine of showing he has not really said anything. The double-think involved in both saying and unsaying the same thing is very tricky and Wittgenstein has provided a highly sophisticated rationale for doing so, but that itself is not an argument that can be given rational exposition and defence. Rather, it has to be accepted as a kind of higher logical illumination. Thus, talking in this paradoxical vein, Wittgenstein declares, 'what the solipsist means is quite correct, only it cannot be *said*, but makes itself manifest.'[2] Apparently solipsism can be meant but not said – that is to say, one can be a solipsist without having to take any intellectual responsibility for it. Frank Ramsay's down to earth comment that what cannot be said cannot be whistled either has a point to it. Ramsay, however, did not realize that he was not dealing with a work that was open to rebuttal. For the *Tractatus* presents itself as a strange mode of ineffable illumination – those who see it accept it, those who do not simply fail to understand. The possibility that anyone might rationally disagree is not open, for no disputation is allowed against that which only shows itself. Wittgenstein made it quite clear in his letters that neither Frege nor Russell, his own teachers, could *see* it; they both failed to understand (see chapter 4).

Lukács' claims for his Hegelian-Marxist philosophy are less abstruse than those of Wittgenstein, but also involve various double-think contortions. Lukács did not maintain that philosophy as such is at an end, since capitalism and the resultant reification had not yet been overcome. But he did argue that his philosophy, Hegelian-Marxism, was the sublation (*Aufhebung*), that is, the cancelling, overcoming and surpassing of all previous philosophies, especially so of the latest and most rationally developed, classical German philosophy, or bourgeois thought in Lukács' terms. However, in the future, following the Revolution and the victory of the proletariat, philosophy would definitely be realized, that is, brought to an end in practice. Tom Rockmore summarizes Lukács' argument as follows:

> The aim of philosophy is to bring about human freedom. But human freedom requires the emergence of the proletariat as the class to end all classes. When this occurs, when the class structure of society has been abolished, the problem of philosophy will have been solved. If Marxism brings this end about, then it also solves the problem of philosophy. In sum, Lukács finds in the concept of the proletariat the resolution of the unresolved problems of classical German idealism. Since the entire philosophical tradition leads up to classical German idealism, which comes to a peak in Hegel's thought, by inference, through the concept of the proletariat the philosophical tradition is brought to a successful close.[3]

But the concept of the 'proletariat', as conceived by Lukács, is itself a highly idealist notion, one that is through and through metaphysical and even theological. Rockmore grants this when he notes that 'in Lukács' reading of Marxism, the conception of the proletariat corresponds to the role of the absolute in speculative idealism . . . Lukács' Marxist conception of the proletariat is as metaphysical as the Hegelian view of the absolute.'[4] And there precisely is the rub: Lukács has to depend on the operation of Hegelian metaphysical machinery to argue for the overcoming of Hegelian metaphysics, and, ultimately, all of philosophy with it. Hegelianism is both employed and abjured at the same time. If the proletariat, as the 'identical subject–object of history', is as Hegelian a concept as is Hegel's absolute, then if the latter is held by Lukács to be mythological, then so is the former. And yet, by a dialectics of double-think, Lukács thinks he can think with Hegel against Hegel. His is a philosophy that tries to jump over its own shadow.

Gentile also tries to think with Hegel against Hegel, but in a much simpler way than Lukács. He merely argues that his Actual Idealism is superior to Hegel's Absolute Idealism because his philosophy is capable of deducing everything from pure thought alone, whereas Hegel must presuppose something, even if only the Idea itself, as prior to thought. Like Marx he tries to go one better than Hegel by inverting him, but not by surpassing the ideal to attain the material, rather by surpassing the ideal to reach the super ideal. For as he puts it, 'the idealism that I distinguish as *actual* inverts the Hegelian problem: for it is no longer the question of a deduction of thought from Nature and Nature from the Logos, but of Nature and the Logos from thought.'[5] Inverting Hegel in this sense by deriving Logic and Nature from thought means in effect going behind Hegel's back: back to Fichte's absolute 'I'; back to Descartes' thought, the *Cogito*; even further back to the neo-Platonic One from which all multiplicity emerges. Gentile's 'thought' is this One, 'it is, therefore, a relation with itself, an absolute, infinite unity, without multiplicity.'[6] Little wonder that 'Croce later characterized Gentile's actualism as a kind of theology, a religion with a kinship to Catholicism that appealed to those unwilling to turn their backs on the vision of mystical unity embodied in the old religion,'[7] as David Roberts puts it.

Heidegger's grappling with the philosophical past, what he calls the Tradition, is as contorted as that of the others. But he does not rely on logic or dialectics for his mode of double-think, instead he claims to elaborate his own peculiar versions of phenomenology and hermeneutics. The term he devises to do away with what he calls 'the history of ontology' is 'destruction':

> If the question of Being is to have its own history made transparent, then this hardened tradition must be loosened up, and the concealment that has been brought about must be dissolved. We understand this task as one in which taking *the question of Being as our clue*, we are to *destroy* the traditional content of ancient ontology until we arrive at those primordial experiences in which we achieved our first ways of determining the nature of Being – the ways which have guided us ever since.[8]

What these 'primordial experiences which have guided us ever since' are we are not told. Heidegger is convinced that there must be such, so he feels no great urgency to specify them; and, indeed, he will change his mind throughout his career as to what they might be. But even apart from this problem of retrieving the so-called 'origins' – which is unsolvable for whatever is specified as the origin there is always something more originary still – there is a further ambiguity in this passage as to what exactly it is that is being 'destroyed'.[9] Is it the thickly encrusted patina of traditional commentary on the original texts that is to be removed? Or is it the original texts themselves that are to be dissolved, or somehow altered and reconstructed? Is Heidegger playing the role of restorer or repainter of the picture? Heidegger wishes one to believe that he can somehow do both at once: both restore the original image to its pristine purity and paint his own version over it in altering it to suit his own tastes. He wishes to be taken as both keeper and reaper of the texts. The former role appeals to conservatives, especially classicists such as his former student Leo Strauss, who saw Heidegger as effecting a 'return to and recovery of classical philosophy'.[10] The latter role appeals to the radicals, such as his present follower Derrida and his myrmidons, the Deconstructionists.

But both roles are mere pretences for, as I shall show, Heidegger relies precisely on the very history of ontology that he claims to be destroying to compose his own text. Without medieval scholasticism, Catholic and Protestant theology, Idealist metaphysics and even a strong dash of mythology there would be neither Being nor Time as Heidegger presents them. *Being and Time* is composed of the very stuff of the 'history of ontology' that Heidegger claims to have 'destroyed'. His 'destruction' is thus really a salvaging and recycling of the discarded materials of the Tradition – which is not to say that he does not succeed in occasionally recovering some long lost treasures of past writing. *Being and Time* is like a palimpsest: beneath the printed text of seemingly modernist philosophy there lie concealed, barely effaced, writings in ancient hierophantic scripts. And something similar is true of the other secondary masterworks as well.

That is, indeed, one of the main reasons why they exert such an extraordinary fascination and capacity to capture and engage attention. But this is also the reason that to be accepted they require a willing suspension of doubt in an act of intellectual double-think. At a time when all open expression of metaphysical, theological, religious and, most certainly, mythological ideas is denied to philosophers and intellectuals in general, works that seem to meet the canons of intellectual rigour and rational thought, yet which at the same time convey, surreptitiously, metaphysics, theology, religion and even mythology, can be intellectually seductive and exercise an extraordinary half-understood appeal. For they satisfy needs produced by the traumas of the times which must remain consciously unacknowledged, at least on the part of intellectuals and students of philosophy. Common folk readily proclaimed their adhesion to irrationalist creeds – provided for them in this period in large part by the totalitarian ideologies – but philosophers could not in good conscience do so at first; not until later when they themselves became totalitarian apologists. Hence, to begin with, highly sublimated and intellectually rarefied forms of double-think evolved to accommodate all these contradictory needs; and these are to be found in the primary masterworks at the highest possible level – the level of 'genius' one might say, if such a word were not so equivocal in this context.

To make this case – that beneath the solid and rational-seeming veneer of these works there are hidden seepages of irrationalist dry rot – will require constant cross-comparisons from one primary masterwork to another. For what is well concealed in one might be more openly revealed in another; and seeing it clearly exposed in the one can help one to detect it in the others. This is so with the first metaphysical concept common to all of them, that of 'totality', for only in Lukács is this openly invoked as a key concept. Yet it is there in all the others as well, only not so candidly proclaimed. For the other common metaphysical concepts I shall unearth Lukács might not be the clearest exponent, one or another of the other malign masters might reveal these more directly and obviously. Thus the conception of a non-egoistic solipsism or subjectless subjectivity is more clearly exposed in Wittgenstein, and that of an inactive activism in Heidegger. These two highly paradoxical notions, together with totality, constitute the triangular metaphysical field of force, so to speak, by which the four primary masterworks are sustained. This is what they have in common beneath their all too evident differences.

That totality is a metaphysical concept hardly requires any special pleading. It is synonomous with what in traditional metaphysics is called Being or Reality or the All or the Whole or the World, or any other such all-inclusive term. To be able to pronounce on everything at once is a characteristic feature of metaphysical thinking. By contrast, scientific thinking eschews any assertions of an undifferentiated generality: a scientific theory is always peculiar to a given field, a scientific concept is always restricted and partial. And the same is true for historical thinking. In this respect concepts of totality in the primary masterworks resemble those to be found in the acknowledged metaphysical works of the past rather than anything else outside these. Though they differ from the metaphysical concepts of the past in that they are disguised by some substantive field of thought, such as Logic or Science or Art or History, ones that had not in the past been regarded as having anything intrinsically to do with metaphysics. This oddity has to be accounted for by the peculiar status of metaphysics in modernist thought, it is usually metaphysics with a bad conscience, one that dares not even speak its own name.

The category of totality is explicitly invoked by Lukács, this being one of the acknowledged highlights of his early work. He states that 'concrete totality is, therefore, the category that governs reality.'[11] But it must be a 'dialectical conception of totality', none other will do; and the 'essence of the dialectical method' is 'the absolute domination of the whole, its unity over and above the abstract isolation of the parts'.[12] Lukács does not stop at any mere understanding or contemplation of the totality of things; he is adamant that this 'category of totality' already contains within itself a directive for action leading to a total transformation of the whole, namely, that it is the augury of a revolutionary messianic age. The 'domination of the whole' in theory is seconded by one in practice as well.

> The category of totality begins to have an effect long before the whole multiplicity of objects can be illuminated by it. It operates by ensuring that actions which seem to confine themselves to particular objects, in both content and consciousness, yet preserve an aspiration towards the totality, that is to say: action is directed objectively towards a transformation of totality. We pointed out earlier in the context of a purely methodological discussion, that the various aspects and elements of the dialectical method contain the structure of the whole; we see the same thing here in a more concrete form, a form more closely oriented towards action.[13]

As this extended quote intimates, everything is to be found in this 'category of totality': it is both a methodology of scientific knowledge and a driving force of revolutionary change; it promotes both total understanding and total transformation; and it is efficacious of itself even before things are known or actions performed according to it. Nothing like it has been entertained in philosophy since Plato's Form of the Good. Little wonder that even his sympathetic biographer, Árpad Kadarkay, states that 'the concept of the social "totality" . . . enjoys something of an ontological status in his work. God is dead, long live the totality!'[14] He, too, points to the obvious likeness to Plato: 'the "totality" was within the grasp of a Marxist intellect, which is the realizer of the wisdom of the proletariat and which, like Plato's philosopher, is exempt from the cave-effect of empirical knowledge.'[15] Lukács himself is, of course, too modest to point out that he is the best candidate in his own time for such a 'Marxist intellect'. But such claims were made on his behalf by his friends and followers.

Gentile is less abashed and somewhat more naive in trumpeting his claims to totality: 'the conception to which I have tried to give expression [is] a conception which resolves the world into spiritual act or act of thought, in unifying the infinite variety of man and nature in an absolute one, in which the human is divine and the divine is human . . .'[16] Gentile's 'absolute one' is also a concept of totality, one that is as conducive to action as to understanding, and, as he claims, to worship as well. It contains and resolves within itself all the fundamental differences: both the theoretical and the practical, both the empirical and the a priori, both the immediate and mediated, both the secular and sacred. It is the unity where all distinctions disappear, all oppositions are reconciled and all conflicts are resolved. It is the whole totality of Spirit, as this is elaborated in his Hegelian 'system of metaphysics'. For Gentile is both more naive and more honest than the other malign masters in proclaiming his work to be no less than a system of metaphysics, but one that is to be the realization, culmination and completion of all previous metaphysics, including that of Hegel.

Gentile's totality is clearly some kind of mystic unity of all things that harks back to neo-Platonic doctrine and to Catholic theology. As Croce saw it, Gentile's conception of totality is 'a sort of ever-present oneness', a 'continuous, ever-present act of thinking'.[17] This appealed to many younger Italian intellectuals, including such subsequently distinguished thinkers as Omodeo and de Ruggiero, precisely because it opened up 'giddy visions of human omnipotence'.[18] Later most of them – with the signal exception of the two mentioned above – would follow Gentile into Fascism, which seemed to promise them some of this 'human omnipotence' through politics.

Heidegger was far more subtle and circumspect than Gentile in declaring his metaphysical affiliations. At first he used this term quite freely for his work, but in his later writings, under the influence of Nietzsche, he became averse to the idea of metaphysics, yet he refused to acknowledge that he had change his mind, pretending that it was what he had intended all along.[19] The metaphysical provenance of his concept of Being is obvious, but the same is also true for his more *sui generis* concept of *Dasein.* These are the two summations of totality in the accountancy of his book-keeping, the grand total and the sub-total respectively. They correspond approximately to what in traditional metaphysics is called God and Soul. In Heidegger's early work it is *Dasein* which assumes priority; in his later work the roles are somewhat reversed and Being takes pride of place.

That *Dasein* is a concept of totality has long been recognized by commentators. Thus Dreyfus and Haugeland write that Heidegger's hermeneutic method is a way of investigating 'the actual totality' that is 'Dasein's Being-in-the-world as a unitary phenomenon'.[20] They spell this out as follows:

> the hermeneutic method is one of finding *interpretations* for the totality; and since the totality has no essence, no determinate 'what it is' that could fix a horizon within which it is ultimately to be understood, hermeneutic interpretations must always be based on (be within the horizon of) such understanding as we already have.'[21]

As they go on to show, it is precisely this totalistic or holistic aspect of Heidegger's hermeneutic analysis that distinguishes it from that of previous philosophies, particularly from the phenomenology of Husserl.[22]

Dasein is a peculiar totality for it is bounded in time. Like Einstein's conception of the universe (which might at the time have influenced Heidegger), *Dasein* is both endless and finite. It is bounded by the finitude of death. But it is also the complete whole and so endless for it contains all time within itself; past, present and future are only modalities of it. How this is possible will soon be better appreciated when it is seen that *Dasein* is a solipsistic totality without a subject or Ego. Everything that pertains to it is always qualified as 'mine' (*jemeinige*), and 'own most' (*eigen*), that is, having the character of 'mineness' and 'belongingness to me'. Yet at the same time, Heidegger denies solipsism – unlike Gentile or Wittgenstein who embrace it – he insists that apart from *Dasein* there is Being and beings in the two modalities of the ontological and the ontic. In this denial he is simply following the traditional precedent of affirming the ontological difference in not identifying God with the world or the Soul.

The totalistic character of Heidegger's thinking is disguised by his continued adhesion to a kind of neo-scholasticism, which derived from his earlier background as a Catholic philosopher, and which he never completely abandoned. As John van Buren states, 'Heidegger wanted to develop a new type of Neo-Scholasticism or Neo-Neo-Scholasticism, which would revive the "ancient wisdom" of medieval Scholasticism and mysticism with the help of modern Christian thought, phenomenology and neo-Kantianism.'[23] In line with this ambition to constitute a contemporary form of neo-scholasticism, Heidegger continued to maintain many of the scholastic ontological distinctions, such as that between Being, beings and human-being or *Dasein*. But these remain purely formal. At least in his primary masterwork, it is *Dasein* that constitutes the whole, for all analyses of everything else are given in terms of it, so that anything else appears as a mode, mood or manifestation of *Dasein*. This will emerge with greater clarity when the solipsistic character of *Dasein*, its subjectless subjectivity, is revealed in what follows.

By contrast to Heidegger, Wittgenstein insists on the solipsistic character of his version of *Dasein*, namely, the totality he considers to be the identity of Self and world. His is the conception of a limited totality, rather than a temporally bounded one as in Heidegger. As I shall presently show, this has to do with the rather different role that death plays in his system. For what is finitude in Heidegger is only limitation in Wittgenstein, since he rejects the idea of death as a final end. The term 'world' is Wittgenstein's primary name for totality. Hence it is the world that is seen as a limited totality: 'to view the world *sub specie aeterni* is to view it as a whole – a limited whole. Feeling the world as a limited whole – it is this that is the mystical.'[24] This open avowal of 'the mystical' points to the religious orientation that is at the heart of Wittgenstein's work. The theology it professes is that of a mystical immersion in the world as an ever-present totality where there is neither a separable Self nor death. His biographer, Brian McGuiness, paraphrases his thoughts on this, to be found in the wartime *Notebooks* as well as later implicitly in the *Tractatus*, as follows: 'the only true life is life in the present. For a man living not the personal but the common life of the spirit, there is no death.'[25] It is understandable that someone facing death daily at the front should have consoled himself with such thoughts, but what has this to do with logic or with philosophy as Wittgenstein understood it? McGuiness provides the answer when he states that 'it is not unfair to see his whole philosophy as a kind of mystic revelation, remembering that mystic *means* what cannot or should not be spoken . . . The reading of the book, then, has a purpose: it is like an initiation into the mysteries, and when they are reached it can be forgotten.'[26] Whether this purpose is attained depends, of course, on who is doing the reading.

Wittgenstein began his work with problems of logic, but very soon this became no more than a screen for his other, more 'mystical', ideas. In one of his *Notebooks* he states, 'Yes, my work has broadened out from the foundation of Logic to the "essence" of the world.'[27] The essence of the world is the subject of metaphysics *par excellence*. The *Tractatus* begins with the eminently metaphysical declaration, 'the world is everything that is the case . . . the world is the totality of facts not of things'.[28] A totality of 'facts' or 'existing states of affairs', as he puts it later, is not the same kind of totality as Lukács', Gentile's or Heidegger's, but it belongs with them in their attempts to formulate 'the essence of the world'. It differs from their metaphysics in that instead of their Parmenidean unity of the One, it follows a Democritean diversity of the Many, in which the totality is made up of 'atoms' of elementary fact, each self-sufficient and independent of every other, like a monad without consciousness. This is an important difference which reflects the origin of Wittgenstein's metaphysics in logic and perhaps goes back to Leibniz through the hand of Russell, but it is not a crucial one as far as relating his work to that of the others goes. Logical atomism is as much a metaphysical postulate as is any other theory of totality.

Logic gave Wittgenstein his point of departure with the formal concept of a 'proposition'. The idea that a proposition mirrors the world if it is true gave him his further concept of a 'fact' or 'state of affairs'. The principle of analysis to ultimate constitutents led him to conceive of elementary propositions and elementary facts. With that in hand he could then construct the world out of these constituents and declare that 'the totality of existing states of affairs is the world'.[29] But this was a patently metaphysical declaration which took Frege by surprise, for he had not been expecting such things from the logician he took Wittgenstein to be.[30] However, Wittgenstein was not content with mere logic, but went on to derive from it everything else, for once he had obtained his initial totality of facts all the other totalities could be generated by the mere process of repeated mirroring or reflection. Thus 'the totality of propositions is language';[31] 'the totality of true propositions is the whole of natural science . . .'[32] 'the totality of true thoughts is a picture of the world . . .'[33] and so on. These totalities cascade one after another: world, logic, language, thought, science each one spills over into the one beneath it, each one is reflected in the clear pools of those behind it like two rows of mirrors facing each other. And so, given that the first, the world, is a limited totality so must be all the others that follow it. Statements to this effect re-echo throughout the work: 'logic pervades the world: the limits of the world are also its limits';[34] 'the limits of my language mean the limits of my world';[35] 'philosophy sets limits to the much disputed sphere of natural science.'[36]

Where did this idea of limits that so pervades Wittgenstein's *Tractatus* philosophy come from and what is its role in the economy of his thought? It sounds like a Kantian principle, and no doubt it was inherited by Wittgenstein as a Kantian legacy through the agency of Schopenhauer and Weininger. Kant had distinguished between limits (*Schranken*) and bounds (*Grenzen*): 'bounds (in extended beings) always presuppose a space existing outside a certain definite place enclosing it . . . limits do not require this, but are mere negations which affect a quantity so far as it is not absolutely complete.'[37] Thus in mathematics and the sciences generally there are limits but not bounds, human reason 'admits that something indeed lies without it, at which it can never arrive, but not that it will at any point find completion in its internal progress.'[38]

Wittgenstein was unlikely to have read Kant, and he uses the two terms *Schranken* and *Grenzen* indiscriminately, though on the whole favouring the latter, also translated as limits in English. However, he arrives at an analogous distinction between limits and bounds. But not for the usual Kantian reasons, the need to circumscribe and critically restrict Reason itself, as for religious ones pertaining to the mystic sense of the world as a limited but unbounded totality. For unlike most mystics who identify Self and God, Wittgenstein identifies Self and World; so that instead of the finite Self being drawn up to infinity in God, it is the world that is drawn down to the finitude of the Self, to its limitations. 'The limits of my language mean the limits of my world,' declared Wittgenstein, but since there is no allowance made for any other language but mine, or any other world but mine, it follows that both language and the world are limited but unbounded because I am so.

But how is it that I am limited but unbounded? At first sight it might seem obvious, I am limited because I am mortal and therefore finite. And at times Wittgenstein does speak as if limitation was finitude. He states, for example, that not only am I finite, but so, too, is the world: 'as in death, too, the world does not change, but stops existing.'[39] But how can the world cease to exist just because I die? When it comes to it, Wittgenstein cannot really accept that the world ceases or that the 'I' does so either. So he affirms a kind of immortality: anyone who completely lives in the present cannot die; for death has no reality for him. This kind of belief in immortality does not challenge the obvious fact that others die; for instance, that soldiers are killed at the front. For it is only, so to speak, the noumenal 'I' which is coextensive with the world that does not die. But this 'I' is not an eternal soul, it is limited, as is the world and everything in it. Since 'I am my world',[40] neither the 'I' nor the 'world' can be finite or bounded, that is, mortal, but they are limited, not eternal or infinite. Thus, in line with Schopenhauer, limitation takes the place of finitude or mortality in Wittgenstein's economy of thought.

But how is it that 'I am my world'? To explain this it is necessary to expound the second common theme, after totality, in the primary masterworks, that of an Egoless or non-egoistic solipsism. Once again it is some of the malign masters, Wittgenstein and Gentile, who openly embrace and express this peculiar paradox, the others, Lukács and Heidegger, seek to disguise it to a greater or lesser degree. It takes a different form in each of them depending on the conceptual apparatus in which it is couched. Thus in Wittgenstein it is stated as an identity of Self and world; in Lukács as an identity of subject and object; in Gentile as the unity of my thought as act and everything that it contains; and in Heidegger, more indirectly, through the interpretation of everything in terms of *Dasein*, the mode of being-in-the-world that comprehends the world. All of these are non-egoistic Subjects, and each one coincides with the totality to which it pertains in its specific philosophy.

It is no mere coincidence that each of the malign masters should have arrived independently at a conception of a subjectivistic but non-egoistic totality. There are good historical reasons for it. Even before the First World War there were strong neo-Idealist and Existentialist currents running counter to the rationalism and scientistic Positivism of the age. The effect of the war on the minds of so many young thinkers was to bring these quasi-metaphysical and quasi-theological *cum* mystical tendencies into prominence. We can see this clearly in the work of Franz Rosenzweig, one of Heidegger's precursors, who, like Wittgenstein, composed his book, *The Star of Redemption*, on the field of battle. Habermas writes of him as follows:

> not only was he one of the first to establish links with Kierkegaard, he also took up motifs of the so-called late Idealism, especially from Schelling's last philosophy; thus he divulged the lineage of existentialist philosophy decades before it was painstakingly rediscovered by the official history of philosophy.[41]

It is not only Heidegger's existentialist philosophy, so-called, which reveals motifs derived from Schelling's late philosophy and its continuation in the work of Kierkegaard, Jaspers' philosophy does so, too. In fact, it was Jaspers who was one of the first to note the strong strain of late Schelling in Heidegger. This was no doubt mediated by Carl Braig, one of his early influences, an exponent of the Tübingen School of South German Catholic theology. Braig was the author of a book entitled *Being: A Study of Ontology*, which clearly shows that Heidegger's preoccupation with Being was simply a continuation of this neo-scholastic and romantic Idealist tradition. Löwith has touched on this in the context of his extended comparison between Heidegger and Rosenzweig. He maintains that

> the philosophy of both men becomes an 'experiencing philosophy' or an 'absolute empiricism', a philosophy of 'revelation' in Schelling's use of that phrase: each wants to reveal the reality of things, their 'positive' character that is always presupposed, but for this very reason is also mere 'existence'.[42]

Zimmerman also takes up this theme and writes that 'in Schelling, whom Heidegger regarded as the most profound of German idealists, we find many of the themes Heidegger discusses in his years at Marburg.'[43] However, in his primary masterwork Heidegger does not make any of this evident. Obviously, proclaiming a return to old Schelling would hardly have redounded to his fame as an original contemporary thinker.

There is an analogous return to Idealism in each of the malign masters. Each one of them went back to one or more of the major Idealist philosophers. Each one was also heavily influenced by one or another intermediate follower or exponent of such an Idealist thinker. I shall explore the influence of these forefathers in greater detail and depth in Chapter 5, here I merely wish to note it in passing as far as it bears on the issue of solipsistic subjectivity.

Only rarely is this reversion back to Idealism openly acknowledged; it is more often tacitly maintained or even disguised altogether. Thus there is nothing in the *Tractatus* to indicate that Wittgenstein was heavily reliant on Schopenhauer and his notorious latter-day follower Weininger. When he hinted at some of this to Frege and later to members of the Vienna Circle, they were visibly shocked. Lukács was more open about his debt to Hegel and the Young-Hegelian Marx, but not so candid about what he owed to Fichte and neo-Kantianism. This reticence still did not prevent him being denounced as an Idealist by the Bolshevik keepers of Marxist materialist orthodoxy. Only much later, towards the end of his life, does Lukács reveal the significance of Fichte for him at the time of *History and Class Consciousness*: 'subjectively, therefore, there was something revolutionary about the impulses that lay behind Fichte's philosophy of history with its definition of the present as the "age of total degradation" poised between the past and a future of which it claimed to have philosophical knowledge.'[44] Gentile alone was not embarrassed by his Idealist antecedents. As Roger Holmes states, 'Gentile draws heavily upon the dialectic of Fichte, for it is in this dialectic and the Hegelian logic for which it is responsible that he finds the answer to his logical, and finally his metaphysical, question.'[45] Gentile is also effusive in his praise for Spaventa, the Italian intermediary of German Idealism. Heidegger, too, was dependent on such an intermediary, but was not so ready to acknowledge this; in his case it was Kierkegaard, who took up where Schelling left off.

This wholesale resurgence of Idealism in its various forms explains the simultaneous attraction to a paradoxical solipsistic subjectivity among the malign masters. It is one of the most peculiar forms of subjectivity ever encountered in philosophy, surpassing even Idealism in its extremist tendencies. For it is a subjectivity that does away with the subject as Self or Ego and, thereby, declares itself to be the opposite of itself, to be at the same time completely objective. The paradoxes that this subjectless subjectivity engender play themselves out in the primary masterworks in ways that are utterly unlike each other, but the *problematic*, so to speak, of each one is very similar. It is as if each one is answering in its own philosophical language, within its specific vocabulary, to the same demand posed by the intellectual pressures of the time for a dissolution or, at least, a radical revision of the traditional subject–object distinction. This distinction was part of the Representationalist Paradigm which was the key feature of modern philosophy since the Scientific Revolution. As I have shown in my book, *A New Science of Representation*, it was the hallmark of modern culture in general since the Reformation. How this issue is dealt with is, therefore, of great consequence not only in philosophy but for modern culture as well.

The wholesale revolt against this culture and its scientific manifestations reveals itself in Lukács' treatment of the subject–object distinction. It is regarded by him as symptomatic of 'bourgeois' philosophy which he seeks to overcome in declaring the proletariat to be the 'identical subject–object of history'. His disciple, Lucien Goldmann, explains this formulation as not entailing a denial of either the subject or the object but merely the affirmation of their identity:

> The use of the concepts subject and object in *History and Class Consciousness* does not imply that Lukács supports their traditional opposition. Lukács does not abolish the existence of the subject and the object, but neither does he separate them in order to oppose them in a rigid distinction. On the contrary, on every occasion he reasserts their identity . . . Every social phenomenon is always one of interconnected praxis, consciousness, action and thought. The subject of this praxis is a collective subject, which acts in relation to the action of other collective subjects; and this subject is part of society, the object of its action, society itself being a part of the subject whose mental categories it constitutes. These categories effect its thought and action, so that the subject is the object, the object is the subject and they can neither be separated nor, with greater reason, opposed. This identity of the subject and the object, as well as the category of totality, constitutes the essence of Marx's thought for Lukács . . .[46]

Whether this complex and paradoxical formulation (for what can it mean for two things to be distinct yet identical?) is really altogether Marx or Lukács, or even partly Goldmann himself, it is not necessary to try to disentangle here. It is enough to note that it is what the latter took the former to be saying.

It is also on this basis that Goldmann goes on to liken Lukács to Heidegger, who supposedly also affirmed a version of subject–object identity:

> The fundamental problem common to Lukács and Heidegger is that of man's inseparability from meaning and from the world, that of the subject–object identity: when man understands the world, he understands the meaning of Dasein, the meaning of his being and, inversely, it is in understanding his own being that he can understand the world. The two thinkers reject, as false ontology, any philosophy which presents a theory of totality or Being based on the opposition between subject and object.[47]

Once again it is unnecessary here to question whether it is quite what Heidegger is saying or whether this is how it appears from a Lukácsian point of view. It is close enough for our purposes here, for a pupil of Heidegger, Max Müller, expresses it in similar terms: 'The figure or shape (Gestalt) that a nation (Volk) must assume is the work. And this shape must be, on the one hand, characteristic of the nation, but, on the other, the contradiction subjectivity–objectivity dissolves in it. It is our shape yet still objective shape.'[48] If one were to substitute proletariat for nation in the above, then it would closely approximate Lukács. If one were to go on and substitute Spirit for shape (Gestalt), then it would equally closely approximate Gentile.

Only Wittgenstein has no such terms, for he affirms neither class nor nation, neither shape nor Spirit, nor any other such concrete or abstract generality. Yet, nevertheless, he also implicitly asserts a variant of the subject–object identity thesis and implicitly denies any fundamental opposition between them. According to Wittgenstein, true solipsism coincides with pure realism. In asserting the truth of solipsism, Schopenhauer and his latter-day disciple Weininger are quite correct, for as the latter puts it, 'man is alone in the world, in tremendous eternal isolation . . .'[49] But so, too, is Frege, the supreme realist, for whom not only things but also numbers were objective and not to be psychologized away. Idealism and Realism are both true; in fact, they 'coincide'. McGuiness tries to explain this paradox by seeing it as a matter of 'identifying with the metaphysical subject, [yet] of seeing the world, one might say, with the objectivity and neutrality of language itself.'[50] Such valiant attempts to elucidate the paradoxes of the *Tractatus* hardly help, for ultimately they must be recognized for what they are – attempts to express a religious attitude. As Monk notes,

> the doctrine might be seen as the philosophical equivalent of the religious state of mind derided by Nietzsche, the morbid sensitivity of suffering which takes flight from reality into a merely 'inner' world, a 'real' world, an 'eternal' world. When this state of mind is made the basis of a philosophy it becomes solipsism, the view that *the* world and *my* world are one and the same.[51]

As McGuiness himself recognizes, Wittgenstein came to his views as a result of his war experiences, which made him adopt 'an attitude to the world which renounces any special position for the empirical self and attributes no value to the holding, or the bringing about, of any particular states of affairs.'[52] We shall see presently what this means for the problem of acting and ethics in Wittgenstein's *Tractatus.*

Gentile also renounces the so-called 'empirical ego' and upholds a similarly paradoxical form of a non-egoistic solipsism. As Roger Holmes puts it, 'Gentile is a solipsist . . .', but his is not the solipsism that is 'defined as that doctrine which asserts that there is no existent except the knowing subject, or Ego'.[53] Gentile opposes any such cruder form of solipsism (and, incidentally, one that is thereby made more comprehensible) for a more sophisticated form (and, therefore, one that is far less comprehensible). For Gentile, too, in some sense Idealism coincides with Realism, for the thought and the thing are one and the same. As he puts it in his own inimitable style:

> And yet, because not thinkable, the thing is thought: the thinking is the thing's very unthinkability. It is not in itself unthinkable beyond the sphere of our thinking; but we think it is not thinkable. In its unthinkability it is posited by thought, or better still, it is as unthinkable that it is posited.[54]

I would not expect anyone to think a way through that thicket of thought and thing, but merely to note that some sort of identification is being invoked. Furthermore, the pure act of thinking in itself does not presuppose any Ego or subject. The Ego comes later, as it were, as an empirical construct of such pure acts of thought. Hence, not even the death of the Ego entails a cessation of Spirit as pure act of thought. In this way Spirit is immortal.

Like Gentile's Spirit, Heidegger's *Dasein* is an impersonal subject of complete generality, it is neither a singular 'I' nor a plural 'we' but somehow indifferently both at once. Though usually in Heidegger's writings it can be taken as either singular or plural depending on the context. Like Spirit, it has no other designations of specificity, it is neither male nor female, nor in any way bodily or biologically determined, nor is it in space or time. It does not have an Ego, neither is it the seat of any kind of consciousness nor centre of perception. Given that it is non-egoistic, is it possible to show that it is also solipsistic? To show this, it is necessary to explore the relation of *Dasein* and Time, for it is this that makes for the solipsistic strain in *Being and Time.* Expounding this relation was apparently Heidegger's original point of departure. According to Thomas Sheehan, 'the original form of SZ [*Being and Time*] emerged as a 6000 word speech delivered before the Theologians' Society of Marburg under the title of "The Concept of Time"':[55]

> Heidegger poses the question of time within the arena of human existence: Could it be that I am the 'now' and that my existence itself is time? . . . It ends with a stirring list of questions which reduce from:

> What is time? to: Who is time? to: Am I *my* time? With the last question, he says, existence becomes questionable.[56]

Heidegger does not go as far as Wittgenstein and say 'I am my world', but rather something closer to 'I am my time'. However, the solipsistic import is not all that different. This is made clear in a statement he made in a work from the period of his first masterwork: 'there is no nature-time, since all time belongs essentially to *Dasein*.'[57] Later in his lectures on metaphysics, he put it even more directly and bluntly: 'strictly speaking we cannot say: There was a time when man *was* not. At all *times* man was and is and will be, because time temporalizes itself only insofar as man is.'[58] Of course, Heidegger never declares himself openly as some kind of solipsist; nor did he continue posing obviously solipsistic formulations of rhetorical, answer begging, questions. He even tended to avoid the ordinary first person pronoun 'I', preferring to couch such issues in a barrage of neologisms or ordinary terms used in a special sense of which *Dasein* is only the most common. But the simple solipsistic drift of the matter remains: Time is somehow a function of *Dasein*; and if 'all time belongs essentially to *Dasein*' then so does everything else.

One basic question still remains: does *Dasein* act, and if so, then what does it do? With that we come to the third, and final, of the metaphysical notions shared in their various ways by the primary masterworks: that of a paradoxical inactive activism. To understand what this means one needs to grasp the peculiarity that though all of these are activist philosophies in principle, in practice they render themselves inactive and impotent when it comes to real practical matters, such as are inherent in ethics, politics or economics. With the possible exception of Wittgenstein, all the other malign masters advocate some version or other of the principle that reality is constituted through activity, or what I referred to in an earlier work as the metaphysics of the Deed.[59] According to this principle of self-activated development, the subjectivistic totality that is invoked in each of these philosophies constitutes itself and its reality through its own activity, in the first place as time and history.

The obvious sources for such ideas are, of course, the Idealist philosophers, especially Hegel. Thus Lukács in his earlier writings gives a completely Hegelian rendering of Marx in precisely these terms of a metaphysics of the Deed:

> Marx . . . took over, as it stood, the greatest legacy of Hegelian philosophy: the concept of development as meaning that the mind develops homogeneously from complete lack of consciousness to a clear, ever-growing self-consciousness . . . But Marx did more than simply take

> over the Hegelian theory of development: he also modified it essentially through his critique – not, as vulgar Marxists assume, by a mere substitution of 'materialism' for 'idealism' (empty phrases), but, *on the contrary*, by deepening the Hegelian concept. The essential feature of Hegel's prodigious world system was its view of nature and history as one great homogeneous process, the essence of which is the development of its ever-clearer consciousness of itself (the Spirit).[60]

Of course, the consciousness that Lukács, following Marx, is most concerned with is class-consciousness. And within class-consciousness, true self-consciousness is 'the class-consciousness of the proletariat, developed on the basis of Marxist theory.'[61] For 'it was in the class-consciousness created by Marxism that the spirit, indeed, the very meaning of social development, emerged from its previous unconscious state.'[62]

In expounding their metaphysics of the Deed, Lukács and Gentile refer themselves not only to Hegel, but even further back to Vico as well. Both quote the Viconian dictum that '*verum et factum convertuntur*'. This Gentile translates as that 'the true is what is in the making'.[63] Lukács invokes the very same idea on the authority of Marx, without going back to its original source in Vico himself. But he also makes it the historical fulcrum on which the whole of modern philosophy turns, for he insists that knowingly or not, 'the whole of modern philosophy has been preoccupied with the problem.'[64] According to Lukács, it is a problem to which only Marxism has the solution, for only in Marxism is the constitutive subject identified as a social and historical one, class, rather than a universal and impersonal subject, as in Hegel and all previous philosophy.

Wittgenstein is the exception to any such metaphysics of the Deed mainly because, following Schopenhauer, he does not recognize the reality of time and history at all. In one of his notebooks he puts it quite baldly: 'what has history to do with me? Mine is the first and only world.'[65] There he briefly toys with the Schopenhauerian notion that the world is my Will:

> As my idea is the world, in the same way my will is the world-will. And in this sense I can speak of a will that is common to the whole world. But this will is in the highest sense my will.[66]

However, he abandons this activist train of thought in the *Tractatus* itself and adopts what one could call a 'passivist' metaphysics, expressed in the sentence 'the world is independent of my will'.[67] From being the All, as in Schopenhauer, the Will is relegated to nothing. Like the Cheshire cat's grin, the Will remains as a mere apparition after the world to which it adheres has been rendered inert. Yet something of the traces of the

Schopenhauerian world-embracing Will still remain, for Wittgenstein grants that the Will is capable of changing the world *in toto*, though not a jot within it, 'it affects the boundaries of the world, not the facts . . .'[68] What this amounts to, we shall see presently.

Instead of Deed or Will, or Spirit or any other such agent of metaphysics, it is logic which assumes in the *Tractatus* the role of 'creative' or, better put, constructive principle. Once the basic 'atomic' facts are given, all else arises through their composition by means of logical constructions. But since the world is identical to a non-egoistic Self, it follows that the logical construction of the world is the self-constitution of the Ego on the basis of logic. Logic, therefore, assumes something of the activistic role of the Deed in the other philosophies. This conception of logic Wittgenstein seems not to have derived from Hegel's dialectic, as one might expect, but from another Idealist source, the minor Schopenhauerian follower, Weininger. According to Allan Janik, in Weininger's work 'the unfathomable mystery which surrounds the "dualism of the world" and permeates its ethical and epistemological character is the result of the peculiar relation between the self and the world. It is the mystery of the self constructing the world and itself on the basis of logic.'[69] It is the very same 'mystery', so-called, that Wittgenstein expounds in the *Tractatus.* 'Logic is the linchpin of Weininger's Weltanschauung';[70] and so it is for Wittgenstein. Weininger 'comes to equate logic and ethics';[71] and so does Wittgenstein. Weininger puts it that 'logic and ethics are fundamentally the same, they are no more than duty to oneself . . . All ethics is possible only by the laws of logic, all logic is also ethical law.'[72] Wittgenstein puts it that 'ethics does not treat of the world. Ethics is a condition of the world, like logic.'[73] But an ethics that is not of this world is a peculiar ethics, indeed, for what can it mean in terms of action and the practical problems of life? I shall return to this problem presently.

Ethics is a problematic issue in all the primary masterworks, as is the whole sphere of what is traditionally called practical philosophy, which includes politics economics, law and in some respects even aesthetics. And this constitutes the nub of the third major feature that they have in common. Precisely because of their elaboration of an activist metaphysics based on Deed, Will or Logic, it is actual acting, willing or practical reasoning concerning the real problems of social and individual life that these philosophies find it next to impossible to articulate. Each issues in peculiar paradoxical formulations that seem to enjoin action, at all times with passionate intensity, and yet deny such action any practical goal or import. What emerges out of them is a peculiar kind of activist inactivity or passive activism. This, as I shall show, relates closely to their quasi-religious character as modes of secular mysticism. It is also what made the malign masters so amenable to the later blandishments of totalitarianism.

This feature of activist inactivity is very pronounced in Heidegger, and is inherent in his key notion of *Erschlossenheit* or Resolution. This concept seems to herald a highly activist philosophy committed to decision, choice and will, but its effect is self-cancelling for it is without any specification of what is to be decided, chosen or willed. It is commitment without being committed to anything specific – as it were, commitment for its own sake. What it encourages is a highly fraught state of anxiety or mood of tense waiting in preparation. For what? For anything or nothing. However, such a charged state of anxiety-laden Resolve cannot remain inert, it will tend to discharge itself into whatever external opportunity offers; and so it can easily be conducted into any cause that provides a purpose and a goal. Karl Löwith has pinpointed this feature in Heidegger, and shown how it led him and others to a totalitarian end:

> The primary attraction of his philosophical doctrine was not that it led his disciples to await a new system, but instead its thematic indeterminacy and pureness; more generally, his concentration on 'the one thing that mattered'. It was only later that many of his students understood that this 'one thing' was nothingness; a pure Resolve, whose 'aim' was undefined. One day a student invented the far from innocent joke: 'I am resolved, only towards what I don't know'. The inner nihilism, the 'national socialism' of this pure Resolve in face of nothingness, remained at first hidden beneath certain traits that suggested a religious devotion . . . in 1925 he saw spiritual substance in theology alone, and even here only in Karl Barth . . .[74]

By 1933 Heidegger saw spiritual substance in Nazism alone, and also here only in Adolf Hitler. For once this 'religious' covering was removed, once the mask of 'religious devotion' was discarded, the grimace of the Nazi death-head soon revealed itself. As Löwith goes on to note:

> One need only abandon the still quasi-religious isolation and apply [the concept of] authentic 'existence' – 'always particular to each individual' – and the 'duty' [Müssen] that follows therefrom to 'specifically German existence' and its historical destiny in order thereby to introduce into the course of general German existence the energetic but empty moment of existential categories ('to decide for oneself'; 'to take stock of oneself in the fact of nothingness'; 'wanting one's own ownmost

destiny'; 'to take responsibility for oneself') and to proceed from there to 'destruction' now on the terrain of politics.[75]

This kind of a move from pseudo-religion disguised as existentialist ethics to the politics of totalitarianism is one that all the malign masters undertook, though each in his own way.

Gentile was the earliest to provide the lead in going from a philosophy of active inactivity into the full brutality of totalitarian violence. His critics castigated him for having expounded a '*filosofia del manganello*' (a philosophy of the blackjack) the favourite weapon of Mussolini's *squadristi.* But it is not quite fair to say that his primary masterwork advocated violence; it did the opposite, since it is hard to see how real action could emerge from it at all. For according to it 'intellect itself is will',[76] so that to think is to act; 'will is the concreteness of intellect',[77] so that to act is to think. Acting is thereby identified with thinking, and all fundamental distinctions between them disappear. What the will acts on is already part of itself. The resistance to the will, such as is felt through suffering and pain, is only apparently outside the self. Moral evil is only practical error, and 'error is only error insofar as it is overcome . . .', hence error is only a stage on the way of progress. 'There is error in the system of the real insofar as the development of its process requires error as one of its own ideal moments, that is, as a position now passed and therefore discounted.'[78] If error is inevitable in the course of progress, and moral evil is only practical error, then it is easy to see how a little moral evil might be justified as the necessary price for progress. And if suffering is nothing outside the mind and it is no more than 'providential pain which spurs us on from task to task',[79] then a little violence might be just what is needed to help those who stumble on the path of progress. Thus a '*filosofia del manganello*' can be made to emerge as the conclusion to Idealist premises which dissolve action in thought and seemingly make it impossible.

Lukács seems to be different from all the other malign masters in this respect, for it is hard to see how his primary masterwork is susceptible to the charge of activist inactivity since it is based on a commitment to revolutionary action as mandated by Marxism and as put into effect by Lenin and the Party. In becoming a Bolshevik he had left behind him his earlier religious phase of mystical contemplation and ethical purity. He had, as it were, stepped closer to totalitarianism than did any of the others at the stage of their primary masterworks. But, as I shall try to show, the traces of an activist inactivity are, nevertheless, still there, despite Lukács' professions of ideological revolutionism. An activism that is quite contrary to the political realism of Marxism and to Lenin's calculating rationality is quite evident in the decisionism that Lukács espouses in this period, immediately after the failure of the revolution in Hungary, when he was advocating world revolution no matter what the objective situation or 'facts' dictated:

> Decisions, real decisions, precede the facts. To understand reality in the Marxist sense is to be master and not the slave of imminent facts. The vulgar Marxist turns helplessly from left to right; helplessly, because facts which succeed one another in isolation necessarily seem to point sometimes in the one direction and sometimes in the other, and because dialectical knowledge is needed in order to come to grips with their labyrinthine complexity. We can tell them straightaway that they will look in vain for a decision emanating from the 'facts'. A situation where the 'facts' point unambigiously and unmistakably to the revolution will never come about . . . the message of reality, meanwhile, Marxist reality, the unity of the historical process, is quite clear: the revolution is here. And every orthodox Marxist who realizes that the moment has come when capital is no longer anything but an obstacle to production, that the time has come for the expropriation of the exploiters, will respond to the vulgar-Marxist litany of 'facts' which contradict this process with the word of Fichte, one of the greatest of classical German philosophers: 'So much the worse for the facts'.[80]

But together with this highly charged activist advocacy of immediate total revolution, there are also quietistic themes of religious messianism which derive from his earlier pre-revolutionary mystical orientations. Later, towards the end of his life, he would criticize his early work and accuse himself of 'relapsing into idealistic contemplation', even while 'proclaiming a total break with every institution and mode of life stemming from the bourgeois world'.[81] This paradoxical position – which he later characterized as an 'idealistic and utopian revolutionary messianism' – is not consonant with an orthodox Marxist conception of 'praxis', and is bound to lead to dangerous results in ethics and politics, for what it is advocating is revolution as an end in itself.

The problem with Wittgenstein's primary masterwork seems the opposite to that of Lukács in that it seems to belie the possibility of any action at all and issues in pure passivity. Yet that impression is deceptive. It is true that the will is denied any efficacy *in* the world. Yet at the same time the ethical will, good or evil willing, is seen as capable of changing the world as a whole: 'it must make the world a wholly different one. The world must so to speak wax and wane as a whole.'[82] This is perhaps less paradoxical if it is recalled that the world and the Self are held to be identical and that a Schopenhauerian conception of a World-Will is being invoked. Hence, what he seems to be saying is that good and evil willing has no effect in the world of facts but it does alter the world as a solipsistic non-egoistic totality. The world of facts, as these are capable of being expressed in language, remains untouched by the ethical will; but the world as a totality which cannot be expressed in language, and must remain perforce ineffable, that world can change its ethical significance, as it were, 'waxing and waning as a whole'.

This can only be understood if it is translated into religious terms. Wittgenstein provides a logical analogue for the religious paradox that the will is powerless in the world – a quietism that is common to many mystical traditions – but at the same time he wants to affirm the possibility of salvation and damnation, that is, of supreme happiness or unhappiness, through the good or bad exercise of the ethical will. This paradox of mysticism is not, however, confronted as a religious issue but as a logical one. It is expressed in terms of the grand distinctions Wittgenstein has elaborated in his work, such as those between the facts *in* the world and the totality of the world; between that which is sayable, pertaining to the former, and that which shows itself, pertaining to the latter; between factual content and logical form; between science and value; and, ultimately, though this is not a distinction made explicitly, between the ordinary will that propels limbs and performs activities and the ethical will, the 'bearer of good and evil'.[83] In all of these distinctions real action – as this functions in time and history, or in politics and practical affairs – is nowhere in evidence. For the ethical will is given no content whatever.

Deprived of any inherent direction or goal orientation, the ethical will which Wittgenstein affirms is just as capable of lending itself to activist decisionism as to quietist passivity. It can just as easily lead to a withdrawal from worldly affairs as to an immersion in them. Wittgenstein himself in his private life took the first course and eschewed the second. However, someone else so inclined might have taken the *Tractatus* ethics in the opposite political direction. Wittgenstein came closer to doing so himself in his later, early 1930s, reflections on ethics. Waismann records the following remarks made by Wittgenstein in commenting on Schlick's book on ethics:

> Schlick says that in theological ethics there used to be two conceptions of the essence of good: according to the shallower interpretation the good is good because it is what God wants; according to the profounder interpretation God wants the good because it is good. I think that the first interpretation is the profounder one: what God commands, that is

> good. For it cuts off the way to any explanation 'why' it is good, while the second interpretation is the shallow, rationalist one, which proceeds 'as if' you could give reason for what is good.[84]

The authoritarian implications of this are expressed in the next remark made on the same day:

> 'Ought' makes sense only if there is something lending support and force to it – a power that punishes and rewards. Ought in itself is nonsensical . . . Reward and punishment. The essential thing is that the other person is brought to do something.[85]

His previous remarks on religion are of a piece with this irrationalist attitude. Religion not only has nothing to do with reasons and beliefs – 'I can well imagine a religion in which there are no doctrinal propositions' – it is, furthermore, essentially wordless or ineffable: 'when people talk, then this itself is part of a religious act not a theory. Thus it does not matter at all if the words used are true or false or nonsense.'[86] An 'ethics' based on sheer command or an ukase from some source of authority backed up with reward and punishment, that is, an 'ought' without reason, and a 'religion' that is wordless or uses words without sense – such sheer irrationalities could easily have been brought to bear on and made use of in a totalitarian politics of 'myth' and violence. Fortunately, nobody thought of doing so, as was not the case with the other primary masterworks which served a political purpose.

All in all, the primary masterworks were expressions of their time. They flashed like streaks of lightning in the turbulent skies as the supercharged intellectual currents discharged themselves in the cultural atmosphere of the revolutionary storms after the First World War. Their success was meteoric and almost instantaneous. With their revolutionary metaphysics they answered to the urgent need among intellectuals for revolutionary thought. Their expectant millennarian hopes made for faiths with no fixed doctrinal content, but with a burning urgency for self immersion in something greater than the Self to the point of self-immolation. Hence the philosophical tendency to a metaphysics of totality, non-egoistic solipsism and inactive activism such as characterize the primary masterworks. For among philosophically minded intellectuals there was an inclination to conceive of a higher Whole or Totality into which the threatened individual Ego could be absorbed and so find safety. A suicidal desire to sacrifice the Self for the Whole became paramount, a need for a *sacrificio intellectualis* such as was exemplified by the religious mystics of the past, or so they thought. In the cruder realities of political ideology in the twentieth century, such impulses among intellectuals led to the self-sacrifice of the intelligentsia on the altar of totalitarian tyranny at the behest of the great dictators. In this way the primary masterworks can be taken as among the finest intellectual instruments of suicide of the philosophically minded intelligentsia as a whole.

With such works behind them, it is little wonder that the malign masters went from totality to totalitarianism. They were drawn to the then nascent totalitarian movements and their charismatic leaders, the future great dictators, like moths to a flame. The absence of any determinate ethical or political content in their '*filosofia teologizzante*' created a vacuum which the totalitarian ideologies were all too apt to fill. All of them read these ideologies in religious terms. Thus for Lukács Bolshevism was a religious movement of 'spiritual' revival rivalling historical Christianity. For Gentile Fascism was a 'totalitarian religious spirit'.[87] Heidegger saw Nazism as a religious movement of salvation from the nihilistic currents of Western rationality and technology. Even Wittgenstein was drawn to Soviet communism because he regarded it as a new 'way of life', a religious and moral passion of which only the uncorrupted Russian 'soul' was capable.

This move from totality to totalitarianism was not, however, logically inevitable. It required the pressures of real political forces, the inducements and attractions of totalitarian blandishments, to bring it about. The abstract totalities of the primary masterworks only contain totalitarianism latently as one of their potentialities. To give it an actual realization and open expression required a period of transition or Turning, which each of the malign masters in fact went through on his way to one or another of the totalitarian ideologies. But these works of themselves did not compel this move; they could, in principle, have led elsewhere. This is even true of Lukács, despite the fact that he was already a committed Bolshevik when he wrote his primary masterwork, for even that work is only implicitly totalitarian, or, better put, it is capable of accommodating the Stalinist totalitarianism to come, as Lee Congdon explains:

> To begin with, *History and Class Consciousness* is not a work of philosophy; it is a *dogmatics* invulnerable to external criticism or argument. No evidence can in principle be adduced to disprove the dogma, which is internally consistent and self-certifying. Second, the book champions a dialectic that is capable of justifying *any* deed, no matter how monstrous, for as Lukács demonstrates, no one armed with a proper 'dialectical' method can ever be put to rout, because any inconvenient circumstance or argument can be declared its opposite. Finally, the book constitutes a blueprint for tyranny. Once condeded that there exists an

> ideal class consciousness independent of historical experience, one is led, step by step, to defend the absolute power of gnostic visionaries.[88]

Suitably adjusted to account for their quite different 'philosophies', this overall conclusion applies to each of the primary masterworks. Each could be transformed into a 'blueprint for tyranny', but it required external events, which as yet were merely in the offing when these books were written, to bring this about.

These events culminated in the rapid slide into totalitarianism that took place from around 1928 till 1934. This was the period when all of the malign masters went through simultaneously, as though synchronized on cue, their so-called Turning or *Kehre*. Intellectually considered, this involved a partial turning against their primary masterworks and a turning towards a new mode of thought that would eventually result in their secondary masterworks. This is the transition from the so-called 'young' to the 'old' philosophies of the malign masters. However, to consider the Turning purely intellectually, as most commentators have so far done for each malign master separately, is to fail to see what they all have in common and what it is that they are responding to which is not in the realm of pure intellect alone. It is to fail to note the real socio-logical pressures that predisposed them all to their *Kehre* at the same time.

2 The Turning (*Kehre*)

The Turning is the period of transition from totality to totalitarianism. It is a complex process involving many internally differentiated stages. It typically begins with an enthusiastic adhesion to a totalitarian ideology and ends in considerable disappointment and disillusionment, but this does not result in outright rejection. To the contrary, the invariable outcome is the attempt to conceive of an ideal, 'philosophical', version of the specific totalitarianism, free of the errors and distortions of the actual regime and the 'mistakes' of its leader – a sublimated image of what it might or ought to become. This idealization – which one might consider a kind of 'private' totalitarianism – is the background to the secondary masterworks following the Turning.

Intellectually considered, the Turning is the process of rethinking that mediates between the primary and secondary masterworks. It manifests a mixture of ideas and themes from both, some harking back to the earlier stage and some heralding the later one in a somewhat confused way. In retrospect the malign masters tended to view this confusion as a process of correction and rectification through which they freed themselves from the supposed 'errors' of the past and began to attain the 'correct' views supposedly contained in their secondary masterworks. But that, as I shall show, is no better than a self-justification which amounts to little more than wishful thinking. For the secondary masterworks are not on par with the primary ones, they evince a decline in intellectual and imaginative powers, as evidenced by the fact that they are generally fragmentary, scattered and often unfinished. The times in which they were produced and their authors' involvements with totalitarianism were hardly conducive to calm philosophical contemplation.

In saying this I am not making a purely psychological observation. The Turning undergone by each of the malign masters individually was not a process that just happened to coincide in all them at the same time. It was as much a common and general reaction to public and political events as the primary masterworks had been in their time. But just as the primary masterworks were quite distinct and unique works, so, too, the *Kehre* undergone by each of the malign masters was characteristically different – as it were, an individual response to a common question posed by the times.

The Turning took place at a time of precipitous decline in European and world history in general. It was when the Great Depression raged in the capitalist West, when many countries turned to dictatorship and a few began external military forays. It was also the time when the revolutionary regimes and movements began their transformations into totalitarianism. In Italy the parliamentary dictatorship of Mussolini began its step-by-step transition into a totalitarian regime. In the Soviet Union Stalin was consolidating his power and embarking on his gigantic programmes of collectivization and industrialization, which soon thereafter would issue in the purges and the Gulag concentration camps. In Germany Hitler was rapidly gathering support from the alienated and desperate, which by 1933 he was able to convert into absolute power, with similar predispositions to terror, and to begin the rearmament programme that almost inevitably led to the Second World War. With such policies the new totalitarian powers were successful in overcoming, or at least tempering, the economic Depression which everywhere else engendered mass unemployment and the kinds of frustration that led to the discrediting of the liberal-democratic, capitalist regimes and the humanist 'bourgeois' culture that upheld these. Intellectuals in particular were prone to grasp at radical solutions, the more extreme the better. The malign masters followed these tendencies in their philosophical turnings.

This period of the late 1920s and early 1930s was a critical time for European culture in general, for it also embarked on a kind of turning away from its history and traditions towards extremist alternatives, initiating a process of cultural disintegration which has still not come to an end. As I showed in my book *A New Science of Representation*, the fate of the Weimar Republic in Germany was paradigmatic for what was to take place in Europe as a whole.[1] Fierce ideological conflicts in politics spilled over into all other dimensions, into the sciences, the arts and philosophy. Everywhere there took place battles between Modernists and anti-Modernists of various colourings. This occurred even in such seemingly abstract and abstruse fields as mathematics and theoretical physics. Each of the malign masters tended to take an anti-Modernist stance of one or another kind depending on the totalitarianism to which he was drawn.

It is little wonder that their philosophies were deeply affected by the conditions of the time, as were those of most other thinkers as well. Under the instigation of these politically fraught changes, each one began a process of revision in his philosophy which might loosely be called a move from totality to totalitarianism. Each was more or less self-consciously aware of doing so. In the process, some, such as Wittgenstein and Lukács, turned almost completely against their earlier work, their primary masterworks, whilst the others not to that extent, Heidegger less so and Gentile almost not at all.

I shall consider Gentile's *Kehre* first because he was the earliest to undertake such a turning, doing so quite self-consciously but very gradually, so much so that he refused to admit that any significant change had even occurred. He thought he was simply applying his earlier philosophy, Actual Idealism, to the new political realities of Fascism. In fact, he thought of this as only a necessary 'logical' progression from totality to totalitarianism. The latter term is, in fact, his neologism, occuring first in such of his phrases as 'the totalitarian spirit of Fascism'. He must, therefore, be granted precedence as the first theorist of totalitarianism. However, despite his own insistence that in doing so he was being completely consistent with his earlier philosophy, scholars such as Harris have recognized that he was subtly changing his philosophy to suit his politics. As a result he devised a specifically Fascist variant of Actual Idealism, which is his late philosophy.

This happened some years after he first became a devoted follower of Mussolini and a member of his first cabinet. He worked out his Fascist philosophy in a series of writings during the period of the late 1920s and early 1930s collected in *The Origins and Doctrine of Fascism*, the work in which he first sought to specify the totalitarian nature of the Fascist State. In this period he was working under the pressure of actual political events, for it was then, and not when he first seized power, that Mussolini and his Party began to consolidate total dictatorial power and to institutionally shape the regime along totalitarian lines. The fact that this occurred more in theory than in practice, that is, more as lofty pronouncements than in actual policy decisions, is due to the peculiar non-authoritarian character of the State in Italy where there were countervailing powers such as the Church, Monarchy and Army which the Fascists never captured. Gentile was sorely disappointed with Mussolini for compromising with the Church; and he might have been ready to proceed further into actual totalitarianism than Mussolini ever contemplated doing, except for the very end, during the so-called Salo Republic in 1944, when he did so under Hitler's instigation, and with Gentile's renewed support.

In 1923 Gentile began his political career as an Idealist philosopher who happened to become a Fascist; by the early 1930s he had ended up as a Fascist who happened to be an Idealist philosopher. In his own words, he had become the 'philosopher of Fascism'. That is a measure of the Turning that he had undergone. Some of the main initiating premisses of his later totalitarian philosophy were already there in his earlier Actual Idealism, but the Fascist conclusions he drew from them required an extensive transition in ideas, a dialectical movement of thought from totality to totalitarianism, as he himself put it. What was there to begin with was a theory of the Ethical State, derived from Hegel but going much further in hypostatizing the State than Hegel ever intended. For Gentile endows his Ethical State with a religious character, because, as Harris summarizes his argument, 'no man can give his allegiance to its institutions or representatives unless he has a religious sense of its law as an absolute limit on his own will.'[2] The Ethical State thereby becomes identified with individual conscience: 'The State, as we know, has its transcendental ground in the relation of the individual and his conscience.'[3] Croce castigated this as a 'governmental conception of morality', and correctly divined where it would lead:

> When morality is conceived as the 'ethical State', and this is identified with the political State or just 'the State', the idea gains ground (and the theorists of the school do not shun formulating it) that concrete morality resides in the governors, in their act of governing, and that their opponents are to be considered foes to the moral Act, meriting not merely punishment according to or exceeding the rigour of the law (as is or may seem reasonable) but also a lofty moral condemnation.[4]

Starting from the basis of this Idealist theory of the Ethical State, Gentile went on to formulate a Fascist theory of the Corporate State. The former was still compatible with a kind of authoritarian liberalism, which Gentile referred back to Mazzini; the latter assumed the full panoply of an all-inclusive power to which he gave the name 'totalitarian' and referred it to the Fascist regime that Mussolini was in the process of establishing. He tried to present the latter as simply a continuation of and realization of the ideals of the former. Thus, as Harris puts it, 'the Fascist Corporate State represented, in his eyes, a closer approach to the democratic ideal than the system of liberal parliamentary government, because parliamentary government belonged to an era in which political rights were the prerogative of a minority who had been educated in the humanism of the classical tradition',[5] whereas Fascism was more democratic because it included everyone in the nation. This kind of double-speak comes into prominence in Gentile's Fascist period for he was simply following Mussolini and the changing dictates of the Party and trying as best he could to justify it intellectually in terms of his philosophy. His philosophy of expressive totality – where every part reflects the whole and where the whole anticipates every part – was well suited to justifying whatever was actually the case. It lacked any capacity for critical distancing, as Croce was perceptive enough to see. But it was no longer the same philosophy as his initial Actual Idealism, in the course of adjusting itself to the Fascist reality it became an ideological world-view. This change is the import of Gentile's *Kehre.*

Lukács' Turning took a very similar course. He, too, had to adjust his thought to the changing reality of Stalin's rise to power and transformation of the initial Leninist dictatorship into a fully-fledged totalitarian state system. Lukács also became very proficient in adapting his initial philosophy of an expressive totality to every totalitarian requirement of the Party at Stalin's behest. Unlike Gentile, who was not excessively pressured or intimidated, Lukács was required to abjure formally his earlier philosophy and to disown his primary masterwork. But that philosophy itself gave him the intellectual justification for doing so – he was most true to his philosophy when he rejected it because the Party told him to do so. For according to it, the Party was the sole standard of validity and truth. In this way, as Kolakowski sees it, Lukács was one of the earliest practitioners of double-think:

> Leninist-Stalinist Marxism expressly justified, at least to a certain extent, the curious epistemology of this apparently impossible phenomenon – sincere mendaciousness. Lukács, among others, was its codifier.[6]

Tom Rockmore maintains that this practice of double-think continued to operate throughout Lukács' life, for once 'he accepted Stalin's view as an intellectual guide' during his *Kehre* he never thereafter completely ceased to do so. 'His servile orthodoxy is apparent even in the philosophical insights he generously attributes to Stalin well after the dictator's death . . . when Lukács had personally nothing to fear.'[7] Seen on the crude political level, Lukács *Kehre* was simply the process whereby he became a Stalinist. And even though he never used the term totalitarian, and denounced all mention of the word with great zeal, he came to condone a far worse form of it than Gentile ever intended. He never ceased to do so, despite his later rejection of Stalinism, to the end of his life. In an interview just before his death, he haughtily declared that 'I have always thought that the worst form of socialism was better to live in than the best form of capitalism';[8] namely, Stalin's Russia was better than, say, social-democratic Sweden. It is, therefore, no surprise to learn that according to Lukács, even at this late stage, 'one must distinguish between "hateful" and "excusable" Gulags'.[9] Presumably Stalin's were the latter. The purges, too, receive some justification. In fact, every policy that Stalin carried out, though not always completely approved of, is always to some extent justified and seen as having also a positive side to it. Little wonder that the wife of Karl Polanyi, Duczynska, both friends of the young Lukács, held that his 'arrogant glorification of evil [was] unprecedented in Western thought.'[10] In him the merely malign at times became fully malignant.

It is evident from this that the Turning, which occurred during the late 1920s and early 1930s, is far more momentous a change, intellectually considered, than his earlier conversion to Bolshevism. As most commentators note, the latter was not a completely abrupt break in his thinking but an extension of it in an extreme political direction: 'his leftism is but the political continuation of his earlier ethical rigorism, the legitimate offspring of his tragic view of the world,' as Michael Löwy puts it.[11] Lee Congdon too stresses that in choosing 'bolshevism and revolution' Lukács was consistent with the choice he had made as early as 1911, when

> he aligned himself with the heretical tradition that stretched back to Jewish apocalyptic writings and the New Testament Apocalypse . . . [with] those who had come to hate the world *as it is* . . . [advocating] the perennial heresy, the belief that heaven, understood as the reign of perfect justice, could be established on earth.[12]

For someone who had begun as an ethical rigorist, given to messianic revolutionary moralism, becoming a servile Stalinist was much more of a change than merely becoming a Bolshevik. How was it possible and how did it happen?

Two key political events served to make Lukács a Stalinist. The first, as I have already mentioned, was the Blum Theses débâcle of 1928–9, when he abjectly had to undergo a process of 'self-criticism' and fall into line with Stalin's new aggressive policy of total non-cooperation with, nay, total opposition to Social Democrats, now renamed 'social fascists'. This, as he declared later in his Introduction to the new edition of *History and Class Consciousness* of 1967, 'changed the whole direction of my later development'.[13] The second major event in Lukács' *Kehre* occurred when he took Stalin's side in the so-called 'philosophy debate' in Moscow in 1930. Stalin initiated a wholesale attack on Avram Deborin and his school. The purpose of this, as Lukács admits in 1971, 'was only to establish Stalin's pre-eminence as a philosopher'.[14] Elsewhere, however, he avows that this played a 'positive role' on his intellectual development:

> Stalin defended an extremely important point of view which played a positive role in my development . . . The way I interpreted Stalin's critique of Plekhanov's orthodoxy was to see it as a view which rejected the idea that Marxism was just one socio-economic theory among others. Instead Stalin saw it as a totalizing world view. This implied that it must also contain a Marxist aesthetic which did not have to be

borrowed from Kant or anyone else. These were ideas which were further developed by Lipshitz and myself.[15]

This 'totalizing world-view' or, in effect, totalitarian ideology, which Lukács had supposedly learned from Stalin, became the mainstay of his later philosophy. It was continuous with, but at the same time different from, his earlier Idealist-Marxist concept of 'totality'. The earlier 'totality' was an intellectual principle of some metaphysical sublety; it was based on the conception of an 'expressive whole' which another kind of Stalinist, Althusser, later quite correctly criticized,[16] but which, nevertheless, allowed considerable scope in interpreting specific social phenomena in relation to society as a whole. His later 'totalizing world-view' had all the marks of a full-blown ideology that supposedly gave answers to all questions. From it emerged the 'Marxist aesthetic' that he no longer had to 'borrow from Kant or anyone else', as well as the critique of Reason, which also bore no relation to Kant's. Lukács' secondary masterwork, *The Destruction of Reason*, began in this period, was a 'critique' of all modern philosophy fully in keeping with his 'totalizing world view'. To what extent it also amounted to a 'destruction of Lukács' reason', as Adorno quipped, I shall leave for later consideration.

But whatever demonstrable effect it had on his reason, it certainly blunted his capacity to do philosophy. For to a considerable extent Lukács' *Kehre* was also a turning away from philosophy – which had become too dangerous after Stalin had asserted his pre-eminence as a philosopher – and a move to literary criticism and aesthetics. But in that capacity, too, Lukács faithfully served Stalin and the Party line, albeit with greater intelligence and cultivation than the other literary hacks. He even attacked avowed communist authors, such as Brecht, who failed completely to heed the latest anti-Modernist aesthetic directives from Moscow. Lukács unerringly complied in enforcing the 'socialist realism' line in Germany before the war (he had been expressly sent to Berlin in the early 1930s especially to do so) and in Hungary, East Germany and throughout the Soviet bloc after the war. As far as matters of German literature were concerned, during this period 'cultural power in Moscow and in the Soviet Zone of Germany often seemed to be wholly in the hands of Georg Lukács, Alfred Kurela and Walter Ulbricht',[17] as John Fuegi, a biographer of Brecht, remarks. Thus another effect of his *Kehre* was his installation as watchdog of aesthetic propriety of German communist literature, a role that was hardly conducive to philosophy or to rational thought in general.

Heidegger's *Kehre*, for that was what he later called it, began almost simultaneously with Lukács', starting with the rushed completion and publication of his primary masterwork *Being and Time* in 1927. In the next year he had gained Husserl's Chair at Freiburg and so attained his own academic and, by implication, also political independence. He then began a dual turning towards Hitler and the Nazis on the political front and towards Nietzsche and his contemporary exponents, such as Spengler, Klages and Jünger, on the intellectual front. But these two fronts were really only two faces of the same totalitarian coin. For Spengler, Klages and Jünger were among the extreme Right precursors of Nazism, and Nietzsche was the acknowledged forefather of the movement, recognized as such by Hitler himself. Thus Heidegger's *Kehre* was a turning to totalitarian Nazism in its two aspects of theory and practice personified by the figures of Nietzsche and Hitler.

However, unlike Lukács, who implied that he had learned from Stalin how to understand Marx, Heidegger would have been too proud to admit that he could have learned from Hitler how to understand Nietzsche. On the contrary, he had hopes that Hitler would learn from him a more authentic interpretation of Nietzsche than the one which had thus far inspired him. As he put it in a lecture of 1936, 'the two men who have led a counter-movement against nihilism, each in different ways, Mussolini and Hitler, have both learned from Nietzsche, both essentially differently. But the authentic metaphysical domain of Nietzsche has not come to validity thereby.'[18] This 'authentic metaphysical domain of Nietzsche' is something that Heidegger thought he alone was capable of providing. Thereby, he believed, he could endow Hitler and the Nazi movement in general with the philosophy it needed to fully realise itself as the most valid 'counter-movement against Nihilism', and so become the saving force of the West that it promised to be. He thought he knew better how the Nazi ideology ought to be articulated than the official ideologists and the other Nazi interpreters of Nietzsche, such as Kriek and Bäumler. This implicit claim to philosophical superiority brought him to some degree of internal conflict within the Nazi movement which he later tried to represent as evidence of disapproval or even punishment for his supposed criticism of Nazism. But all it indicates is that he tried to concoct for himself a kind of 'private Nazism' – which is the gravamen of the charges levelled against him by the official Nazi ideologists.

The same is true of his supposed confrontation with Nietzsche and his claim to have criticized and surpassed him. As I shall show in the next chapter, Heidegger's so-called 'criticism of Nietzsche' is really an absorption and internal adjustment, an acceptance of what Nietzsche puts forward, but translated into different terms, Heidegger's own terms. 'Surpassing Nietzsche' also means placing himself in relation to Nietzsche as his sole heir and successor. Thus Nietzsche is presented as the last of the metaphysicians, the culminating figure in the history of Western philosophy, and Heidegger himself appears as the first of the post-metaphysicians, the only thinker of Thought. Even this degree of difference only made itself manifest late in his voluminous lecture series on Nietzsche which constitutes his secondary masterwork. It is of a piece with his so-called 'criticism' of Nazism and, by implication, of Hitler himself.

To begin with, at the start of his *Kehre*, Heidegger completely and uncritically embraced Hitler and Nietzsche together. He declares his belief in force and power (*Kraft und Macht*) as early as his 1929–30 lectures on *Die Grundbegriffe der Metaphysic*, lashing out at his humanistically minded contemporaries he states, 'we believe it is no longer necessary in the fundament of our being to be strong . . . We concern ourselves only with acquired talents and skills, however, force and power can never be replaced by the accumulation of competencies.'[19] Force and power – to which he later also added struggle (*Kampf*), storm, work and other Nazi sanctioned terms – became the key themes of his *Rektoratrede*, the climactic moment of his *Kehre*, and the other speeches of the period in which Nietzsche and philosophy and Hitler and ideology are completely merged. He so fused and confused his terms that, as Löwith comments sarcastically, it was not clear to his hearers whether they ought to begin reading the pre-Socratics or to join the SA. Heidegger had become an expert in double-think and the double-talk that went with it, a master of equivocation.

During the course of his *Kehre* Heidegger began the process of elaborating a contorted eschatology of history based on the vicissitudes of Being, a *Heilsgeschichte* drawn largely from Nietzsche but with some input from Hölderlin and other poetic mythologues. This he continued to do throughout his life. I shall examine it in more detail in the next chapter, however, a few indications of its critical steps are in order here since they belong to his *Kehre*. The main change that had occurred was that Being became the main agent of history rather than *Dasein*, which was the active totality of his earlier work. Like a *deus absconditus* Being concealed and revealed itself in a series of epiphanies that constituted the essence of true history. Thus the nihilism that Nietzsche mooted became for Heidegger a self-occlusion of Being giving rise to an age of technology. The only way out of this nihilism is through a recall of Being which can only take place in German through the German nation, the only extant metaphysical people. According to this eschatological schema the Nazi movement under the leadership of Hitler assumes a providential role in this confrontation with nihilistic technology. To himself, as the sole contemporary thinker of Being, he assigns an equally providential part, which he leaves largely implicit as he was perhaps too modest to spell it out in full. However, as he did speak of himself as the 'shepherd of Being', and as, according to his philosophy of language, this was only possible because he spoke in German, *ergo*, we might see him assuming the role of the German shepherd of Being.

As the watchdog of language, which is the House of Being, Heidegger began to elaborate a new surrogate religion during his *Kehre*, which he continued to do throughout his life. He had turned away from Existentialist theology and moved to neo-pagan mythology in keeping with Nazism seen as a religion. This received various subsequent formulations of which the most explicit is contained in his posthumously published manuscript *Beiträge zur Philosophie.* Here I shall consider its initial stage only which is a mystical conception of primal origination revolving around a quartet of terms: Being, Time, Language and *Dasein* (Man). These, according to Heidegger, are not mere concepts or categories, and he explicitly states that Being has a different kind of meaning than any other word.[20] Obviously, they are symbolic notions that cannot be analysed, rationally discussed or questioned, despite Heidegger's fondness for putting things to the question.

What Heidegger elaborates is a kind of theogony, a myth of the origination of things. At first it seems that Being, the supreme notion, should come first in order of precedence, but on closer examination it soon reveals itself that it is as dependent on the others as they are on it – they circle around each other in a dance of mutual involvement. Hence, in a way, all these 'gods' are equally primordial. First we are told that without Being or, more specifically, the 'meaning of Being', there would be no language: 'let us suppose that this interminate meaning of being does not exist and that we do not understand what this meaning means . . . There would be no language at all.'[21] Next we are told that if there were no language there would be no Man (*Dasein*), for Man is human 'because in his essence he is a speaker, *the* speaker'.[22] But if there were no Man there would also be no Time for

> strictly speaking we cannot say: There was a time when Man was not. At all *times* Man was and is and will be, because time produces itself only insofar as Man is. There is no time when Man was not, not because Man was from all eternity and will be for all eternity but because time is not eternity and time fashions itself into a time only as a human, historical being-there [*Dasein*].[23]

Obviously the facts of evolution matter little to Heidegger, as does any anthropological science of Man or history.

But just as Language, Man and Time depend on each other and all ultimately on Being, so, conversely, does Being depend on them. It is not only that if there were no Language, Man and Time there would be no 'meaning of Being', but also if there were no 'meaning of Being' there would be no things in being and no Being itself. Existing things, such as are in being (or essents as the German *Seiende* is technically translated), are so only when they are disclosed in words and through our understanding of meaning, 'for the much-vaunted particular essent can only disclose itself as such insofar as we already understand being in *its* essence.'[24] Later in Heidegger this insight is expressed more 'poetically' and so allegedly more profoundly:

> Language is the precinct (*templum*), that is, the house of Being. The nature of language does not exhaust itself in signifying, nor is it merely something that has the character of a sign or cypher. It is because language is the house of Being, that we reach *what is* by constantly going through this house. When we go to the well, when we go through the woods, we are always already going through the word 'well', through the word 'woods', even when we do not speak the words and do not think of anything in relation to language.[25]

Or as he puts it more succinctly elsewhere: 'the being of anything that is resides in the word. Therefore this statement holds true: Language is the house of Being.'[26] In some ineffable sense, therefore, things depend on words – things themselves, not merely the 'meanings' of things or their symbolic significations. Thus in explicating the last line from Stephan George's poem 'The Word', 'Where word breaks off no thing may be', Heidegger explains the relation between words and things in general as follows:

> here the relation between thing and word comes to light, and further, that thing here means anything that in any way has being, any being as such. About the 'word' we also said that it not only stands in a relation to the thing, but that the word is what first brings that given thing, as the being that is, into this 'is', that the word is what holds the thing there and relates it and so to speak provides its maintenance with which to be a thing.[27]

Or, as he puts it more poetically, 'no thing is where the word breaks off'.[28]

According to Heidegger, then, both beings and Being somehow or other depend on Language. But this Language is 'not a mere human faculty',[29] but the deliverance of Being itself. It is the favour that Being itself grants to Man (*Dasein*) in order that Being can in turn make itself manifest through Man, that is, through Man's raising of the question of the 'meaning of Being' and so initiating original thinking and thanking at once (pun intended):

> Original thanking is the echo of Being's favour wherein it clears a space for itself and causes the unique occurrence: that what-is is. This echo is man's answer to the Word of the soundless voice of Being. The speechless answer of his thanking through sacrifice is the source of the human word, which is the prime cause of language as the enunciation of the Word in words.[30]

To explain what he calls Language Heidegger offers a peculiar version of Christian theology, of the enunciation of the Word (Logos or the Christ) in words (mundane speech). Obviously, he is not interested in any naturalistic explanation for the origin of language since only a theological cause will do: Language is the incarnation of the speechless Word of Being in words given to Man. This is not only the source of Language but it is also the original Event (*Ereignis*) that brings Time into being as well, for before Man and Language there was no Time and there were no things. Being temporalizes itself in this unique occurrence that gives rise to Time. But, conversely, Time, by permitting a temporalization of Being, gives rise to Being itself. Thus Being, Time, Language and Man are all interdependent.

It is pointless trying to unravel the countless involutions and convolutions of the varied Heideggerian expositions of the mutual interrelationships in his theogony of Being, Time, Language and Man. This fourfold is not, however, a quartet of separate gods, such as the Hindu trinity of Brahma, Shiva and Vishnu, but more like the Christian hypostasis of the one God with three natures, Father, Son and Holy Ghost. Being plays a role analogous to God the Father; however, it has become a *deus absconditus* distinct from but not transcendent to the beings which depend on it – there is an ontological difference separating them, but no division. Language as the Word is like the Son, the Logos incarnate in mere human words and in temporal life. Time is like the Holy Ghost spiritually informing everything with its presence – though here the analogy is not so exact. Man or *Dasein* is fallen humanity that has to be saved by thinking or 'thanking through sacrifice', as he puts it. The fourfold has an origin, but not in time, since Time itself originates thereby. This supreme Origin is the Event (*Ereignis*) wherein Being 'clears a space for itself and causes the unique occurrence: that what-is is'.[31] The Origin is thus more than God's creation of the world in Christian theology, it is, as it were, the self-creation and instantiation of the whole fourfold at once through a kind of mutual self-begetting.

Apart from this primordial mystical origination in the Event, which is outside time, Being has, so to speak, a second origin in human history as well, at the dawn of the West when the Greek thinkers first inquired into the 'meaning of Being'. At this point of his hermeneutics of Being Heidegger does venture some historical assertions, but these are not open to correction for they consist mainly in interpretations of the illusive fragments from the pre-Socratics, above all Parmenides and Heraklitus. According to Heidegger, Heraklitus 'says the same as Parmenides. He would not be one of the greatest of the Greeks if he had said something different.'[32] The early thinkers can no more differ from each other than the Evangelists. But the Evangelists were eye-witnesses to a Revelation, but what was it that gave the early thinkers such a unanimous access to the truth of Being? All Heidegger can say in answering this further historical question is to launch into his peculiar version of the etymology of the different verbs signifying 'to be' in the Indo-Aryan languages, above all in Greek, Sanskrit and German, with the occasional reference to Latin as well. From these studies into the supposed *Urgrund* of the meaning of the word 'being', 'we derive the three initial concrete meanings: to live, to emerge, to linger or endure'.[33] It can hardly come as a surprise that these meanings had already been found to be inherent in the basic concepts of early Greek philosophy, in *physis* and *ousia.* This last term Heidegger interprets as *parousia*, the usual New Testament expression for the Revelation, which is thereby projected backwards to the early Greek philosophers. These meanings of 'being' have remained permanently fixed ever since, and they are the secret source of the 'hidden history' of the West:

> Accordingly, 'being' has the meaning indicated above, recalling the Greek view of the essence of being, hence a determinateness which has not just dropped on us accidentally from somewhere but has dominated our historical being there (Dasein) since antiquity. At one stroke our search for the definition of the meaning of the word 'being' becomes explicitly what it is, namely, a reflection on the source of our hidden history.[34]

So it is thanks to the Indo-Aryan system of conjugations that the Greeks owe their philosophy, and all the history of the West, indeed, of the world ever since, is determined by it. As the coming of Jesus is foretold by the prophets, so is the coming of Being prefigured in the Indo-Aryan verb formations. The Nazis ascribed everything good in history to an original pure Indo-Aryan race; Heidegger improved on that formulation: everything in history originates from the purity of Indo-Aryan words. Hence if Being revealed itself first in Greek, it can only be 'repeated' and so come back again in German. Between these two chosen languages there stretches the nihilistic hiatus of inferior languages through which fallen Being had to pass in the foreordained eschatology of *Seinsgeschichte*. I shall examine this in detail in the next chapter.

Heidegger's 'philosophy of language' is thus a racist mythology of grammar that parallels Nazi racist ideology. It is the basis of the 'hidden history' of the West, just as in Nazi ideology race is the key to history. The common source of these ideas both for Heidegger and the Nazis is to be found in Nietzsche. In the next chapter I shall examine Heidegger's variant of Nietzsche's mythology which constitutes his secondary masterwork, for that takes us beyond the period of his *Kehre*.

Wittgenstein's Turning cannot be treated politically as easily as that of the others, for he was not actively involved in any totalitarian movement. However, the rise of totalitarianism during the period of his *Kehre* was not the mere coincidence that his pupils and followers make out. Wittgenstein was not a political thinker, far from it, from all accounts he was politically naive, and he has next to nothing of interest to say about the major political events of his time. Nevertheless, these events, as Nyiri contends, must be considered a major factor in Wittgenstein's *Kehre*:

> It appears that Wittgenstein's return to philosophy, and the emergence of his later mode of thinking, must be regarded in a broader historical context, the context of the heyday and collapse of Austrian and German neo-conservatism between 1927 and 1933. The economic and political causes of the relevant development – the economic crisis, beginning in 1929 and culminating in 1931, and the political defeat of the German neo-conservatives with Hitler's rise to power – can only be mentioned here.[35]

Though Wittgenstein never discusses such things, it can be deduced that he was strongly influenced by them, perhaps even more than he was himself aware, or willing to acknowledge. Thus his biographer Ray Monk reports that it was no doubt the Nazi rise to public prominence and eventual power in Germany during the early 1930s that released in Wittgenstein a sympathetic outburst of virulent anti-Semitism, one that fell little short of Hitler's racial ideology:

> Many of Hitler's most outrageous suggestions – his characterization of the Jew as a parasite 'who like a noxious bacillus keeps spreading as soon as a favourable medium invites him', his claim that the Jews' contribution to culture has been entirely derivative, that 'the Jew lacks those qualities which distinguish the races that are creative and hence

> culturally blessed', and, furthermore, that this contribution has been restricted to an *intellectual* refinement of another's culture ('since the Jew . . . was never in possession of a culture of his own, the foundations of his intellectual work were always provided by others') – this whole litany of lamentable nonsense finds parallels in Wittgenstein's remarks of 1931. Were they not written by Wittgenstein, many of his pronouncements on the nature of Jews would be understood as nothing more than the rantings of a fascist anti-Semite.[36]

Why the name Wittgenstein should absolve these 'rantings of a fascist anti-Semite' from being in fact taken as the rantings of a fascist anti-Semite is hard to fathom, unless a misguided sense of loyalty blinds one to the obvious. Remember, of course, that it was not the Italian Fascists, but the German Nazis who were the anti-Semites. It is true that Wittgenstein made no public profession of his anti-Semitism. All his anti-Semitic remarks he consigned to the privacy of his notebooks, suitably disguised in code. It might not have done his career at Cambridge any good to have said any of this aloud especially among his communist friends. However, one cannot but wonder what effect such secretive thoughts on race had for his philosophical thinking in this crucial period of his *Kehre*. We know from the work of Schopenhauer and Weininger, who influenced him, that such anti-Semitism cannot be regarded as a personal quirk separable from a general philosophical outlook. Indeed, Wittgenstein's anti-Semitism emerges very clearly in his self-hating view of himself and his own analytic philosophy as no more than 'reproductive', like the Jewish 'pseudo-science' of Freud, psychoanalysis; and most likely also in his hostility to the new transfinite mathematics of set-theory and mathematical formalism founded by the Jew Cantor and pursued by so many other Jews, such as those members of the Vienna Circle whom he particularly disliked (I shall argue this in greater detail in a forthcoming paper).

However, unlike Heidegger, Wittgenstein could not have become a Nazi since he considered himself 'racially' a Jew. But at the start of his *Kehre* he was a right-wing revolutionary-conservative anti-modernist, heavily influenced by Spengler, as he himself admits, and possibly also by Austrian neo-conservatives of the 1920s, as Nyiri argues. Nyiri maintains that this influence played a part in predisposing him towards certain intellectual themes in his philosophy that first came to prominence during his *Kehre*, themes such as 'following a rule', conforming to a tradition and subscribing to collective authority:

> That one must 'recognize certain authorities in order to make judgements at all', or that one cannot err – that is, that one loses altogether

the capacity for rational thought – if one does not judge in conformity with some group or other: such views, worked out in detail in his later philosophy, were, obviously already characteristic of Wittgenstein in the twenties.[37]

At the same time in the late 1920s Wittgenstein returned to Cambridge and resumed contact with Moore, and through him with traditions of English, or rather, British, conservatism, since its original sources were mainly Scottish, a conservatism that placed great emphasis on common sense and on the adherence to conventions, which he absorbed into and interpreted in terms of his conception of common language. It was this side of his later philosophy that made him so appealing in the English universities and led directly to the Oxford school of linguistic philosophy with its own specific conservative biases which I cannot explore here.

But in England, too, Wittgenstein came into close contact with a large variety of Marxists sympathetic to the Russian Revolution and what was then occurring in the Soviet Union under Stalin. In 1931 he is reported to have said: 'Russia. The passion is promising. Our waffle, on the other hand, is impotent.'[38] For reasons that are not altogether clear, he began making extended and concerted plans to emigrate to the Soviet Union, plans that he only abandoned for practical reasons after the *Anschluss* in the late 1930s. He was not at all inhibited by the ever more obvious signs of the repressions and rigours of Stalinist totalitarianism. As he told his disciple Rhees, 'tyranny doesn't make me feel indignant.'[39] The purges and even the Nazi–Soviet pact made no difference to him in his regard for Stalin: 'people have accused Stalin of having betrayed the Russian Revolution. But they have no idea of the problems that Stalin had to deal with, and the dangers he saw threatening Russia.'[40] The elite of 'Red Cambridge' attended his lectures and constituted his circle of friends and followers.

He was strongly drawn to Bolshevism and the Soviet Union because he felt that only there might an antidote to the cultural poison of the nihilistic West be sought. His revolutionary conservatism led to a cultural pessimism that made him condemn all manifestations of modernism, science and liberalism. In these respects he was like the other malign masters, who similarly despaired of the 'depravity' of modernity. But unlike Gentile and Heidegger, he did not seek a solution to this problem of the age in right-wing totalitarianism; more like Lukács, he sought an answer to his revolutionary conservative cultural problems in left-wing totalitarianism. But unlike Lukács, he did not go over completely to Stalinist communism; though presumably he was prepared to do so had he gone to live in Russia.

In Cambridge he maintained some reserve and in Vienna gave no hint of any of this.

This peculiar combination of revolutionary conservatism and Bolshevism inevitably makes one think of the National Bolsheviks of the 1920s, thinkers such as Ernst Niekisch and Ernst Jünger, especially the latter, a war veteran whose writings Wittgenstein must have known or heard of, and, incidentally, also a friend of Heidegger. It is possible that Spengler, who preached a similar right-wing version of Prussian socialism, also one of the precursors of National Socialism, was an influence in favourably predisposing Wittgenstein towards the far left. However, it is doubtful whether Wittgenstein was capable of developing a coherent political ideology such as those of the above thinkers. It is more likely that he was simply drawn in contradictory extremist directions without fully realizing the inconsistencies involved. In other words, he was simply politically naive and confused. His regard for the Russian Revolution was as much conditioned by its being *Russian* – with all the romantic connotations of the Russian 'soul' drawn from the great Russian novelists – as by its being a *Revolution*, with the obvious Marxist signification. His adherence to Bolshevism was, nevertheless, sincere.

For in Bolshevism he also saw the promise of a solution to the 'problem' of philosophy, because the 'passion' of communism was perhaps the only way of satisfactorily countering the 'waffle' of philosophy. Or as he put it at some time in the early 1930s: 'the sickness of a time is cured by an alteration in the mode of life of human beings, and it was possible for the sickness of philosophical problems to get cured only through a changed mode of thought and life not through a medicine invented by an individual.'[41] And where, at the time, was there any attempt to change thought and life but in Soviet Russia? In condemning 'a medicine invented by an individual' he was implicitly rejecting all positivistic claims to have 'solved' the problems of philosophy, such as those of his teacher Bertrand Russell and the members of the Vienna Circle. He might even have been referring self-critically to his own 'medicines', both the *Tractatus* mode of logical analysis and the later therapeutic method of the linguistic 'dissolution' of problems partly modelled on the psychoanalysis of Freud. This, he believed, was only a treatment of mere symptoms, not an eradication of the underlying causes: 'I am by no means sure that I should prefer a continuation of my work by others to a change in the way people live which would make all these questions superfluous,'[42] he said disparagingly of his own philosophy. But since any 'alteration in the mode of life of human beings' or 'the way people live' could only be politically achieved, at this time by the Russian Revolution, it follows that he placed more faith in

Bolshevism than in philosophy. Even the best philosophy, his own, was but a palliative not a cure of the 'sickness of the time'.

Wittgenstein's new 'therapy' of linguistic-analysis involved a reconception of language away from the views he had held in the *Tractatus.* This was the main intellectual transformation brought about during his *Kehre*. His new view of language was subject to both kinds of ideological influences at once, the conservative and the radical. As I have already indicated, in accordance with his conservative sources he drew a highly traditionalistic picture of language as common and governed by tacit rules and 'grammars'. From his Marxist sources, chiefly through the critical agency of Sraffa, he drew a 'praxis' picture of language. This latter became encapsulated in his anthropological fiction of the 'language game', which, as I shall show, is not only a game theory but also a labour theory of language, with pronounced work as well as play aspects.

If the work aspects of language have a Marxist source, then the play aspects derive from the opposite conservative leanings, specifically from the work of Friz Mauthner. Mauthner developed his 'critique of language' on the basis of ideas derived from a most unusual collocation of late nineteenth-century sources: Nietzsche, Mach and the *Völkerpsychologie* of Lazarus and Steinthal and the so-called new-Grammarians. Wittgenstein had referred to Mauthner in the *Tractatus* by name, only to dismiss him without any indication of how much he had learned from him: 'all philosophy is a "critique of language", (though not in Mauthner's sense)'.[43] Later during the period of his *Kehre* he was to return to philosophy as a 'critique of language' precisely in Mauthner's sense, but without admitting this even to himself and without even once mentioning him or in any way adverting to his work. Yet the similarities between the two, which cannot be coincidental, have been extensively explored by Gershon Weiler and acknowledged by Wittgenstein's disciple Stephen Toulmin, and his disciple Allan Janik. They write as follows:

> All the same, regarded as a general philosophical critique of language, Wittgenstein's later writings revived many positions and arguments already put forward by Mauthner in 1901 – for example, the view that the rules of language are like the rules of a game, and that the very word 'language' is itself a general abstract term, which we need to unpack by looking to see how, in actual practice, men put the expressions of their languages to use, within the contexts of all their varied cultures.[44]

What Wittgenstein took over from Mauthner is a series of metaphors which he literalized. Mauthner's view that language is like a game be comes in Wittgenstein the full-blown phantasy of the language-game. Mauthner's conception of grammar as like the rules of a game becomes in Wittgenstein the idea that the meaning of a word is the rules for its use – as in chess where the powers of a piece are the rules governing its movements. Mauthner's likening of logic to grammar becomes in Wittgenstein a tacit assertion of their identity in his notion of 'logical grammar'. Mauthner's view of language as like a set of games becomes in Wittgenstein the idea that a language is a collection of language-games. Mauthner's image of the cultural development of language as being like the growth of a city is taken over by Wittgenstein in the picture of different language-games as like the parts of a city. All of these are perhaps suggestive as metaphors but completely wrong-headed as conceptions of language, as I have shown in my book *A New Science of Representation.*

If this can be shown then the view of philosophy as 'critique of language', whether in Mauthner's sense or Wittgenstein's, is based on a completely erroneous 'theory' of language. It is premissed on a confusion between language and culture, between a system of signs and a system of symbols and representations, which has the effect of making language coextensive with culture. This is expressed in Wittgenstein's oft-quoted dicta to the effect that a language is a whole 'form of life', namely, a cultural complex. Language is thus stretched to embrace everything that falls under the heading of culture, so that science, myth, philosophy, religion and all other symbolic forms of discourse characteristic of given cultures become incorporated into so-called language.

But at the same time as being stretched to take in all of culture, language is also contracted and reduced to the level of a game. For each of Wittgenstein's initial language-games is no more than a primitive communication system or signalling activity. As I argued at length in my book, a language is not reducible to systems of signals or language-games because there is an evolutionary discontinuity between such primitive systems of communication – which even some animals can master and children do so routinely prior to learning language – and language proper. And for similar reasons, no game can ever even approximate to a language. Hence all attempts to liken languages to games, which are very common and to be found in many quarters, are at best metaphorically suggestive and at worst dangerously wrong. The errors this can lead to are typically exemplified by Wittgenstein's later philosophy of language.

The two main themes of labour and language, which I have located in Wittgenstein, are equally characteristic of all the other malign masters during the period of their *Kehre*. It is, of course, a reflection of their totalitarian involvements, for the ideologies of both opposed modes of totalitarianism preach the supreme importance of labour and language, though not in the same proportions. To some extent the emphasis in the left-wing ones is on labour and in the right-wing ones on language, but each contains something of both themes. They are a legacy of nineteenth-century political movements and the kind of thought they propagated. Among these there is a rough separation between socialist and pragmatist movements and their ideologies which stressed labour, and Conservative and Nationalist ones which stressed language. But labour and language are often to be found together in thinkers drawn from both kinds of movements. In Marx, the leading theoretician of labour, there is also a recessive strain of language philosophy inherited from his German philological heritage.[45] And, conversely, in Nietzsche, one of the main nineteenth-century exponents of a philosophy of language, there is also a distinctive pragmatist emphasis on labour. The totalitarian movements of the twentieth century were all based on an ideology of labour, drawn from the socialist sources of the nineteenth century from which they all derived. But they all also appropriated the theme of language: the right-wing nationalistic ones from the start, and the left-wing Bolshevist ones not till later when Marr and other Soviet linguists, above all Stalin himself, were given official standing in the state-sponsored ideology of Marxist-Leninism-Stalinism.

Heidegger, for whom neither of these themes had much prominence in his primary masterwork, *Being and Time*, became obsessed with them during his *Kehre* as a function of his deepening involvement with Nazism and with the nationalistic intellectual currents that flowed into it. He became preoccupied with the proto-Nazi thought of Ernst Jünger with its talk of the *Gestalt* of the worker. This symbolic figure is, however, far less that of the socialist labourer than that of the nationalist soldier; it is more charged with the impulse to destruction than construction; all of which was in keeping with the new militarism of Germany. The theme of work climaxed in Heidegger's *Rektoratsrede*. There he asserts that labour – not contemplation as the classical philosophers believed – is the essence of science, that *theoria* is 'the highest mode of energeia', of Man's 'being-at-work'.[46] Karsten Harries summarizes his views at this time as follows:

> In the *Rektoratsrede* Heidegger suggests that this world is established and reestablished by human work. Authenticity depends on such establishment. Thus it demands of those who lack the strength to create their own work the subordination to the work of a creative leader which assigns them their place and joins them in a community.[47]

From this it is apparent that this philosophy of work leads straight into an ideology of submission to the will of the leader characteristic of Nazism.

Later in the speech Heidegger even alludes to the *Blut und Boden* themes of Nazi ideology: 'and the spiritual world of a people is not a superstructure erected by culture . . . but it is the power which most deeply preserves the forces stemming from *earth and blood* as the power which most deeply moves and profoundly shakes our being.'[48] Thus Heidegger holds a highly elitist conception of work from the start. This becomes more pronounced later in the works written after his resignation from the Rectorship of Freiburg; in these it is the elect creative work of the thinker, artist and statesman alone that counts for anything. And, furthermore, 'the work of the statesman is given privilege place in that it "grounds and preserves" the work of other creators.'[49] It alone 'lets a people discover its own essence and destiny and thus itself as a people'.[50] And it is no mystery to divine which statesman's work of state creation Heidegger is alluding to, for, as Harries states, 'the connection between these ideas and Heidegger's turn toward National Socialism cannot be denied.'[51]

The Nazi ideas of *Volk* and *Gemeinschaft* (community) as transcending mere 'culture' which Heidegger voices relate closely to his concurrent preoccupation with language – the German language, above all, but due acknowledgement is also made of Greek, the founding language of philosophy. Heidegger's involvement with the theme of language during his *Kehre* is focused on his study of Nietzsche and Hölderlin, whom he saw as the German philosopher and poet *par excellence*. From both he derived the idea that the initial emergence of Being in the West was mediated by the Greek language, the great original Aryan language. The subsequent history of Being, or *Seinsgeschichte*, was seen by him as a degeneration into the inferior languages, such as Latin, French and English, through which it passed, that is, into which it had been translated, in the course of its fall and decline into nihilism. It seems both logical and providential to assume that the new recapturing or repetition (*Wiederholung*) of Being, the emerging recapitulation of the Origin in Heidegger's eschatological schema of history, could of necessity only take place in German, the only original Aryan language of equal worth to Greek. This was in fact taking place in the course of the renewal of the German Volk and German Thought, of which Hitler and Heidegger were joint instigators – the statesman and the poet-thinker joining hands to save the West. Unfortunately, Hitler spoiled things by his refusal to grant Heidegger his providential role as the German shepherd of Being.

By comparison Gentile is far more sober and restrained in his treatment of labour and language. This is because his conception of both is also more tradition-bound, and sometimes expressed in a way that is reminiscent of the moralistic platitudes of Catholic pastoral teaching. His first statements on language go back to his early work on education. With its emphasis on Italian, Latin and Greek, his approach to language at this early stage is part of a traditional philological approach. It was only later, beginning with his *Prolegomena to the Study of the Child* (1921), that he began to develop a more original conception of language. It was part of his own unique theory that 'the individual contains society in himself', as he puts it.[52] Harris comments on this view of language as follows:

> For him language is not simply the garment in which thought is clothed; it is bodily substance through which it is expressed. Thought must be individualized in order to be concrete; hence language is the most primitive form of human personality. Yet this language, which is the ground of our possession of everything that is most truly ours because through it we give determinate form to our own thoughts and feelings, is at the same time essentially public and communicable.[53]

It is readily apparent how such a conception of language lends itself easily to a denial of individual autonomy and to a conception of this 'internal society' within the individual as an inner conscience representative of community, nation and State. And this is exactly how his theory of language as *societas in interiore homini* is utilized in his final work, *The Genesis and Structure of Society*:

> The language that every man uses is that of his fathers, the language of his tribe or his class, of his city or his nation. It is his and not his; and he cannot use it to say 'This is *my* view' unless at the same time he can say 'this is *our* view'. For at the root of the 'I' there is a 'We'. The community to which the individual belongs is the basis of his spiritual existence; it speaks through his mouth, feels with his heart, and thinks with his brain.[54]

This is the simplest and clearest statement of the totalistic collective communalism focused on language to be found in the secondary masterwork of any of the malign masters.

It was in this final work that Gentile made his culminating statement on labour as well. However, both his statements on language and labour, as Harris notes, go back to earlier works, most characteristically those of his *Kehre*, but even as far back as his studies of Marx at the start of his career. His final statement on the so-called 'humanism of labour' is worth quoting at length for it sums up the whole trend of his thought:

> For the humanism of culture, which was indeed a glorious step in the literature of man, there succeeds today or will succeed tomorrow the

> humanism of labor. For the creation of great industry and the advance of the worker onto the great stage of history have profoundly modified the modern conception of culture. The word used to mean intellectual culture, and especially art and literature; it left out of account the vast segment of humanity who do not rise their eyes toward the free horizons of the higher culture, but labor at the foundation of human culture. There at the foundation man is in contact with nature, and *labors* on it; but he labors *as a man*, he is aware of what he is doing, aware of himself and the world in which he is incorporated . . . The peasant labors, the artisan labors, and so does the master craftsman, the artist labors and the scholar and philosopher.[55]

This simple, and in its own way beautiful, statement of the dignity of human labour, no matter what form it takes, is not far removed from traditional pieties. Though it seems revolutionary in style, it is traditionalist in substance – more or less as is Italian Fascism in general. It does not entail any real social change. For no sooner having advanced in the revolutionary manner the idea that 'the creation of great industry' has brought 'the worker onto the great stage of history', Gentile retreats to an implicitly hierarchical social order in his discussion of the peasant who is 'at the foundation . . . in contact with nature'. Gentile places the peasant or labourer at the bottom of the work and social hierarchy, above him are all those who labour not in matter but spirit. For labour only begins as material but ends dematerialized as spirit:

> Gradually the material through which man puts himself to the test in his labors grows lighter, and as it were, dematerialised; so that the spirit is released to fly freely in its own air, outside of space and time. But matter is already conquered when hoe bites the earth, breaking up the ground and making it play its part in the pursuit of human ends. From the very beginning of his labors man is human; he has risen into the kingdom of the spirit, where the world is his world, the creation of his thought, or in short his own self.[56]

Hence, if the peasant is at the bottom of the social pyramid, in direct contact with matter, the philosopher is at the very apex in the 'kingdom of spirit' of which he, surely, is king in spirit. For only the philosopher recognizes that 'the world is his world' because it is a world of thought. However, Gentile does compromise with realities, for in the world of real politics in contemporary times it is the Fascist Corporate State, or totalitarianism, which can best realize the 'humanism of labour'.

Surprisingly so for a nearly life-long Marxist, Lukács' conception of labour is not so well developed, and of language hardly at all. It was not till his dying days that he began to explore philosophically the nature of work in his unfinished *Ontology of Social Being*, an attempt at what one might call a Marxist metaphysics to which I shall return in chapter 3. Right throughout he does acknowledge the Marxist orthodoxies concerning production and economics, but without elaborating these to any marked extent. This omission has also partly to do with his predominant aesthetic and cultural orientation. His Hegelian approach with its focus on consciousness also did not lend itself to any detailed consideration of the material factors of society, apart from his very general conception of reification and its relation to the commodity form of capitalism. He tried to remedy this lacuna in his Moscow years in his book *The Young Hegel*, which 'is the first detailed study from any angle of vision of the relation of philosophy and economics in Hegel,' as Tom Rockmore remarks.[57] But, as he goes on to point out, 'this treatise . . . shows clear traces of Stalinist orthodoxy . . . it is marred by an unpleasant form of Marxist orthodoxy.'[58] It does not really go beyond the stock Marxist doctrine of labour. Hence, there is not all that much to say on Lukács' view of work during his *Kehre* that is at all distinctive, and almost nothing to be said about his view of language.

With Wittgenstein it seems the other way round as compared to Lukács, his whole concern seems to be with language and not at all with work. However, it has not been noted that at least implicitly during his *Kehre* he turned to labour as well. In fact, the two themes are inextricably bound up with each other in his conception of the language-game, which is in effect a kind of 'labour theory of language' in miniature. This is evident from the fact that most of the language-games he depicts, either in his early *Blue and Brown Books* or in his later *Philosophical Investigations*, are more like working situations, and are not recognizable as games in any accepted sense. Each might be better designated as work with language or a language-*work* rather than a language-*game*. Thus the initial one of the builders passing bricks and slabs is obviously an activity that takes place at a building site, there does not seem to be any discernible play element in it.

This 'labour theory of language' is part of Wittgenstein's general praxis approach to language, the view that 'meaning is use', and that 'use' refers to a practical function in an everyday context. Meaning is taken as literally word-work. Words themselves thus come to be likened to tools and instruments; the fact that there are different kinds of words is likened to there being different kinds of implement, each with its own mode of use. Metaphors of this instrumentalist view of language proliferate in his later work. They are accompanied with the conception of word-work as a collective enterprise. Work activities require groups of workers and cannot usually be performed by a single person, so language, too, comes to be seen as such a collective activity which the single individual cannot carry out alone.

It is not necessary to argue here at length against this 'labour theory of language' and the techno-ergonic biases it creates. The argument against it is simply an extension of that already invoked against the whole idea of the language-game. Here I shall merely point out how it leads Wittgenstein into ideological value judgements which have a very damaging effect on his conception of philosophy, and by implication on all theorizing. Wittgenstein is continually driven to judge modes of language use that have a practical everyday function, or working words, in a very positive light and to treat those which do not negatively. Words that are idle, that have gone on holiday, are bad; as it were, they are not proletarian words. Philosophical, especially metaphysical, uses of words are particularly prone to such charges of parasitism, of not doing a proper job, of being the lumpenproletariat of language.

Wittgenstein's bias against so-called idle words is part of his stand against philosophical discourse and intellectual theorizing in general. This anti-intellectualism he shares with the other malign masters, and it is a reflection of their extreme hostility to the modern world which I shall explore in the next chapter. Wittgenstein's rejection of intellectuals and theorizing of any kind comes to the fore in the period of his *Kehre*. To the members of the Vienna Circle, intellectuals *par excellence*, he expostulates vehemently: 'if I were told anything that was a *theory*, I would say, no, no! That does not interest me . . . *For me* a theory is without value. A theory gives me nothing.'[59] This is at one with his later statements in the *Philosophical Investigations* that philosophy must avoid all hypotheses and explanations and only engage in pure description. It is to be undertaken as a kind of practical therapy, a treatment of linguistic problems reminiscent of Freud's 'talking cure' (though, as usual, Wittgestein was very ambivalent about being likened to Freud or his philosophical therapeutic approach to psychoanalysis). In this general anti-intellectualism both sides of his ideological extremism, the neo-conservative and the incipiently Marxist, join hands. For he is also against theorizing and intellecting from his conservative point of view. As I have already noted, his preference for common language with its everyday, practical and communitarian orientation also fits in with a certain kind of British common-sense conservatism.

Common or ordinary language is an extremely multivalent expression in Wittgenstein's work which encapsulates both conservative and revolutionary impulses at once. It is a little like that ideologically charged symbol 'the People', which can stand for the Volk in conservative politics or the masses in radical politics with all kinds of variants in between. Common language is closely related to 'the People' in all its senses. It can stand for conservative values of community, custom and common-sense deriving both from the Austrian and British traditions. This spectrum of values easily shades into populist notions of ordinariness, basicness and naturalness as espoused by the Tolstoyans and the Narodniks in Russia. On the other extreme, common language can stand for the values of practicality, work, effectiveness and even vigorous vulgarity characteristic of radical approaches. Like the term 'the People', 'common language' cannot be given any specific definition, it is a value-laden symbol whose meaning shifts depending on the ideological context in which it is embedded.

At one point, which might be dated towards the end of his *Kehre*, Wittgenstein asks himself quizzically whether his approach is a Weltanschauung: 'The concept of a perspicuous representation is of fundamental significance for us. It earmarks the form of account we give, the way we look at things. (Is this a "*Weltanschauung*"?)'[60] The answer to this question is difficult because Wittgenstein was forbidden by his anti-theory stance and hostility to all explanation from exploring self-consciously his own *Weltanschauung*. He frequently gives the impression of not having one and not needing one. But behind the cover of this denial he could selectively pick and choose elements from the ideologies that were close to hand, utilizing these out of context as he felt inclined and not feeling bound to own up to what he had taken. A good example of this is his approach to language which contains many contradictory cross-currents drawn from the opposed ideologies of Marxism (the pragmatist labour theory of language) and neo-conservatism (the rule-bound traditionalism of custom and game) brought together under the general rubric of common language. This notion has little to do with actual languages as these are studied in any science of linguistics or semiotics. It is a kind of ideological construct which might in this sense be called a *Weltanschauung*, but one that is not conscious of itself as such.

One element that is most characteristic of Wittgenstein's *Weltanschauung* is its extreme anti-Modernism. It is generally assumed that because he seems to be attacking what he calls 'metaphysics' – like the Positivists, though with different weapons – he is, therefore, against traditional philosophy. But the opposite is the case, he always defends tradition against its modernist philosophical critics and invariably praises the metaphysical philosophers of the past, above all, Plato, Augustine and Kierkegaard. Late in his life he declared to his friend Drury, 'don't think I despise metaphysics or ridicule it. On the contrary, I regard the great metaphysical writings of the past as among the noblest productions of the human mind.'[61] (At the same time he almost boasted to Drury, 'here I am a one-time professor of philosophy who has never read a word of Aristotle'.)[62] In his characteristic way, Wittgenstein wants to have it both ways: to praise the metaphysics of the past and yet to dissolve and dispose of the so-called 'problems of philosophy' which are generally metaphysical. He tries to console himself with the thought that 'what we are destroying are nothing but houses of cards (*Luftgebäude*) and we are clearing up the ground of language (*Grund der Sprache*) on which they stand.'[63] But are these 'houses of cards' the structures of traditional metaphysics or are they something else? And if the latter, then what are they? This is the same ambivalence we have already encountered with Heidegger's 'destruction' of the 'traditional content of ancient ontology', which can be taken as either the classical texts of metaphysics themselves or the 'hardened tradition' of commentary which has come to surround them.[64] It is the typical predicament of conservative revolutionaries who want both to destroy the past and preserve it.

None of these problems arises for Wittgenstein or Heidegger or the other malign masters when they attack their own Modernist predecessors or their rival contemporaries. Destroying the depraved present and its intellectual expressions in philosophy suits both their conservative and radical impulses. Thus Wittgenstein practises most of his 'dissolving' techniques against the thinkers of his own time or those of the preceding generation in the period immediately prior to the First World War. The 'problems' he selects for dissolution are mostly derived from Russell, Frege or Moore and sometimes only slightly further back from William James. He is most critical of the mathematical formalists of his time, above all Cantor, Hilbert and Gödel. He is absolutely scathing of scientists. The various schools of contemporary psychology from the Behaviourists to the Gestalists receive extensive critical attention. All in all, one can conclude that Wittgenstein's destructive animus is mostly directed against the intellectual manifestations of contemporary modernity. As against these intellectuals he pitted ordinary people (Tolstoy's peasants) and their sound common language which is less prone to the diseases of the intellect that manifest themselves as 'problems of philosophy' or so-called conceptual problems. But perhaps in some utopian future a 'new life', such as was already beginning to arise in the Soviet Union, would establish itself and do away with the need for philosophy and for further treatment of language, as he sometimes fondly imagined.

Given his faith in the soundness of common language, Wittgenstein could not elaborate a political programme, since language is not a directly political matter. This is part of the reason that he did not develop a totalitarian conception of politics, as all the other malign masters did. Yet he thought politically about other things apart from politics. Thus in discussing his differences with Ramsay concerning logic and mathematics he couches it in a simple political metaphor that reflects the ideological conflicts of his time in which he casts Ramsay in the role of 'bourgeois thinker' or reformist and himself by implication in that of anti-bourgeois or revolutionary thinker:

> Ramsay was a bourgeois thinker. I.e. he thought with the aim of clearing up the affairs of some particular community. He did not reflect on the essence of the state – at least he did not like doing this – but on how *this* might reasonably be organized . . .[65]

The sad, unwitting irony of this remark is that Wittgenstein thought even less about the essence of the real political state than did Ramsay who was, after all, a mathematical economist. But all the other malign masters did think about the essence of the State and invariably defined it in totalitarian terms. In that respect they were self-consciously totalitarian thinkers in a way that Wittgenstein was not.

Gentile thought about the essense of the State most explicitly and therefore most ably. He is the only one with any claim to being a political philosopher, perhaps because he had not totally abandoned the categories and problems of traditional practical philosophy. As is well known, he put forward a quasi-Hegelian theory of the Ethical State and set out the institutional arrangements of Corporate Fascism. Heidegger's unacknowledged political philosophy is not far removed from this view of the Ethical State, though it is expressed in very different terms. Both conceptions were based on idealizations of the Greek polis. But, as Karsten Harries argues, 'the attempt to reconstruct the modern state in the image of the polis will tend to totalitarianism.'[66] This must be so because under modern conditions of society and economy any attempt to impose a comprehensive communal solidarity, in which the public and private, the political and ethical, the secular and religious are all unified, will inevitably entail controls exercised by a State, and in practice by a party and its leader.

Lukács' advocacy of his party and its great leader derived from quite different theoretical presuppositions and amounted to another kind of totalitarianism. This was partly disguised by his continual espousal of 'proletarian democracy', which, of course, in no way detracted from the simultaneous demand for a 'dictatorship of the proletariat'. However, from 1933 onwards when Stalin changed his line and advocated a Popular Front policy, Lukács went along enthusiastically as it seemed to vindicate the stand he had taken in the 'Blum Theses' débâcle of 1928 when he incurred the wrath of the Party. Thus, whereas for Stalin and the Party the Popular Front was nothing but a tactical ploy to be abandoned at any convenient opportunity, for Lukács it was more than that, for as Isaac Deutscher maintains, he 'elevated the Popular Front from the level of tactics to that of ideology; he projected its principle into philosophy, literary history and aesthetic criticism.'[67] It was in this spirit that he was able to reconcile himself with the 'bourgeois' Thomas Mann as against the avant-garde communist Brecht, and in general with classicism and realism as against Modernism. By this round about route Lukács also ended up as a traditionalist of sorts. By espousing classicism and realism he was able to reconcile himself to and articulate better than anyone else the new traditionalist aesthetic requirements of the Party and so survive the murderous purges which consumed many of his Hungarian colleagues and rivals in the mid-1930s.

At this period all the totalitarian regimes were well installed and engaged in purges of a greater or lesser terror. The need for philosophers was over. They had served their purpose and were of no more use. By 1935 Herman Finer was perceptive enough to see that Gentile had been 'squeezed dry and the peel thrown away'.[68] Much the same could have been said of the others. Even Wittgenstein must have realized by then that life in the Soviet Union was not quite what he imagined it to be and that there was no place for him there, despite the offer of a chair of philosophy at Kazan University, Tolstoy's Alma Mater.

Their response to this setback took two characteristically opposed forms: Heidegger and Wittgenstein withdrew from any further political involvements into a quietistic state of resigned disengagement – these one might call the despondents; Gentile and Lukács took the opposite course and threw themselves all the more desperately into political commitment, 'despite all' – these one might call the desperados. The philosophical reaction of the despondents during their post-*Kehre* retreat was to preoccupy themselves with other-worldly philosophical concerns, which took characteristically different forms. Heidegger busied himself with his own concocted hermeneutic interpretations of past philosophy, mainly the pre-Socratics and Nietzsche. In the course of that he built up his increasingly more elaborate mythological schema around the terms *Ereignis, Gelassenheit, das Ruf, das Geviert*, etc. Wittgenstein withdrew into the philosophical purism of the problem of language mainly focused on the detailed analysis of the concepts of so-called 'philosophical psychology', which he derived as a residue of real psychology drained of all its empirical and theoretical content. By contrast, the desperados reaffirmed their adherence to their totalitarian faith and clung to it all the more tenaciously. Gentile elaborated ever more idealized forms of Fascism totally remote from what Mussolini was actually doing. Lukács, too, according to his disciple Ferenc Feher, 'tried to reveal the "ideal type" of the system as opposed to its empirical reality'.[69] But since this was 'a procedure barely tolerated by the system itself', he had perforce to content himself with the more prudent course of adopting the negatively critical role of attacking its enemies or its friends who did not quite measure up by Stalinist standards.

For all of them the Turning was over. Each one withdrew from active political involvement and retired to one or another kind of academic refuge. Heidegger preferred the security of his native Freiburg to the tempting but dangerous offers from Hitler of a Chair in the exposed position of Berlin. He tried to justify this with mawkishly sentimental effusions on rural life in the provinces. Wittgenstein eagerly sought the Chair vacated by Moore in Cambridge, which he gained largely through Keynes' patronage. Despite his constant and unceasing animadversions against academic life, he kept it till 1947. Gentile withdrew from Fascist politics to an academic Chair in Rome and eventually to the directorship of the Scuola Normale Superiore in Pisa. At the same time he preoccupied himself with the academic politics of numerous institutes and committees, in the course of trying to set himself up as the 'cultural dictator' of Italian academic life.[70] Lukács in Moscow withdrew into the Soviet Academy of Sciences, but continued to engage in the internecine politicking of Stalinist cliques of Russian philosophers and German-speaking émigré intellectuals and artists. In these retreats, while all around the world steadily slid into the turmoil of total war, the malign masters worked on their secondary masterworks.

3 The Secondary Masterworks

Out of the experiences of the *Kehre* and its aftermath emerged the secondary masterworks: Gentile's *Genesis and Structure of Society*, Lukács' *The Destruction of Reason*, Heidegger's *Nietzsche* (Vols. I–IV) and Wittgenstein's *Philosophical Investigations* (together with various other volumes of *Nachlass*). All of them show the scars of the painful operations of their grafting onto and subsequent, unsuccessful attempts at partial detachment from totalitarianism. The symptoms of mingled hope and despair, aspiration and despondency are evident in them.

Mainly produced during a period of academic withdrawal before, during and after the Second World War, the more academic character of the secondary, as compared to the primary, masterworks is also markedly evident. They are on the whole works of exposition, commentary and detailed but frequently trivial analyses. Each is a scattered and fragmented compilation, and, apart from Gentile's brief essay which needs to be supplemented with his other works, they are huge tomes without much order or coherence. Those of the despondents, Heidegger and Wittgenstein, are collections of lectures or notes that remain unstructured and unfinished. Those of the desperados, Lukács and Gentile, though formally complete, are still fragmentary since there is so much that they leave out. Both of these were intended to justify and uphold the totalitarian beliefs of their authors and to provide propagandistic support for their masters at critical political junctures.

All these works are obviously secondary in quality when compared to the primary masterworks. They lack the imaginative vision of totality, the apocalyptic élan, the seriousness of subject matter and the completion of form and presentation that is generally to be found in the latter. This degeneration in the thought of the malign masters has frequently been acknowledged by independent scholars who are not disciples or followers. The famous economist von Hayek, who knew Wittgenstein well and who at one time soon after his death intended writing his biography, until foiled by the disciples, in 1984 commented as follows:

> I have known him longer than any person still living and was sixty years ago very much impressed by his first book. But his later works meant little to me and I have never quite understood the enormous

> admiration he has gained in Cambridge. Crudely expressed, he always seemed to me the maddest member of a highly gifted but somewhat neurotic family, always on the verge of actual madness and not to be taken too seriously. These may be my limitations, but I just did not find it worthwhile to spend too much time on them, they certainly do not fit my system of thought.[1]

Unfortunately, this later work has been taken all too seriously first in Cambridge, England, then in Cambridge, Massachusetts, and subsequently throughout the Western world. Much the same kind of verdict applies to all the other malign masters as well. It is generally acknowledged, even by disciples such as Hannah Arendt, that Heidegger never wrote anything as masterful as *Being and Time*. Lukács' primary masterwork is the one still widely read now; few, except for disciples or commentators, bother with his later masterwork. Gentile is now hardly read it all, so it is difficult to say how his two masterworks compare in this respect; but in its time it was the primary one that had a world-wide influence among Idealists, the secondary one is yet to attract any interest outside the narrow circle of Gentile scholars; its Fascist bias has condemned it to sterility.

Despite the inherent superiority of the primary over the secondary masterworks, in some cases it is the latter which have exerted a greater influence and provoked more academic commentary and debate. This is clearly so in the case of Wittgenstein's *Philosophical Investigations*, which is considered the dominant text in philosophy departments in Anglo-Saxon and allied countries. It is starting to happen with Heidegger's work as well, as his later work in general is arousing greater scholarly effort than his early work, though this is not yet focused on his Nietzsche studies. It seems that it is precisely the disjointed, fragmentary and unfinished state of the late works, as well as their more pronouncedly academic character, that has prompted scholarly interest. Such works demand commentaries and analyses to be made generally available, and these in turn call forth commentaries on commentaries and analyses of analyses in a perpetual self-renewing cycle of scholarly activity. For the more uncertain a text, the more it serves as a pretext for countless other texts. The only precondition for such a new scholasticism or neo-Talmudism to obtain is that some texts should be canonized as authoritative and that there should be many scholars who need to publish. The 'open-ended' texts of eminent modern authorities – and some of the malign masters have already achieved that status, especially the two despondents, Wittgenstein and Heidegger – fulfil these requirements to perfection. They also permit schools of rival interpretations to be founded and orthodoxies and heterodoxies to be contested.

The works of the desperados, Lukács and Gentile, do not lend themselves so well to such scholarly needs, even apart from their ideological odium which was so abhorrent to Western universities during the period of the Cold War. This is one of the main reasons why these works have been so much less successful.

Yet notwithstanding all the reams of commentary that have been heaped upon them, there is still no proper appreciation of how the secondary masterworks relate to the careers of their authors and to their political experiences in the troubled times surrounding them. For just as the primary masterworks might be said to be an expression of the First World War, so the secondary ones bear an analogous relation to the Second World War; to the period of heightened ideological conflict leading up to it, the war itself and the period of Cold War following it. And just as the primary masterworks breathe a spirit of radical revolutionary optimism, so do the secondary ones evince the opposite attitude of pessimism and despair. This is true both of the work of the despondents and the desperados. The despondents openly express their disillusionment: Wittgenstein speaks of 'the darkness of these times' and Heidegger of 'the darkening of the world'. The desperados are too ideologically committed to say openly anything as pessimistic as that, but one can glean something of the nature of their despair by the effort that they have to make to deny it. Both Gentile and Lukács seem to be whistling in the dark to keep their spirits up, the one well aware that the cause of Fascism was in its last gasp and fighting for its very life, the other that Bolshevism, having barely survived the Nazi onslaught, was faced with an even more menacing enemy.

In his final work, which he sensed would be his last and which he wrote as an *apologia pro vita sua* as a Fascist, Gentile was not inclined to dwell on the negative prospects facing Italy or himself. Nevertheless, he was fully aware of them. He saw his beloved land surrounded by the 'decadent materialism of the industrial democracies or the military materialism of the USSR',[2] just as Heidegger saw Germany, the central nation, caught in the vice between the same two alien forces. The nation where the saving Fascist spirit was nourished was facing invasion from the outside and insurrection from the inside; for the Anglo-Saxon liberal democrats and the Russian communists were not only foreigners besieging her gates, but were also present within the polity itself among those Italians who yearned for their alien gods. This was the negative foil of the pall of darkness against which he desperately tried to project his bright image of light. For as he put it in the Preface to his book, he was writing it 'as a relief to my mind in days full of anxiety for every Italian, and to fulfil a civil duty, since I saw no other course open to me in my concern for that Italy of the future for which I have laboured all my life.'[3] This Italy of the future was simply his ideal version of Fascism.

Lukács did not dare expound any such ideal vision of Bolshevism for his position as an officially accredited ideologue was insecure and fraught with the continuing danger of charges of heresy such as he had already experienced in the past. In Stalin's time this would have been fatal. There is some suggestion that he began with the intention of writing a positive exposition of his views, but that he gave it up for reasons of prudence. Thus he tells us that when he first arrived in Moscow, 'it was my intention at the time to publish a statement of my new position. My attempt to do so proved a failure, the manuscript has since been lost.'[4] Lost or destroyed, who will ever know the real truth? Instead Lukács retreated to the safety of the past, to Hegel and classical German literature, and to the less liable to be denounced course of attacks on all forms of German thought that were not in accord with the orthodoxies of Marxist-Leninism as interpreted by Stalin. But these works of German thought were precisely the formative background of his own development as a thinker, from which he now tried to distance himself as far as possible. He charged them all with the sins of 'irrationalism' as defined by the orthodox Marxist-Leninist canon. Not even his teachers and personal friends, Simmel and Weber, were spared. But the central focus of his animus was Nietzsche, the arch-irrationalist and precursor of Nazism and every other form of 'reactionary' thought: 'Nietzsche, who became the paradigm in content and methodology of irrationalist philosophical reaction from the USA to Tsarist Russia, and whose influence would not and cannot be rivalled even approximately by a single other reactionary ideologist.'[5]

Heidegger was precisely one such 'reactionary ideologist' whom Lukács had in mind. Heidegger no doubt agreed with Lukács that Nietzsche was the most important thinker of the time, but for exactly the opposite reasons. Heidegger became almost obsessively concerned with Nietzsche from the first moment of his *Kehre*. His secondary masterwork, *Nietzsche* (Vols. I–IV), is almost a record of this continuous involvement in its various phases, ranging from total acceptance to partial withdrawal. For his attitude to Nietzsche changed in keeping with his changing relation to Nazism and by implication to Hitler himself. At first during his *Kehre* when he was totally involved with Nazism, he was a complete Nietzschean *sans reserve*. As he retreated from public life and grew somewhat distant from the regime, without ceasing for a moment to believe in it, his critical separation from Nietzsche also became more pronounced, but also without ever withdrawing from him. Throughout, he held that Nietzsche alone had stated the problem of history to which Hitler alone had any kind of an answer. The parallels between his attitude to Nietzsche and to Hitler always remained close. He never ceased to regard the one as the greatest modern philosopher, save himself, and the other as the greatest modern statesman. Nietzsche was the culmination of the whole history of metaphysical philosophy since Plato, the great thinker of the idea of Nihilism; Hitler was the leader of the greatest modern movement, Nazism, the only one that could stand up to this Nihilism.

As is clear from the numerous lecture series on Nietzsche which he gave from the late 1920s onwards till the end of the war, his attitude to both Nietzsche and Hitler waxed and waned together, depending on his own standing within the regime and on the changing fortunes of the regime itself. This is perhaps not always apparent from the four volumes of Nietzsche studies as finally published in 1961, for, as is his wont, Heidegger has adjusted the texts to make them conform with the post-war political realities which he could not ignore; something which has only become apparent with the posthumous publication of the original versions of his lectures. From these in their chronological order it can be deduced that Heidegger went through approximately four distinct phases in his interpretation of Nietzsche, changing in conjunction with his varying attitudes to the Nazi movement and Hitler and the vicissitudes of the regime. The initial phase from 1929 to early 1933 is a preparatory one, when in a hesitant conservative revolutionary manner he begins to adopt a tentative Nietzschean terminology and moves closer to Nazism. The second phase from early 1933 to sometime in 1935 is when he became an active Nazi and Nietzschean and began to interpret the one in terms of the other. The third phase from sometime in 1935 to early 1943, when the defeat at Stalingrad took place, reflects a dual movement of partial withdrawal from total identification with Nazism and Nietzscheanism and also at the same time the attempt to place both of these within his own schema of things; thus Nietzsche's eschatology of history is transformed into a Heideggerian *Seinsgeschichte,* the details of which I shall explore in what follows. The final phase, from the defeat at Stalingrad to the defeat of Nazism itself, is one of resignation in despair accompanied by a call for sacrifice according to which it is clear that Nietzsche and Hitler are seen in defeat as precursors for something more momentous which is yet to come. Heidegger now allots himself and his own philosophy a larger role in this future coming, and his own mythology now comes to the fore.

Later, after the war, Heidegger tried to make out in the course of his forced recantation that he had engaged in a critical confrontation (*Auseinandersetzung*) with Nietzsche and by implication with the Nazi regime itself, and that he had spoken against it in the veiled terms he had to employ for his own self-protection. It is true that he criticized Nietzsche, but only in the sense that he saw him as a mere precursor to himself and tried to place Nietzsche's scheme of things in a subordinate position within his own. But this does not mean that he turned against the regime or its goals of conquest. As Domenico Losurdo shows, 'the fact remains that Heidegger to the end continued to identify himself with Germany at war.'[6] Losurdo argues that 'his criticism of Nietzsche's nihilism seemed at times to envision a new ideological platform to justify the desperate effort of the German army in the East.'[7] After Stalingrad, Heidegger no longer saw the German warrior as a Nietzschean *Übermensch*, the exponent of a ruthless active nihilism, but as 'the desperate custodian of the truth of Being'.[8] Germany itself 'no longer represents active Nihilism, which fights for a different configuration of Being, but is the country that fights and sacrifices itself for "the truth of Being"'.[9] In defeat Heidegger put a different gloss on the destiny of Germany and its Nazi regime, that is all that his self-confessed 'opposition' amounts to.

However, Germany's approaching defeat and his efforts to accommodate it intellectually did push him more and more into his own philosophically devised mythological scheme of things. This became even more pronounced after the war when this mythology was endowed with ever greater religious significance, eventually returning to the kinds of mystical speculations with which he began his career. As Richard Wolin states, 'his thought seeks refuge in a recrudescence of myth: "openness for the mystery", "the remembrance of Being" and "the mirror-play of the four-fold" (gods and mortals, heaven and earth) becomes the mystified scheme around which his later thinking revolves.'[10] The peculiarity of this myth-making is that it combines in a peculiar collocation themes and metaphors drawn from Christian theology and from Greek and Germanic neo-pagan sources. At this stage Heidegger is elaborating a private religion that no longer has much to do with Nietzsche.

Wittgenstein's thinking was also deeply affected by the Second World War. As the war proceeded he grew ever more pessimistic; after the war he became positively misanthropic. His philosophy suffered accordingly; most of the key ideas of the *Philosophical Investigations* had already been arrived at in the 1930s; after the war he busied himself with elaborations of these in ever greater detail. In this period Wittgenstein seems to have given up his earlier political hopes. He no longer believed in Russia, and, by inference, in Bolshevism either, for the behaviour of Russian troops in Vienna, which he had witnessed on a brief trip there, shocked him. Not that it was all that outrageous for an army of occupation after such a war, and it hardly measured up to the practices of the German army, which the

Austrians in this period shared, but for Wittgenstein, who operated something of a double standard in these matters, it was enough to shake him out of his former illusions about the 'Russian Soul' and Bolshevism as a 'new passion'. As von Hayek reports, 'he was reacting to having encountered the Russians in Vienna in a manner which suggested that he had met them in the flesh for the first time and that this had shattered all his illusions.'[11]

His deeply despairing pessimism during this time is openly expressed in his Foreword to the *Philosophical Investigations,* which seems to have been written shortly after the end of the war. By contrast to the Foreword of the *Tractatus,* where he states that in principle he has solved all philosophical problems, he even despairs of what his own philosophy amounts to and what it can accomplish. The times are dark, dominated by a shallowly rationalistic 'soapy water science' and 'clever' scientifically minded intellectuals.[12] At his most misanthropic, he even welcomes the atom bomb, for its destructive power might just serve to do away with this hated scientific civilization: 'the bomb offers a prospect of the end, the destruction of an evil – our disgusting soapy water science.'[13] He makes it clear that his own work is not addressed to present benighted humanity, among whom he doubts there is even one brain into which his illuminating light can penetrate. By implication, we are given to understand that his work will only be understood by the better people of some future humanity. In a letter to Drury he writes, 'my type of thinking is not wanted in this present age, I have to swim so strongly against the tide. Perhaps in a hundred years people will really want what I am writing.'[14] He did not have to wait so long. It is ironic to note now just how much the people who mattered in philosophy, mainly philosophy professors, wanted just his type of thinking.

Prior to the war Wittgenstein had sustained considerably more hope. The diseases of the time are not incurable, the neuroses of language can be relieved through his language-analytic treatment. The sicknesses of the understanding, which manifest themselves as problems of philosophy, can be dealt with by clearing up the muddles and confusions of the grammar of language, and so these problems can be dissolved. For Wittgenstein all problems are focused on language, for like a kind of linguistic Midas, everything he touches turns to words. Language assumes something of the protean multipurpose role that logic had held in the *Tractatus.* It becomes the omnibus term for nearly everything, for any subject or field of discourse or mode of representation is always considered as 'the language of such and such' or the 'concept of such and such'. This panlinguistic holism, so to speak, provides Wittgenstein with the illusion that he can cope with anything at all in his own terms and within the limits of his approach; which gives him the satisfaction of believing that he can deal with all problems as long as they are 'conceptual'. And this in turn gives him a large measure of his confidence in what his philosophy can accomplish.

In the aftermath of the war, Wittgenstein lost much of this confidence. He ceased to place his hopes on anything in the public world, including politics. He largely withdrew into himself and the circle of his closest disciples. His last work reflects this for he became more and more preoccupied with a few issues which he had already raised much earlier, such as his curious comments on the Gestalt theory of perception, which is not explicitly identified or discussed as such, or on such oddities as Goethe's 'theory' of colours and Moore's remarks on knowledge and belief. These he pursues with an almost obsessive intensity, repeating over and over again a few points in ever varying formulations. He had given up the attempt to pull all his accumulated notes together into the one structured work, as he had done with the *Tractatus*. Apart from the opening torso of the *Philosophical Investigations*, all he left behind was a huge bulk of *Nachlass* notes.

I shall presently return to a more detailed discussion of *Philosophical Investigations*, but prior to that I should like to consider the other three secondary masterworks. What I will provide are quick sketches of bulky tomes intended to convey in barest outline the essential nature of these works. Their character as works of philosophy is conditioned and informed by their ideological orientations and by the circumstances of war in which they were produced. Each embodies these features in a distorted and usually concealed fashion. I shall attempt to reveal this in my reading of these works, beginning with Heidegger's *Nietzsche*.

The key to understanding Heidegger's secondary masterwork – the numerous volumes of Nietzsche studies as well as the other works of his later philosophy – is to grasp his eschatological schema of history, the *Seinsgeschichte*. This he took over unquestioningly from Nietzsche, even while he made out that he was deeply interrogating Nietzsche's philosophy, indeed, criticizing it. Heidegger's unthinking resort to Judaic and Christian theological concepts and patterns of eschatological thinking, largely in order to denounce and renounce Judaism and Christianity and elevate the Greeks and Germans, is precisely the kind of self-contradictory trap into which an erstwhile Christian theologian turned latter-day pre-Socratic philosopher might fall. In doing so, he was not even pursuing an original path, but simply following in Nietzsche's footsteps. In what follows I begin with Nietzsche and then return to Heidegger to show that the eschatological pattern is the same in both, the only difference being that what is clearly expressed in Nietzsche is obfuscated by being translated into ontological terms in Heidegger.

In Nietzsche's philosophy the basic eschatological drama of historical time is presented as a Zarathustran cosmic battle between the good and evil principles of the master and the slave, that is, essentially of the Aryan and the Jew – and Nietzsche is not squeamish in depicting this struggle as one for racial supremacy. In my book *The Ends of Philosophy* I have shown in some detail how this eschatology goes through five phases: Origin, Fall, Decline, End and Return. Thus, to take morality as an example, the 'original' master morality based on the opposition of good and bad (morality of Greeks, Romans and other conquering people) is inverted and perverted into the slave morality based on the opposition of evil and good (morality of Jews and Christians). This fatal step constitutes the falling away or Fall from the Origin which initiates the nihilistic decline of Christian and subsequent Western culture. The Decline reaches bottom, as it were, and attains its End in the full Nihilism of Modernity's devaluation of both evil and good, the levelling and equalization of all higher values that takes place in contemporary culture (egalitarianism, democracy and socialism). But a Return to the master morality principle of good and bad is foreshadowed in the re-emergence of a new master race and a reassertion of the pathos of distance between superiors and inferiors, in short in the overcoming of Nihilism. It goes almost without saying that this eschatology derives from the very Judeo-Christian traditions that Nietzsche so vehemently inveighs against.

In my book I also show how the same five phases of Nietzsche's eschatology reappear in his account of the history of philosophy, which is even more important for Heidegger.[15] At the origin of Western culture, in Homer, the tragedians and the tragic philosophers, the pre-Socratics, there is an incipient conception of 'another world' as opposed to 'this world', but this 'other world' is no more than a dim realm of shades and shadows. But along came Plato and inverted and so perverted this 'natural' relation, declaring 'this world' to be nothing but an 'apparent' world and the 'other world' to be a 'true' world:

> And behold, suddenly the world fell apart into a 'true' world and an 'apparent' world . . . And behold, now this world became false, and precisely on account of the properties that constitute its reality: change, becoming, multiplicity, opposition, contradiction, war. And then the entire fatality was there . . .[16]

This fatality is the Fall of philosophy into metaphysics, 'the greatest error that has ever been committed, the essential fatality of error on earth'.

The Fall works itself out as a gradual Decline through the subsequent history of Western philosophy. It reaches its End in modern Nihilism brought about by the corrosive acids of science, Positivism and the other 'moraline' agents of devaluation which reveal the 'true' world of the metaphysicians to be a mere fiction or 'false' world. As a result, its contrasting opposite, 'this world' or the 'apparent' world, also comes to be seen to be false and valueless. Thereby a general condition of Nihilism ensues. In this parlous state along comes the new Zarathustra, alias Nietzsche in disguise, and begins a counter-movement of Return back to the Origin in a new revaluation which will eventually overcome Nihilism and begin the eschatological cycle again in an eternal recurrence of the Same.

Löwith is quite emphatic that 'Nietzsche's historico-philosophical construction of the decay of supersensible values ('How the "true world" finally became a fable') is adopted without reservation and simply paraphrased [by Heidegger]'.[17] Thus Heidegger explicitly takes over this five-stage eschatology of History and interprets it as a *Seinsgeschichte* or history of Being in which Being itself becomes the active agent of its own revelations and occlusions. Man or *Dasein* is passive, becoming the mere recipient of what Being chooses to give or to withhold, to present of itself or to conceal. Heidegger openly admits in some places that what he has in mind is an *Eschatologie des Sein*: 'das Sein selbst ist als geschichtliches in sich eschatologisch,'[18] he declares. But he does not simply repeat Nietzsche's version, he seeks to go one better than it in that he also locates Nietzsche within it as the precursor to himself. Nietzsche is merely the penultimate stage in the history of philosophy, the culmination and completion of Nihilism. Nietzsche merely inverts and overturns Plato and so cannot escape from the history of metaphysics. The real overcoming of metaphysics is reserved for Heidegger. In a nutshell, Plato is the first metaphysician; Nietzsche is the last; and Heidegger is the first post-metaphysical, or as he also sometimes puts it, post-philosophical thinker of Thought.

As the first metaphysician, Plato is responsible for the fall into nihilism: 'the essence of Nihilism is historically as metaphysics, and the metaphysics of Plato is no less nihilistic than that of Nietzsche. In the former, the essence of Nihilism is merely concealed; in the latter, it comes completely to appearance.'[19] Plato's metaphysics is thus a falling away from the original revelation of Being as this was first thought by the pre-Socratic philosophers, especially Heraklitus and Parmenides. Plato treats truth or *alytheia* as *orthodes*, that is, correctness and by this move he brings about the first fall from Being into beings, the initial forgetfulness of the ontological difference between Being and beings that is the start of the oblivion of Being.

'What happens is the history of Being, Being as the history of default'[20] – Heidegger makes it quite clear that the subsequent phase of Nihilism in *Seinsgeschichte* follows from this Fall. As he puts it, 'the essential unfolding of nihilism is the default of Being as such . . . The default of Being is its withdrawal, its keeping to itself with its unconcealment, which it promises with its refusing, self-concealing.'[21] In an earlier work Heidegger expostulates on the Fall as a continuous Event in history:

> And should we not say that the fault did not begin with us, or even our immediate or more remote ancestors, but this is something that runs through Western history from the very beginning, a happening which the eyes of all historians in the world will never perceive, but which nevertheless happens, which happened in the past and will happen in the future? What if it were possible that man, that nations in their greatest movements and traditions, are linked to being and yet had long fallen out of being, without knowing it, and that this was the most powerful and most central cause of their decline?[22]

Out of this Fall comes the Decline: from this original error or fault, as Heidegger calls it, the whole history of metaphysics unfolds as the gradual but ineluctable descent into a history of errance, the sinking into a forgetfulness of Being. Descartes and modern subjectivist philosophy is the crucial half-way stage of modernity in this ontological amnesia which is really a self-concealing of Being from *Dasein*. The final stage of this is reached with the subjectivist philosophers of Will culminating in Nietzsche, whose Will to Power Heidegger interprets as a 'will to will'. Will to will is also the essence of Technology, the final stage of the end of metaphysics as complete nihilism. The overcoming of metaphysics and consequently the move beyond this nihilism is the task reserved for his own Thought which makes the attempt to recollect or repeat or retrieve (*wiederholen*) the original thought of Being and so in effect to return back to the Origin; and thereby it promises what Heidegger, somewhat incautiously at times, refers to as a 'new dawn of Being'.[23] Thus Heidegger's eschatology does not fundamentally differ from that of Nietzsche and is open to the same criticisms.

The eschatological nature of Heidegger's later thought is not something that Heidegger scholars have failed to note. But they do not make it a basis for criticizing Heidegger. Indeed, some of them praise him for it. Thus John van Buren declares approvingly that 'there lies in it perhaps the most ingenious account of the "history of ideas" and culture that has ever been put forward.'[24] Apart from failing to see that Heidegger's 'ingenious account' is only the latest in a long line of eschatological speculations of which Nietzsche's was the more original, he fails to note how utterly self-contradictory it is, for it is Judeo-Christian theology used to attack Judeo-Christian theology. That it is Judeo-Christian theology van Buren has no doubt and, indeed, he brings out the specifically theological flavour of Heidegger's language, drawn largely from the New Testament, with unerring accuracy. His account is worth quoting in full if only to show that I have imposed nothing on Heidegger that is not there.

> In the late thirties, forties, and fifties, this mythos of origin, fall and second coming of the *arche*/kingdom-come was worked out in other versions of Heidegger's notion of the destined 'history of being'. Though it was a reinscription of his earlier model of Christian parousiology and kairology, Heidegger's account of this history nonetheless often seems to fly in the face of his early warnings against eschatological speculation. According to this *Geschichte,* this history/story, which Heidegger constantly revised right into the sixties and seventies, the first beginning (erstes Anfang) and first arrival (parousia, Anwesen) of the poetic truth of being took place with the pre-Socratics and the Greek tragedians, who at least implicitly experienced it. The falling away from this original dawn into the 'western land of evening' (Abendland), which has its Lutheran analogue in the *status corruptions* of original sin, began with Plato and unfolded in the long history of the 'oblivion of being', culminating in the 'world-night' of the departure of the gods and the 'wasteland' of the epoch of modern technology. In this ongoing night of 'homelessness', where we are 'too late for the gods and too early for beon', 'commemorative thinking' must 'wait' for the uncertain *Eschaton* of the technological epoch and for the address of the second arrival of being in the other beginning (anderes Anfang), which will come incalculatively like a thief in the night, releasing the 'saving power' of poetic dwelling in the fourfold of the 'arrival of the [new] god'.[25]

This 'most ingenious account of the "history of ideas" and culture that has ever been put forward', as van Buren puts it, is not only eschatological but through and through political as well. It is, as it were, the continuation of politics by other means, for it completely backs up Nazi ideology in its war against Jews, Modernists, liberal-democrats, communists and all its other enemies. For the high-point of the eschatology is to identify the Germans as the chosen people of history, and the German language as the favoured 'House of Being'. According to the schema of Origin, Fall and Second Coming, it is the Germans and their unique language who repeat at the end of the history of the West that which the Greeks initiated at its origin. In between the Greeks and the Germans there stretches nothing but the historical graveyard of Nihilism in which all other nations, languages and philosophies are buried. The Greeks and Germans mirror each other across this gap of time, the one the predestined reflection of the other. A former Heidegger pupil, Rainer Marten, has noted this forced analogy and the purpose it serves in Heidegger's historical scheme:

> There are many reasons why it is expressly 'the Greeks' that Heidegger needs for his design of an inverted Utopia of Being itself and of an intellectual, German definition (of essence). To return eschatologically to the Greek intellect, this must be reflected in an inceptive destiny. And where could this reflection better succeed than in the beginnings of philosophy, when the imagined intellect is one that is through and through philosophical.[26]

Heidegger has obviously borrowed Nietzsche's estimation of the Greeks, especially of the pre-Socratics, but he has used it, in a way that would have been abhorrent to Nietzsche, to endow the Germans with equal status. And furthermore, he has used it politically to support the Nazi totalitarian revolution and its leader. The Nazi movement is the only one to provide a counter-movement to Nihilism and Hitler is the only leader capable of awakening the German nation to its historical task at the culmination of the eschatological moment of fulfilment. At the same time, and not coincidentally, Germany has produced the one thinker able to recall and repeat the original manifestation of Being in Greek philosophy in another beginning, a second dawn of Being after the long dark night of Nihilism. That thinker, who is no longer a mere philosopher, is, of course, none other than the German shepherd of Being himself, the guardian of the House of Being.

Lukács' *The Destruction of Reason* is also a kind of *Heilsgeschichte*, a sacred theology of historical time, but couched in secularized Hegelian-Marxist terms. It is presented as a critical history of modern, largely German, philosophy and related intellectual concerns, which, by extension, can be seen as a critique of Modernity in general. Lukács is mainly concerned with criticizing the negative aspects of Modernity, but by implication these are set against the background of the positive aspects which are largely presupposed and left tacit. Thus for Lukács history gradually divides into two mutually opposed currents, the one leading to salvation and the other to damnation. The positive current has its source in early bourgeois philosophy, mainly in Kant, and leads through Hegel to Marx, then on to Lenin, Stalin and, presumably, culminating in Lukács himself, though he is too modest to say so openly. The negative current takes off from the same bourgeois sources, but leads through the reactionary Idealists, such as Schelling and Schopenhauer, and then on to Existentialism and *Lebensphilosophie*, such as that of Kierkegaard, Dilthey and Nietzsche, finally debouching into Racism and the proto-Nazis, such as Spengler, Klages and Heidegger.

The division between the two streams is by no means even, for the one is narrow, though presumably deep, the other is very wide, though presumably shallow, it takes in everything else that the Marxist tradition excludes, all that is non-Marxist. The point of crucial separation and polarization of the two streams is the 1848 Revolution, which for the first time separates the revolutionary sheep from the reactionary goats in Europe. In Russia, however, by special dispensation, the date is shifted forward to the 1905 Revolution, which leaves most Russians on the correct side of history, unlike most nineteenth-century Europeans. Lukács thereby made his concession to the Russian chauvinism that Stalin had made mandatory for all communists after the Second World War.

According to Lukács, History purifies itself by precipitating into an ever clearer separation, not only, as Marx would have it, between the bourgeois and proletarians, but also between the irrationalists and upholders of Reason. He took great pride, and regarded it as an original departure within Marxism, to have chosen Reason as the shibboleth of revolutionary rectitude. And obviously he saw himself as the great upholder of dialectical Reason, the philosophical successor to Hegel and Marx. His antitype he saw in Nietzsche, the Great Irrationalist, a kind of fallen angel of German philosophy who has led all the others since into the bottomless pit of Nazism.

With the defeat of Nazism, Lukács made a belated attempt to extend this *historia sacra* to the new exigencies of the Cold War. In the later parts of the book the Western powers opposed to the Soviet Union are incorporated into the irrationalist side, frequently retrospectively so. Thus nineteenth-century American Pragmatism as well as British Empiricism are cast together with twentieth-century Positivism and Existentialism as the progeny of the very same diabolic irrationalist paternity that spawned Nazism and Fascism. However, since Lukács' knowledge of Anglo-Saxon philosophy is so much weaker than his knowledge of German philosophy, he has nothing worthwhile to say concerning it. On German philosophy he is often critically acute on points of detail, even when his overall case is insupportable.

For Lukács there is but one right Marxist road, the only one that is straight and true, all others, no matter what their points of origin, are destined to end in Nazism or American imperialism. In the irrational night of non-Marxism all cows are equally black: Simmel is as responsible for

Nazism as Spengler; Jaspers and Heidegger are equally to blame; Dilthey is at one with Nietzsche in this respect. There is but one correct line of succession in philosophy and politics, anything that departs from it is irrational. The irrational is not simply that which is mistaken or in avoidable error and, therefore, subject to correction, it is that which is totally opposed to the truth and has no share in its heritage. The irrational is to be strenuously rejected and cast into the rubbish bin of history. By the time he had come to write *The Destruction of Reason* Lukács had abandoned every vestige of the Hegelian view of the dialectic according to which the truth is arrived at through the clash of contradictory concepts, so that opposed positions cannot be simply dichotomized as wholly rational or irrational. Instead he had adopted a Party-line approach to truth such that some positions, the Marxist ones, are objectively true and all opposed or even differing ones are simply false, that is, irrational.

Oddly enough, in the light of Lukács' Marxism, in his diatribe against German philosophy he ascribes to it far too much influence and importance as a causative agent of history. Apart from the usual blanket materialist explanation that monopoly capitalism is behind everything, there is little sense that there are any other robust causes at work in German history except philosophical ideas. There is no developed sociology of philosophy in Lukács which would have enabled him to more appropriately judge what part philosophical ideas played in political developments and what other factors were at work as well. His doctrinaire Marxism allows him only to view philosophy as ideology which subserves class interests, primarily that of the bourgeoisie; or as reflecting the predicament of a class given its position within the social whole in relation to the other classes, particularly that of the bourgeoisie in its defensive stance as against the rising proletariat. Any other approach which could provide a more nuanced explanation of the social and political role of philosophy is not even recognized as requiring to be argued against, it simply does not exist by the Stalinist canons with which Lukács operates. His study of the history of philosophy in *History and Class Consciousness*, where he was still able to utilize the social theories of his teachers, Simmel and Weber, no matter how distorted to make them consonant with Marx, was intellectually much more subtle and not as bereft of original insights as it later became in the *Destruction of Reason.*

By contrast to the previous two secondary masterworks, Gentile's *The Genesis and Structure of Society* is not cast in the form of an *a priori* history but more like an *a priori* social psychology. It purports to deal with the formation of the Self, Society, the State and other such grand abstractions of politics, but it does so in the speculative manner of Hegel rather than that of any modern empirical political sociology. Of any such sociological approaches Gentile is quite oblivious. His work is far from being even historical in the manner of Croce. He is more intent to provide an apologia for his Idealist conception of Fascism and, thereby, also to justify his actual current support for Mussolini's faltering regime in the closing stages of the Second World War.

It makes no sense to compare Gentile's account of the nature or structure of Society and the State or of economics and ethics with that of a real sociologist such as Weber. To criticize him in Weberian terms would be easy but pointless since he belongs to the quite different tradition of metaphysical thought on such subjects. At best, his abstract conjectures would have to be reinterpreted and given some theoretical specificity before they could even be referred to real history or society. This might yield some general ideas for social psychology. Hence it is with some justice that Harris compares Gentile to the older-style philosophical social psychology of G.H. Mead. Gentile's underlying purpose, as is Mead's, though for quite other reasons, is to provide a social psychological dissolution of the Self, that is, of the individual, which is seen by him as wholly a function of society, as a *societas in interiore homini.* Any sense of opposition, conflict or contradiction between Self and Society is thereby abrogated for it becomes theoretically impossible, and the phenomena which manifest such differences are explained away.

Gentile's aim in making the Self totally dependent on Society, unlike Mead's, however, is to make it also totally subservient to the State. The Subject is literally a subject of the State, for the State assumes the full force of the moral law, and in an ideal guise it becomes the very voice of conscience within the individual. If any given individual is obstreperous enough not to harken to his ideal conscience and obey the State, then it ought to compel him or her to do so, with violence if necessary. The amount of violence to be exerted to bring recalcitrant subjects into line is up to the Statesman, the *Duce*, to decide in each given case; and if it requires concentration camps for political re-education, then that is what the higher will of conscience within the individual demands. Furthermore, if this coersion takes place within the confines of the Fascist Corporate State, then it amounts to the highest realization of freedom and democracy. At the end of his life Gentile had produced an idealized version of the *filosofia di manganello* (blackjack philosophy) of which his opponents accused him earlier, not altogether unjustly as I previously showed.

In his *Philosophical Investigations* Wittgenstein avoids the pseudo-history or sociology of the others and chooses instead pseudo-anthropology in which to couch his philosophy. For that is what his language-games, which feature so prominently throughout the work, amount to in reality. They are no more than spurious anthropological fictions, as I have amply demonstrated in my book *A New Science of Representation*. They cannot possibly function as languages or parts of language in any way that is acceptable in linguistics. Yet Wittgenstein bases the whole approach of his later philosophy on such impossible *Gedankenexperimente*. In order to deal with any philosophical problem he adopts a two-step strategy of first, reducing the problem to an issue concerning the meaning of ordinary words; and second, of explicating this meaning in terms of the supposed language-game in which the word functions, asking rhetorically: 'What is the original language-game in which the word finds its home?' He then proceeds to devise a fanciful language-game activity in which the specific features of the meaning Wittgenstein wishes to project onto the word are supposedly instantiated. This is what passes for conceptual analysis. Such analysis is a kind of conceptual shadow-boxing in a magic ring of anthropological make-belief. It is a naive, linguistic fairy tale. For, as I have shown, the whole 'theory' of the language-game is a complete misconception of the nature of language. Furthermore, the misapplication of this model of meaning to theoretical and philosophical concepts leads to the reduction of such intellectually sophisticated ideas to the status of the meanings of ordinary words. Both of these moves are wholly indefensible and need to be unequivocally rejected.

As against the first move, I argued in my previous book that language cannot be conceived of in terms of language-games since no congeries of language-games can ever amount to a language as this figures in any real society. A language-game as Wittgenstein describes it is no better than a signalling system or signals code, which can either be pre-linguistic, occurring among animals or very young children, or it can be a system of codes that human beings who already speak a language employ. In the first case language-games fall far short of being languages themselves; in the second case they are dependent on and so parasitic on real languages. In fact, the very term 'language-game' is well nigh a contradiction in terms for games cannot be languages, and languages are not games. 'Language' and 'game' are opposed concepts in this respect.

As against Wittgenstein's second move, I argued that theoretical concepts and philosophical notions are not inherent in language as such. Languages in themselves contain no beliefs or complex ideas or theories or *Weltanschauungen*, for these belong to the narratives and texts of culture and are not purely linguistic. The fundamental separation of language and culture is one that Wittgenstein, together with the other malign masters and many other modern philosophers, was unable to acknowledge.

Yet, as I show, it is a fundamental and necessary distinction insisted on by many linguists and some anthropologists. It is the distinction between the verbal syntactic and semantic structures, on the one hand, and the cultural forms of myth, religion, science and philosophy, on the other. Consequently, philosophical problems have nothing to do with language *per se*, but only with philosophical theories and ideas that arise in the cultural context of historically specific modes of discourse, those of intellectual debate concerning systems of ideas.

The discussion of such philosophical problems only rarely touches on disputes about the meaning of ordinary words. It mainly concerns the interpretation or explication of theories and sophisticated ideas, that is, of concepts in that intellectual sense. The ordinary concepts, if they can even be called that, amounting to the simple meanings of ordinary words, are not really involved in such an intellectual activity. Wittgenstein's belief that an investigation or analysis of the meanings of ordinary words 'dissolves' philosophical problems by showing that they amount to no more than 'grammmatical' misconceptions, or, in other words, his so-called therapeutic 'method' of philosophizing, can be shown to be largely an illusion produced by a trick of meaning reflection. Sophisticated meanings are projected into simple words and then discovered in those words by this process of pseudo-analysis. But all that is ever found is what was put there in the first place. Language is a faithful mirror; the philosopher who looks into it will always see his own visage.

As I show in my book *A New Science of Representation*, language-analysis is by no means the asceptic, value-neutral, purely descriptive activity that its followers, especially the Oxford linguistic philosophers, took it to be. There is a *Weltanschauung* behind it, as, indeed, Wittgenstein himself half-admits. This *Weltanschauung* is ultimately a political ideology, albeit a very confused one, which is what makes it so difficult to identify. It contains both conservative and radical features at once, as in his notion of 'common language' or the ordinary language of the 'people' in all the varied meanings and values that this expression can connote in different ideologies.

One way of locating Wittgenstein's *Weltanschauung* is to see it in terms of the goal for which it aims: it is that of a cultural cure of the 'conceptual' sicknesses of modernity. This is the linguistic utopian project of preparing the basis of a sound culture in some indefinite future society. Wittgenstein is characteristically ambivalent as to his own role in all this. Sometimes he sees himself as merely another Freud of culture, who can at best provide a palliative for cultural corruption in treating the neuroses of language, releasing the cramps of the understanding by means of his language-analytic techniques. His Spenglerian assessment of the magnitude of the problem, the decline of the West no less, and his own anti-Semitic sense of himself as a Jew incapable, therefore, of any 'original' thought, make him despair of what he can achieve. Spengler's view of the role of Jews as mere cultural scavengers, feeding off the dead body of a once living cultural organism, re-emerges in Wittgenstein's estimate of the role of Jewish intellectuals and artists in modern society and to some extent of himself as well. In his self-abnegating moods Wittgenstein despairs of anything that an individual can do, and places all his hopes on a collective change in the way of life, such as was supposedly taking place in Russia under Bolshevism. However, in his more self-confident moods he does affirm the capacity of his philosophy to change the way things are seen and understood. He also believes it could have a profound effect on culture through its destructive critical potential. But its usefulness cannot be apparent to the dim minds in the dark times of the present, only to new generations of the future who will be free of the corruptions of modernity.

Modernity itself is Wittgenstein's great ideological antagonist. He is especially hostile to modern science and intellectualism, to Modernist art, to contemporary irreligious morality and, more vaguely, to Anglo-Saxon liberal democratic politics. In his reactionary conservative mood, he speaks as if these problems of modernity are so big and all-encompassing as to be well nigh insurmountable. At times Wittgenstein expresses himself as if he were a latter-day Hamlet for whom 'the time is out of joint'. But he does believe that he can set something right, for he has developed a technique for dissolving problems of language and these for him are the same as problems of culture.

Language and culture are identical for Wittgenstein. Hence the problems of modernity appear to him as problems of language. He followed the teachings of Karl Kraus, who held that cultural corruptions manifest themselves in language, for example, that a person's moral, intellectual and general character failings are revealed in his or her style and diction. Wittgenstein translated this sort of literary 'le homme c'est le style' snobbery from the personal level to the social, and ultimately to that of culture and history. Hence, he came to hold that the failings of a culture reveal themselves as unclarities of language and the philosophical problems to which these give rise. He deluded himself with the thought that he had in his own hands the means to tackle the cultural problems of modernity through his techniques of clarification of language and the dissolution of philosophical problems. And it seemed to him that all he had to do to achieve this was to provide a simple and clear description of the facts of language usage. This is why he asserts that 'the concept of a perspicuous representation is of fundamental significance for us' and wonders whether 'this is a *Weltanschauung*'.[27]

Indeed, as I argued in the previous chapter, it is a *Weltanschauung*, but not of the kind that Wittgenstein himself assumes it to be. It is not a self-aware philosophy of culture and language but engages in a series of surreptitious borrowings from various opposed and contradictory ideologies. Most of them involve an illicit identification of culture and language and the vague sense that a return to common or ordinary language can be culturally salutary. A Tolstoyan course of returning to the soundness and sanity of ordinary working people and common language seems to Wittgenstein the only way that the disease and madness of modernity can be cured or at least alleviated. What this amounts to in philosophical practice is simply an analysis of verbal usages in an attempt to provide a perspicuous representation of the supposed 'ordinary' meanings of words.

But once culture is distinguished and separated from language, once the concept of 'common language' is shown up for the ambiguous ideological construct it is, once philosophy is freed from any inherent relation to any kind of language analysis and placed within the realm of theoretical thought where it belongs together with science, once the anti-theoretical bias is removed, once all such Wittgensteinian moves are retracted, then his *Weltanschauung* shows itself for what it is – a confused medley of cultural-political ideologies. Its sole cultural function can only be academic, to found a school of philosophy – which is precisely what Wittgenstein said he did not wish to do. It is of no use in dealing with any of the cultural problems of modernity. On the contrary, any such attempts are always counter-productive. The whole linguistic movement in philosophy instigated by Wittgenstein can itself be viewed as one of the intellectual diseases of our time. Kraus's jibe at Freud's psychoanalysis, that it is itself the disease of which it claims to be the cure, can with more justice be applied to Wittgenstein's later philosophy.

Having concluded the survey of the secondary masterworks, I can now return to my previous consideration of how these emerged out of a *Kehre* and how they relate intellectually to the primary masterworks. I have spoken of all this in very general terms as a movement from totality to totalitarianism, but that is no more than a shorthand expression of a complex and convoluted series of transitions at once philosophical and political. The philosophy and the politics are not separable. The late works of the malign masters are neither works of philosophy nor works of politics in any traditional sense; one cannot, for example, refer to them as political philosophy. To consider them ideology or even mythology is not altogether correct either. The only way one can account for them is to see them as works that have emerged from a philosophical matrix but moved in a political direction. To understand how these peculiar intellectual hybrids arose one needs to trace their concepts and ideas as the outcomes of a series of characteristic transformations. This requires seeing the late work in terms of the early work, and the early work in terms of the previous philosophies from which the malign masters originated, as I shall do in the next chapter. But before going on to that, I shall briefly summarize the main differences between the early and late masterworks in each case.

Heidegger's move from the totality of his primary masterwork to the totalistic *Weltanschauung* (a term he himself strenuously rejected) of his secondary one can be expressed as the transition from Being and Time to Being and Language. But it is not the same notion of Being in both instances. In the early work the 'meaning of Being' is invoked at the start, yet left rather vague, for it is the hermeneutics of *Dasein* that preoccupies most of the work. *Dasein*, as I have shown, is a subjectivistic totality, a kind of non-egoistic solipsism, whose modes and moods, such as the oppositions potential–factical, authentic–inauthentic, etc. are collated into an Existentialist system. In the late work, by contrast, it is Being itself that becomes the main subject, the agent of history that discloses and occludes itself at its own behest, without *Dasein* being able to compel it to do its bidding in any way. Thus a totalistic *Weltanschauung,* based on the *Seinsgeschichte* which I previously examined, develops, one that traces the epiphany of Being in language seen as the 'House of Being'.

But language is no longer the individualistic speech and understanding of the early work, it is the collectivist voice of a nation. And, of course, it is only in the languages of the 'chosen people', the Aryan Greeks and Germans, that Being reveals itself. In the language of the Greeks – starting from the very root etymologies of basic words such as '*on*' and continuing in the words of philosophy such as '*alytheia*' – Being first discloses itself at the very start of the history of the West. And in a parallel and symmetrical way, at the end of the history of the West this origin of Being is once more recaptured, that is, recalled and repeated, in the no less original language of the Germans; whose etymology is as decisive for Being as that of Greek, and whose philosophers are, as it were, reincarnations of their ancient originals.

The transition from early to late Wittgenstein is also a transformation in the conception of language: from language as the totality of propositions to language as the form of life that is given to a group, that is, as the totalistic *Weltanschauung* of a community. In the *Tractatus* language is an atomistic totality coextensive with the world of atomic facts to which it is correlated. The relation between language and the world is a matter of the isomorphism of logical form, a 'picturing' relation that shows itself but cannot be stated. This *Tractatus* metaphysics of the relation between language and the world, which gives rise to the mystical ineffability of logical form, gives way in the *Philosophical Investigations* to a consideration of so-called logical grammar. This is an equally mystified conception of 'grammar', especially as so-called 'deep' grammar, which takes over the quasi-metaphysical role of determining the nature of things: 'essence is expressed by grammar,' states Wittgenstein.[28]

'Grammar', however, is not a metaphysical ultimate but is itself determined by the 'rules' governing language-games. And these, in turn, are based on natural 'agreements' which reveal themselves in the common uses of words and which are in conformity with very general facts of nature. Language-games are thus anthropological givens which cannot be questioned, refuted or refused; they are the *Urphänomena* of human culture. Only a change in the very general facts of nature on which they are based can alter them. They are impervious to the reformist zeal of intellect alone. Hence philosophy can only describe language, but change nothing in it of any consequence.

Wittgenstein's imaginary conception of language reflects a totalistic *Weltanschauung* just as much as Heidegger's. But it does not entail a direct move to totalitarianism. Rather, it implicitly recommends the more conservative course of a return to the original language-community in which our language-games supposedly have their home. The recovery of such a *Gemeinschaft* in some future society is the hidden political goal towards which Wittgenstein's late philosophy points, as I have previously explained. Thus his political ideology is at once a conservative and radical linguistic utopia, a striving for a total change in culture which will recover a lost age of uncorrupted language. For, as Gellner puts it, 'the primitive functional community, to which one was by implication advised to return under his guidance, would, then, from its own resources, solve or "dissolve" all problems which have been engendered by the mysterious and misguided striving for a universal and philosophically justified way of thought.'[29] In Gellner's view what this amounts to is regressive: 'Wittgenstein's programme recommended a collective infantile regression for all mankind.'[30]

In his primary masterwork Lukács had affirmed totality as the 'absolute domination of the whole, its unity over and above the abstract isolation of the parts'.[31] Despite Sartre's later admonition, with Lukács plainly in mind, that 'totalizing is identical with terror [in its] inflexible refusal to differentiate', it is not quite true that Lukács' 'absolute domination of the whole' is necessarily totalitarian.[32] However, it did become so once this 'whole' or 'dialectic of totality' became – in the course of Lukács' *Kehre* – the totalizing world-view of his political ideology, namely, Stalinism. For all his talk of reason, objective truth, reality and realism was simply a philosophically elevated way of expressing the Party line as dictated by Stalin, whose views, as Lukács held even towards the end of his life, always had a positive side. His biographer, Árpad Kadarkay, concludes bluntly that 'the concept of "totality", as understood by Lukács, spoke not on behalf of literary truth, but on behalf of totalitarian socialism.'[33] The distinction between his two masterworks is this basic difference between a metaphysics of totality and a totalizing worldview that amounts to totalitarianism.

In Gentile's late work there is a much more open and honest defence of totalitarianism, bereft of all subterfuge, than there is in any of the other malign masters. The pretence only comes in when he claims that this is simply a working out and application of his early Actual Idealism to practical political reality. However, as Harris and other commentators from Collingwood onwards have noted, there is a world of difference between the Act of Pure Thought as an abstract totality and the Fascist Corporate State as an actual totalitarian reality. Even when he tries to present the latter in an ideal form in the theory of 'transcendental society' of his final work, it still departs markedly from his early philosophy. It is true, as Harris states, that 'the doctrine that the State is immanent in the consciousness of the individual citizen can be found in his earliest writings, and is the foundation stone of his whole social theory.'[34] Harris concludes from this that 'since this immanent State is clearly identified with the Kantian moral will, it is fair to say that when he talks about "the State" Gentile usually means, or ought to mean, what we call "conscience".'[35] All this is dangerous in the extreme, but it still would not have led him to totalitarianism unless he made, what Harris calls, the 'mistake' of confusing 'the transcendental State with the actual structure of governmental authority'.[36] That is, the 'mistake' of endowing Mussolini's regime with the moral trappings of the Idealist conception of the Ethical State.

The main differences between the primary and the secondary masterworks can perhaps best be summed up by examining the transformations that had taken place in the three features identified in chapter 1 as characteristic of the metaphysics of the former, namely, totality, subjectless subjectivity and inactive activism. Such an estimate will provide a measure of the intellectual distance travelled by the malign masters in the course of their *Kehre*. At the same time, it also shows what their early and late philosophies still have in common despite all the differences.

In all the late works of the malign masters there takes place a transformation of the totality invoked in their early work for instead of a pure metaphysical totality, the abstract totality of the primary masterworks, there emerges in the secondary ones a much more concrete, but tenuous and indefinite, totalistic world-view of things. Ontological purity gives way to a historically and politically conditioned conception of reality as a whole. This is what Lukács called a 'totalizing world-view' and Wittgenstein referred to as his *Weltanschauung*. Obviously, each malign master's world-view is different, just as the politics of each is different. The totalizing conception in Gentile focuses on State and Nation, in Lukács on Reason or the Marxist conception of History, in Heidegger on *Seinsgeschichte* or the eschatological schema of the history of Being, and in Wittgenstein on language and linguistic clarity to counter the tendency to 'grammatical' confusion. However, despite these enormous differences, there is a common impulse at work, the propensity to propound a vision of salvation for mankind that will rescue it from its fallen state in modern times. And this promise of redemption is almost invariably expressed in the political terms of an ideal totalitarianism.

Wittgenstein seems the only exception to this, for his is an implicit advocacy of a linguistic Utopia, instead of an actual totalitarian system. But the two are not unrelated. Wittgenstein is implicitly advocating a return to an original 'language-community' whose language is not yet corrupted; that is to say, whose language-games have not been rationalistically intellectualized by philosophy and science. But since no such 'language-community' can be located anywhere in the actual historical present, it can only be projected into some revolutionary future when 'people will be different'. What is clearly apparent in Wittgenstein is that it is not only the first theme, that of totality, which has undergone a transformation in moving from the primary to the secondary masterwork, so too have the other two themes, that of non-egoistic solipsism and that of inactive activism, these have also been subjected to a thorough revision. Whereas in the former there is an abstract subject correlative with the world, 'I am my world', in the latter there is the concrete social subject of an actual group or community. Such an impulse to transform the subject in a collectivist direction is also apparent in the other malign masters, where it is more obviously in keeping with their totalitarian ideologies. In each of them there arises what Wolin, referring to Heidegger, has called 'a collective megasubject'.[37]

In late Heidegger the collective megasubject is most often called *Dasein*, but it no longer carries the connotations of an individualistic, private being that it had in his primary masterwork. It is either given the collectivist feature of Man, meaning by this Western mankind, that is, primarily Aryan Man, or it has a distinctively German look and becomes synonomous with the chosen Volk. Heidegger's so-called anti-humanism notwithstanding, *Dasein* as Man or some such term remains as a collective megasubject throughout his later work. It is only its relation to Being that changes, there it becomes more a case of Man proposes but Being disposes.

In his early work, despite his doctrinaire Marxism, Lukács did maintain a strong sense of subjectivity as consciousness, developing on Hegel, Fichte and early Marx. After the *Kehre* most of this disappears. As his old friend Bloch complained, 'everywhere, Lukács proposes a closed, integrated reality that leaves no room for subjective idealism'; and he avers that 'it is possible, however, that Lukács' concept of reality, the transposed totality, is not really objective.'[38] This is putting it very mildly. 'Subjective idealism' was the pejorative term Lukács brandished to attack all 'bourgeois' manifestations in philosophy and literature; most frequently linking it to the term 'irrationalist'. 'Objective' and 'realistic' became the contrary terms of praise for works that embodied the 'socialist' sense of 'totality' that was currently approved of and sanctioned.

In Gentile the collective megasubject is clearly stated to be the community as Nation organized in a State. The individual subject is attenuated to the point of extinction, becoming submerged in the communal according to his doctrine of *societas in interiore homine*. As he puts it in simple grammatical terms, 'at the root of the "I" there is a "we"'.[39] The change from the early to the late philosophy of the subject is quite marked, as Harris explains: 'roughly speaking, we may say that this "renunciation of solitude" is the great novelty of Gentile's last work. Even the second volume of the *Logic*, in which the theory of the *alter* as *socius* briefly appears, is dominated by the doctrine of the "eternal solitude of the Spirit".'[40] Gentile travelled from solipsism to an almost subjectless anti-individualist communalism, from one extreme to the other, without a proper appreciation of individual subjectivity which is, as it were, lost en route.

The third paradoxical factor, that of inactive activism, would seem to have been resolved in totalitarianism. The highly fraught tension of will, decision and resolve of the primary masterworks seems to have been discharged in the secondary ones through active participation in an ideological cause. The acquisition of a Party card would appear to have been the answer to philosophical quandary for three of the malign masters, and the fourth made his choice clear even without formal Party membership. However, this outcome, though perhaps satisfactory in practice, was far from being so in theory. For once they became committed to a totalitarian movement, the malign masters no longer bothered to think through philosophically the basic issues in politics, ethics and the other fields of practical reason. It is significant that none of them produced a work dealing with such matters. Lukács attempted it only in his old age when it was too late, and he left his work unfinished.

I have emphasized the differences that separate the early from the late works of the malign masters. But that must not be taken to imply that there is a complete break or total gulf between them. The late works do not develop a wholly separate philosophy, a completely different approach, they are merely transformations of the original approach in the general directions previously specified. This means that there are also continuities between the primary and secondary masterworks. The malign masters themselves insisted on these continuities. Thus Wittgenstein in his Foreword to *Philosophical Investigations,* Heidegger in his Preface to Father Richardson's book *From Phenomenology to Thought* and Lukács in his belated Introduction to the 1967 second edition of *History and Class Consciousness* all make a point of emphasizing that their late works must be read against the background of their early works; and, furthermore, that their primary masterworks are not to be dismissed as wholly wrong, despite the fact that they had turned against them during their *Kehre.* Partly, of course, this sort of disclaimer of a complete break between early and late philosophies must be seen as a salvaging operation to ensure that the early works, which had in the meantime become universally famous in their own right, will not be neglected or discounted. But partly, too, it is perhaps an unconscious tribute and acknowledgement of the superiority of the early works with which they made their careers.

The continuities between the *Tractatus* and *Philosophical Investigations* have been set out by Hao Wang under six points derived from the preface to the *Tractatus:*

> W1. The goal is to deal 'with the problems of philosophy'. W2. The way to attain this goal is 'to set a limit to thought'. W3. The way to do this is to set a limit 'not of thought, but to the expressions of thought', i.e., to language. W4. The reason why the problems of philosophy ('metaphysical' problems in particular) are posed is that the logic of our language is misunderstood. W5. What 'can be said at all can be said clearly, and what we cannot talk about must be consigned to silence'. W6. Wittgenstein believed himself 'to have found, on all essential points, the final solution to the problems' (of philosophy).[41]

According to Hao Wang, the late philosophy of Wittgenstein continues to maintain points W1–W5; there is only some ambiguity about W6, since it is not the case that late Wittgenstein believes himself already to have solved all problems of philosophy, but merely to have invented an analytic technique whereby problems can be solved or 'dissolved' as they happen to arise, like an itch that continually has to be scratched anew.[42] If this is indeed Wittgenstein's basic programme of philosophy, then the main difference between his early and late work is simply that the former addresses itself to the problems in the philosophy of logic as these arise out of the issues broached by *Principia Mathematica*, whereas the latter generalizes this approach to all philosophical problems whatever. The former claim to have solved all problems makes some sense when applied to these logical issues; the latter claim to be able to 'dissolve' all problems makes no sense whatever when referred to the metaphysical traditions of thought. For these latter are not problems that can be solved or dissolved; they are paradoxes that arise out of metaphysical systems and have no meaning apart from them. They cannot be lifted out of their texts and treated as simple problems on their own. They have to be understood in their context and interpreted in terms of and in relation to the systems of thought out of which they arise; which Wittgenstein fails to do, and refuses even to consider.

The continuities between *Being and Time* and Heidegger's later writings have also been often noted. In particular, it has frequently been remarked that in the second half of this work there is already prefigured what would become his later political commitment in the themes of belonging to a community, choosing a tradition, responding to the call for heroism and leadership, and the idea of Destiny, all of which were to play such a nefarious role later. Heidegger does not distinguish between the individual and social levels, the concept of *Dasein* obfuscates this distinction, so that what appears on the individual level in the early work is often referred to society and history in the later work. Thus the early themes of anxiety, the call, care, concern, conscience and finitude often recur in the later work applied to the Volk or the history of the West. Another kind of continuity is Heidegger's annoying habit of playing on the root meanings of words, an age-old technique of didactic preaching. He seems to have acquired from Nietzsche the further idea that ontology recapitulates philology, namely, that the concepts and categories of philosophy are versions of the basic meanings and grammatical forms of words in Greek. Later Heidegger was to apply this to German as well and make a fetish of breaking up and playing with the syllables of words. The confusions concerning language that underlie all this, I have already explained.

The continuities between the early and late works of Gentile and Lukács seem less of an issue for they both claimed to hold a consistent philosophic line from start to finish. For Gentile this was his Actual Idealism from which he never deviated and never turned against his earlier work. For Lukács it was his Hegelian-Marxism; though he did turn against his earlier work under Party pressure. He later claimed that his rejection of *History and Class Consciousness* was sincerely meant and, what is more, that it was justified. To what extent this is true and to what extent Lukács practised his habitual form of double-think is now difficult to establish.

One cannot take Lukács' words about his past at face-value. Nevertheless, even if he did sincerely reject his earlier masterwork this still does not create any serious difficulties about the continuity of his overall *œuvre*. In fact, many of the themes which he first broached in his youth, especially during his Heidelberg period, he took up again in his old age. These works of his old age, and how he came to write them, require further consideration.

It was only after Stalin's death and Krushchev's disclosures at the Twentieth Party Congress concerning Stalin in 1956 that Lukács finally found his own voice again. After his notable part in the Hungarian uprising which followed, and from which he barely escaped with his life, he once more returned to philosophical work in his retirement and produced his last works. This was no mean achievement at his age and raises the question whether he, unlike the other malign masters, had entered a third period after the second, following his *Kehre*. Is the developmental pattern, which I inductively derived from the lives of all the malign masters, incomplete in Lukács' case? Gentile and Wittgenstein can hardly be said to have had a third period after their secondary masterworks because they died too soon for that to be possible. Only Heidegger is potentially another candidate for a third period, for he continued writing and lecturing long after his secondary masterwork had been finished (though not published) and was active well into old age. I shall consider his claim after I have dealt with Lukács' first.

Lukács' disciples, Agnes Heller and Ferenc Feher, write of his work in old age as if he had indeed entered a new phase of his career, the equivalent in my terms of a third period. Thus Feher states:

> The mid-1950s, the period after Stalin's death, prompted a change in Lukács' political and aesthetic position, even if not a 'radical' one. The change in Lukács was slow and gradual (the old reverberations of 'anti-realism' cropped up in his writings in the most unexpected places); it involved a return to the (Jacobin-proletarian-monolithic) radicalism of the 1920s, it did not imply a radical renunciation (either political or aesthetic) of the premises that had guided him since the Hungarian Revolution in 1919.[43]

In the course of this by no means 'radical' change Lukács set about writing his last works. Of three projected masterworks only the one on aesthetics, *Das Eigenartige des Aesthetischen,* was completed and published in 1963 when Lukács was 78. Of the other two, *On the Ontology of Social Being* is a large but incomplete fragment and the *Ethics* barely exists at all. What is one to make of these works: are they the ripe fruits of a mature old age, the intellectual equivalent of Verdi's last operas, or are they merely an old man's 'theoretical autobiography', as Ernst Joos maintains? According to Joos, 'his ontology comes close to Bergson's *évolution créatrice*'.[44] This work has even incurred the criticism of Lukács' own close disciples.

However, Tom Rockmore has very recently come out with a very different opinion. According to him, 'this study represents a new high point in Lukács' Marxist period because of its theme, its intrinsic quality, and its revised understanding of Marxism.'[45] He makes it clear that in this work, Lukács had finally regained his freedom to think and was no longer following a narrow orthodox Marxist line. He goes on to compare favourably Lukács' treatment of reason as against that of Habermas, arguing that 'Lukács offers a wider, theoretically more powerful analysis of the specific differences between the older view of reason and a proposed Marxist alternative as well as a more detailed account of the philosophical tradition from this new perspective.'[46] All this might well be true, but is it enough to constitute a new departure? Without a close study of the *Ontology* it is difficult to substantiate any definite point of view, but on balance it seems to me unlikely that this work, though obviously of great interest, is unprecedented, being more of a scholastic attempt to synthesize various kinds of twentieth-century metaphysics.

That only leaves the *Aesthetics* about which opinions also differ. According to Georg Lichtheim, it is 'an exposition of aesthetic principles largely derived from Weimar culture.'[47] Its premisses are those of classical aesthetics from Aristotle to Hegel. As Lichtheim sees it, 'he has done for his chosen topic what Dilthey did for Kant and Hegel: he has systematized a body of ideas, that was once novel and revolutionary, and rendered it fit for academic consumption.'[48] But even this, as Lichtheim makes evident, is a no mean achievement in this day and age. However, it does not amount to another breakthrough, a third period. It seems rather a desperate attempt in old age to accomplish what Lukács had failed to achieve in his youth. Lukács seems to have returned to the grant projects he had hatched in partnership with Bloch and to the incomplete work of his Heidelberg period during the First World War when he was also Weber's unofficial student and friend. Politically, he seems to have returned to the youthful romantic Bolshevism that immediately followed with Kun's Hungarian Revolution. There is an element of nostalgia about it all that precludes it from being a new departure.

Something similar holds for the works that Heidegger wrote in his old age. In these works Heidegger seems to be returning to the religious mysticism and a generalized version of the theology of his Catholic youth. As John Caputo states, 'these writings are marked by Heidegger's deeply

– albeit generically – religious discourse of giving and receiving, grace and graciousness, saving and danger, address and response, poverty and openness, end of time and new beginning, mystery and withdrawal, and by a new thematic of the truly divine God.'[49] This has been of interest to post-Bultmannian theologians, but it has little to offer to philosophers. Even one of his younger American followers, Gerald Bruns, admits that 'what goes on in the writings of the later Heidegger cannot truthfully be called reasoning of any sort.'[50]

In very late Heidegger poetry has assumed the role of a kind of secular mysticism. This leads him to a strangely mystified conception of language. Language, on this view, is neither representation nor expression of things that pre-exist it. Rather it is a 'primordial naming' which brings things into presence and calls them into the world. Language is no longer something spoken by people; but, to the contrary, it 'speaks' them. This hypostatization of language is not without its hidden political implications. Allan Janik summarizes Robert Minder's argument to this effect; referring to the Hebel lecture he concludes as follows:

> Heidegger does indeed seem to reify the notion of language and, what is worse, to shroud it with mystery in the manner of just those Romantic authors who were most appealing to the Nazi ideologists. Moreover, his reference to dialect (*Muttersprache*) as the origin (early in the lecture as the *Quelle*), as Minder emphasizes, is typical of *völkisch* rhetoric. The same is true of the peculiarly repetitive usage of *Sprache* and its cognates.[51]

As we now know from the detailed investigations of Farias and the belated admissions of Heidegger's own pupils, he never abandoned key elements of the Nazi ideology, just as Lukács, too, retained his Bolshevik faith till the end. All in all, in Heidegger's case, even far less so than in Lukács', there can be no question of a third period.

This concludes my account of the major works of the malign masters. Having completed a study of the texts in this Part I, I can now turn in Part II to an examination of the contexts in which these were produced. I shall be mainly intent on the background influences behind the primary masterworks, in particular on the fathers, grandfathers and earlier forefathers. The influences behind the secondary masterworks, some of which have already been cursorily mentioned, cannot be studied here to any extent and will have to be considered elsewhere.

Part II
Influences and Confluences

4 Fathers and Sons

'The philosopher must dare to become a father-killer,'[1] Heidegger told his students in his lecture-course of 1924–5. He proved himself true to his word just a few years later when he carried out his own act of parricide. By that stage all the other malign masters had already disposed of their paternal mentors. By this Oedipal deed each sought to establish his independence and, indeed, superiority as a philosopher and take the place of the slain father. The philosophical public cheered: the master is dead, long live the master.

But who exactly were these fathers who were so unceremoniously dispatched without a twinge of guilt or later remorse? Each of the malign masters began as the beloved pupil, close collaborator and intimate friend, that is, as the son and hoped-for heir of an older thinker of the pre-1914 generation. Such was the relation between Lukács and Weber, Heidegger and Husserl, Wittgenstein and Russell, and Gentile and Croce. Croce considered Gentile his younger partner in thought with whom he carried on an extended dialogue, a *concordia discors*, for nearly a quarter of a century. Weber saw Lukács as 'a potential companion and ally in the field', as Eva Karadi states; he assiduously groomed and promoted him for a position at Heidelberg in succession to himself and quotes him in his great speech 'Science as a Vocation' as if he were already an established master thinker.[2] Husserl said to Heidegger repeatedly during the 1920s, 'you and I are phenomenology', and he helped set him up on his own Chair in philosophy. Russell not only saw Wittgenstein as his successor, but made haste to vacate his place for him; under Wittgenstein's withering criticism he abandoned his project of 1913, 'Theory of Knowledge', and commented, 'well, well – it is the younger generation knocking at the door – I must make room for him when I can, or I shall become an incubus.'[3] All of these fathers were to be sadly disappointed with their sons and heirs presumptive.

At first it looked as if the sons had fulfilled their fathers' hopes in writing their primary masterworks. Two of them, Gentile and Heidegger, dedicated their works to their teachers – dedications that were later prudently omitted when political realities intervened. The other two, Lukács and Wittgenstein, might easily have followed suit, had not political differences in the former and personal loyalties to a dead friend in the latter made that impossible. Despite such testaments of loyalty and devotion from their sons, the fathers soon realized that these works produced under their aegis, and for the most part only published because of their support, were foreign to their minds and antithetical to their own work. They had reared cuckoos in their swallows' nests. At first each of them confessed himself baffled by the metaphysics of totality that their sons had espoused. This bafflement soon turned to rage when they realized that these works were a fundamental betrayal of all that they stood for and valued.

Initially, Croce reacted to Gentile's new philosophy of Actual Idealism more in resigned sadness than in anger, criticizing it as a 'mystical mish-mash in which clear thinking dissolved'.[4] In 1918, in an essay entitled 'On the Survival of Theologizing Philosophy', Croce wrote as follows:

> The mind thus bewitched by the old metaphysical reasoning, in its zealous striving to possess what one Italian philosopher, Spaventa, actually invoked as a 'brain above brain', runs perforce into one of two blind alleys, the first being, so to speak, a hunt for unity on the hither side of the process of distinction, and the second a hunt on the yonder side . . . The effort, then, pursued along the first blind alley, leads to metaphysics and mythologism, and if refuge then he sought in the second blind alley, one is back in the arms of mysticism . . . In fact, it is no historical or critical urge that foments this zealous hunt for unity, but the incessant religious urge for an escape, a beatification, a pacification in a mythical image or a mystical sensation of God.[5]

At this stage Croce had little inkling where this craving for unity would lead. But in the 1920s, when Gentile began to put this philosophy to practical political effect, Croce gradually turned against him; he complained of *troppo filosofia* and took to biting criticism of every one of Gentile's ideas. Soon after Gentile became a Fascist a complete breach opened between them, and there ensued 'twenty years of bitter hostility and violent polemic', as Harris notes.[6]

Weber was already dead when Lukács' primary masterwork appeared in print, hence we do not have his reaction to it. But we know what he would have said had he been alive. In a letter to Lukács of March 1920, soon after Lukács had taken part, and nearly lost his life, in the failed Hungarian revolution, Weber writes more in sorrow than in anger:

> Most esteemed friend, of course, we are separated by our political views! (I am absolutely convinced that these experiments *can* only have and will have the consequence of discrediting socialism for the coming 100 years) . . . I cannot help feeling bitter about this senseless fate . . . Everything will be reactionary for decades to come.[7]

Before he died Weber had read three of the articles which later in revised versions appeared as chapters in *History and Class Consciousness.* Hence many of the critical asides Weber makes in his late work refer explicitly to Lukács' views. For example, in *Economy and Society* he speaks of the 'pseudo-scientific operation with the concepts class and class interest which is so frequent these days and which has found its most classic expression in the statement of a talented author that the individual may be in error concerning his interest but that the class is infallible about its interests.'[8] He countered Lukács' 'ethics of conscience' with his own 'ethics of responsibility'. He was appalled by Lukács' 'claim that the Communist Party resides in the sphere of morality',[9] insisting that a political party is an organization for domination. And he countered Lukács' view of the Revolution as an apocalyptic event in history with his own sober assessment of plebeian revolutions as charistmatic movements fuelled by *ressentiment.* At first Lukács responded to Weber only obliquely and indirectly. Much later Lukács attacked Weber directly and listed him among those 'preparing the ground of German barbarism'.[10] We know what his brother, Alfred, who was also attacked by Lukács, felt about that, and Max would if anything have reacted even more strongly had he been alive.

Husserl was slow in grasping the full import of *Being and Time* when he first published it under the auspices of his journal and continued to support Heidegger in his academic career. But as soon as he read it with any care and attention, he realized how opposed it was to his own work. He accused it of the mortal sin of phenomenology, 'anthropologism'. His attitude to the work is recorded in the marginal notes he made in his copy, now preserved in the Louvain Archives. Thus he refers to Heidegger's hermeneutic of *Dasein* as 'the way to an intentional psychology of personality'.[11] Thomas Sheehan states that 'Husserl would later attribute Heidegger's divergence from his own work to Heidegger's theological prejudices and the disorienting experience of the war and its ensuing difficulties [which] "drive men into mysticism".'[12] What Heidegger thought of Husserl is ironically conveyed by Löwith's note written in 1939: 'in 1938 Husserl died in Freiburg, Heidegger proved that "Admiration and Friendship" (the terms in which he dedicated his 1927 work to Husserl) by wasting no words of remembrance or sympathy either public or private, oral or written.'[13]

Russell was even slower than Husserl in realizing the hostile tenor of Wittgenstein's work to his own. He, too, found the mysticism resulting from war experience somewhat disconcerting. Nevertheless, he ensured the publication of the *Tractatus* and wrote an Introduction to it, which Wittgenstein accused of such a gross 'failure to understand' that only with great qualms did he bring himself to suffer it appearing together with his work. Russell did not take this as badly as he might have and in 1930 intervened decisively in securing Wittgenstein's appointment at Cambridge. Only much later did it become clear to him that Wittgenstein's 'new philosophy' was the antithesis of his own. Wittgenstein considered Russell mentally dead and never ceased to belittle him in private to his disciples; though outwardly in Russell's presence he maintained a hypocritical façade of respect. When Russell finally decided to retaliate, so as to scotch the influence Wittgenstein was having on the young after the Second World War, it was already too late to have any effect. Towards the end of his life he declared vehemently, 'I detest linguistic philosophy more and more as time goes on and I am sorry that at one time I thought well of Wittgenstein.'[14]

It must not be supposed that the fathers' typical reaction to the work of the sons was simply a case of jealousy, of old men not appreciating the achievements of young 'geniuses', as the disciplines of the malign masters make out. Nor was it a matter of resentment that the sons abandoned the ways of the fathers. For at no time did the fathers treat the sons as mere disciples, in the way that the sons were later to treat their own pupils. The fathers regarded the sons more as friends and collaborators from whom they were prepared to learn as much as they were teaching them. Thus Croce writes much later in his *Autobiography*:

> I came into direct touch with Hegel through the friendship and collaboration of Gentile, in whom the tradition of Spaventa came to life again, more flexible, more modern, more open to criticism and self-criticism, richer in spiritual interests; and in this way, in spite of occasional differences between the paths which we respectively followed, Gentile and myself came to influence each other and to correct each other's faults.[15]

Much the same might have been said by Weber about Lukács, Husserl about Heidegger and Russell about Wittgenstein. Weber owed to Lukács the incentive to a more critical ethical and aesthetic thinking and a deepened appreciation of the great Russian novelists, Tolstoy and Dostoevsky, about whom Weber was planning a book at one time. Husserl owed to Heidegger a sense of the 'everyday', which he went on to examine phenomenologically as the *Lebenswelt.* Russell owed to Wittgenstein his philosophy of Logical Atomism which he briefly entertained during his First World War period. These debts were generously acknowledged in each case.

In all these respects the ethics of the fathers was very different to that of the sons. This was not just a matter of a difference of personal character, it was a measure of the changed moral climate of two epochs, that before and after the First World War, the initial calamity in Europe's moral decline. The fathers imbibed the atmosphere of an antedeluvian Europe with its humanistic, rational-scientific, culturally modernist and politically liberal spirit, the very opposite of the spirit that their sons were later to manifest. The fathers practised the traditional norms of scholarly intercourse and free communication which their sons abandoned. Croce, Weber, Husserl and Russell were not altogether foreign and hostile to each other's work in the way that Gentile, Lukács, Heidegger and Wittgenstein came to be. The fathers strongly opposed their sons' totalitarian involvements. Croce was a life-long enemy of Fascism; Weber opposed both nascent Nazism and Bolshevism; Husserl could obviously have no truck with Nazism or even with revolutionary conservatism; and Russell already realized the dictatorial reality of Soviet Russia in the early 1920s under Lenin and never ceased to inveigh against it. All these ethical, cultural, scientific and political differences between the generations are encapsulated in one famous debate, in 1929 at Davos, between Cassirer, a representative of the old and fading ethos, and Heidegger that of the new about to come to power. As Habermas sees it:

> The theme was Kant but in truth the end of an epoch was up for discussion. The opposition of the schools paled beside that of generations. Cassirer represented the world in which Husserl belonged against his great pupil – the cultivated world of European humanism against a decisionism that invoked the primordiality of thought, whose radicality attacked the Goethe culture at its roots . . . The discussion came to an end with Heidegger's refusal to take Cassirer's outstretched hand. What Heidegger announced four years later, at the Leipzig election rally of German scientists in the name of Hitler's party, reads like a continuation of these events.[16]

As such events reveal, the generational break was a breakdown in all those values that had constituted European culture, including such basic norms as ordinary civility. Now more than half a century later we can begin to appreciate better the cultural loss this entailed. The achievements of the fathers were not to be equalled by anything that came later, and certainly not by the work of their sons. There is nothing to match the full corpus of Weber's sociology, with its universality of scope, detailed empirical research or methodological sophistication. Russell and Whitehead's *Principia Mathematica* is a milestone in logic. Husserl's foundation of phenomenology as a *strenge Wissenschaft* and the body of work he accomplished on this basis is still exemplary. Even Croce's work in history, criticism, aesthetics and practical philosophy, though not perhaps as great or original as the others, is still worthy of attention and study. Some Italian philosophers are beginning to recognize that fact, including the Heideggerian philosopher Gianni Vatimo, who states: 'now that the anti-Idealist wave of the postwar period – inspired by Existentialism, but above all by neo-Positivism and Scientism – has exhausted itself, we are in a better position to resume contact with the work of Croce.'[17] As I maintain in what follows, re-establishing contact with the fathers in general would seem to be the best course on which philosophy can now proceed. Philosophy might advance by returning to the fathers and by-passing the sons en route. The starting point from which the sons began, and from which they then deviated by strange turnings and returnings, might also be our own new point of departure from which we might take a new bearing on the future. 'Back to the fathers' is the slogan that philosophers might now adopt on the model of the earlier 'back to Kant'.

The malign masters were like prodigal sons, heirs to a rich legacy which they squandered, first in the pursuit of metaphysical and theological will-o'-the-wisps, later in reckless political gambles, following an uncharted course from totality to totalitarianism that inevitably ended in shipwreck on the hard rocks of political reality. They began with the ideas of their fathers but utilized them to serve strange ideologies which were antithetical to the values of the fathers. The ideas, methods, philosophical approaches of the old masters were both systematically appropriated and distorted by their successors. At first this misuse of their predecessors' work was more or less hidden under a disguise of respect and reverence which suited their ulterior goals. For on the one hand, the sons could present themselves to the public as the designated heirs of their fathers achievement and so profit from the already established reputations that the latter had accrued. On the other hand, they could go behind their backs and claim to have gone beyond them and surpassed them, and so be credited with even greater originality than their fathers were granted. They were dwarfs standing on the shoulders of giants but pretending to soar high above them by flapping their hands, which, of course, raised them not a whit higher, except in the estimation of their applauding students and followers.

I shall now proceed to examine the relation between the work of the fathers and that of the sons in some detail. Not every primary masterwork of one of the malign masters relates to an old master's work in quite the same way, or can even be accounted for in quite the same terms, but there are close parallels in all cases even though the details are very different. What the sons took from the fathers they invariably simplified and distorted to serve their own purposes. In general, the sons were intent on appropriating just those aspects which would serve their early predisposition towards totality, non-egoistic solipsism and active inactivity, the main features of their primary masterworks. All else was tacitly abandoned or subjected to criticism. Since I cannot provide here full-length studies of all these relations, I shall confine myself to a few leading pointers in each case.

In a recent work, the logician Hao Wang explains how Wittgenstein transformed Russell's work and made his own seem so much more impressive:

> how he took on Russell's problem and modified it; how he selected from Russell's wealth of suggestions, modified them, and carried them to their logical extremes; how his influences on Russell and the logical positivists and [later] on the ordinary language philosophers are to be understood in terms of his cryptic style, serious distortion of his views, and a predisposition to certain rigidified beliefs.[18]

Wittgenstein was able to accomplish this by a few grossly simplifying moves:

> Wittgenstein transformed the program [of Russell] by dropping the theory of knowledge and concentrating on a theory of the world. Two strong oversimplifying (and mistaken) assumptions were made concerning infinity and atomicity. The result was the awe-inspiringly brief and elegant *Tractatus.* This seminal work appeared to give a surprisingly simple and compelling theory of logic and its sharp separation from science. An astonishing episode in intellectual history is how this powerful book misled Russell and the logical positivists, who were largely familiar with and greatly interested in mathematics, to adopt an obviously unreasonable and trivializing conventionalist conception of mathematics.[19]

An astonishing episode in intellectual history, indeed, especially given that Wittgenstein himself hardly knew enough mathematics for the job he was undertaking. His biographer, McGuiness, now states that his knowledge was no better than that of a sophomore student: 'his mathematical education and sophistication barely qualified him to discuss the foundations of mathematics in the way he did.'[20] Hao Wang himself provides the explanation why so many distinguished philosophers allowed themselves to be so easily misled. Wittgenstein's simplifying assumptions 'promised to supply or strengthen the missing or fragile link in the neat and alluring picture of knowledge and the world, which the logical positivists were striving to complete'.[21] In other words, it promised to provide a total picture of the world all in one neat expression. The lure of totality – of having the full picture and being able to supply all the answers to all problems – proved irresistible even to seasoned minds such as Russell's.

Lukács' appropriation of Weber was much more surreptitious than

Wittgenstein's of Russell, for as a Bolshevik revolutionary activist, subject to Party discipline and the ever watchful critical eyes of Lenin and the others, he could no longer openly admit his derivation from Weber, who was regarded as a bourgeois German nationalist and enemy of the Revolution. After Lenin's criticism of Lukács, as exemplifying the 'infantile disorder of left-wing communism', in 1920, he knew he dare not put a foot wrong, left or right. To have admitted to any residues of Weberism would have been enough to have warranted his expulsion from the Party, which was more than he could bear. But denying his Weberian heritage did him no good anyway, for at the fifth Comintern Congress in 1924 he was denounced as a 'revisionist' by Zinoviev, and the forbidden Weberian influence was detected by Deborin, on whom Lukács would wreak his revenge later under Stalin.[22] This was the background to his first 'self-criticism' which made him abandon *History and Class Consciousness* till the very end of his life.

Only at the end did he begin to admit what he owed Weber. In 1967 Lukács stated that his early work *A History of the Development of Modern Drama* (written in Hungarian and not yet translated) already contained elements of Marxism, but of a Marx 'seen through the spectacles tinted by Simmel and Max Weber'.[23] The same might be said of all his work down to and including *History and Class Consciousness.* Many of its supposedly purely Marxist concepts, such as reification (*Versachlichung*), objectification and alienation, reflect a distinctively Weberian colouring. In regard to the first concept, it is clear that Lukács' whole conception of reification is largely dependent on Weber. It has been extracted from Weber's complex sociological theory of historical rationalization, with its numerous distinctions and typologies, but linked holus-bolus to simpler Hegelian and Marxist assumptions. Thus it is imbued with the quasi-Idealist Young-Marx idea of alienation as well as the Old-Marx theory of commodification. As a result, what emerges is a confused amalgam which serves indifferently as a critique of science, technology, the factory system of production current in the 1920s, that is, Fordism and Taylorism, and the economics of commodity production and wage-labour in general. These are all supposedly the progeny of capitalism, the Devil who fathers all evils. Weber's careful differentiations and exploration of the quite separate historical trajectories of these social forms is abandoned, for Lukács' yen for totality makes him see all these things as one. The upshot is that each one of them comes to seem a wholly negative phenomenon, which is completely against Weber's intent.

Something similar happens to some of the fundamental themes of Weber's methodology of the social sciences, which Lukács also appropriates for his own political purposes. Weber's notions that history can only be studied from a given point of view which is guided by the historians' fundamental value orientation, and that causal links in the social sciences cannot be simply inductively discovered but must be imputed (*zugerechnet*) on the basis of objective possibilities are taken over by Lukács to establish the sole and only priority of the proletarian point of view and the imputation of a proletarian class consciousness (*zugerechnetes Bewusstsein*) that is quite indifferent to what actual proletarians think and feel. Putting the two together we get Lukács' unstated but strongly implied view that the Marxist philosopher – by implication meaning himself – alone can know what is proletarian consciousness. And that in turn allows him to know the final truth of history. His disciple Lucian Goldmann explains it as follows:

> Every group does not understand the result – the totality – and, consequently, every group understands itself and its situation, the goals and the action of other groups, only up to a certain point, from a viewpoint determined by its objective situation. It can be – and very often this is the case – that no group can have a consciousness vast enough to achieve this totality. Writing from the orthodox Marxist viewpoint, Lukács believed that the proletariat, by its privileged situation, could achieve a transparent consciousness and find itself at a moment of history in which it was on the verge of doing so . . . This consciousness which is essential for praxis and for its understanding, a non-conscious consciousness, one might say, the mental structure Lukács calls *zugerechnetes Bewusstsein* . . . is determined by objective possibility, which constitutes this possible consciousness while being constituted by it.[24]

Though derived from Weber, nothing could be further removed from Weber than this; it is a complete travesty of what Weber either preached or practised.

Goldmann, who fails to note how closely Lukács follows Weber, thinks that Heidegger follows Lukács. But the evidence he provides for Lukács' priority in certain respects only shows that both belonged to the same intellectual milieu in Germany and imbibed its leading ideas. Weber's friend, Rickert, who taught Heidegger, was also the teacher sought by Lukács, on Weber's advice. Husserl, Heidegger's main teacher, was well known to all of them. It was as a pupil of Husserl that Heidegger first presented himself. Thus at the start of *Being and Time* Heidegger goes to great lengths openly to acknowledge himself as a phenomenologist and, therefore, the faithful exponent and heir of Husserl's philosophy.

But as Hubert Dreyfus shows, 'Heidegger succeeds in taking over Husserl's definition of phenomenology and totally transforming it for his own ends, making "phenomenology" mean exactly the opposite of Husserl's proposed method for spelling out the intentional content of his own belief system and thereby arriving at indubitable evidence.'[25] Dreyfus, who is very sympathetic to Heidegger, believes that this distortion of Husserl is all to the good. It seems to him, as to many others, that Heidegger is carrying the phenomenological approach much further forward, and exploring regions of being inaccessible to Husserl's '*strenge Wissenschaft*'.

But is Heidegger a phenomenologist at all? For no sooner having declared himself to be one he launches into his favourite etymological game of breaking up the Greek word into its two root-meaning constituents, '*phenomena*' and '*logos*', so as to discover their supposedly 'original' meanings and thereby to arrive at a more primordial 'ontological phenomenology'.[26] It was to be a new 'genuine beginning' of phenomenology itself, which was understood not merely 'in its *actuality* as a philosophical movement', but 'as a possibility of showing thé things themselves',[27] as John van Buren puts it. From this it very quickly emerges that he is really concerned with an 'interpretation of the meaning of being', which is metaphysical hermeneutics rather than phenomenology. For if phenomenology is concerned with the interrogation of phenomena given to consciousness then Heidegger's claim, in his 'My Way in Phenomenology', that 'the distinction worked out [in Husserl's Sixth Investigation] between sensory and categorical intuition revealed itself to me [after 1919] in its scope for the determination of the "manifold meaning of being"',[28] no longer refers to phenomenology. The problem of the 'manifold meaning of being', which Heidegger in his youth discovered in Brentano, goes back to Aristotle's 'Metaphysics'. It is precisely the kind of neo-scholastic problem that Husserl held in highest contempt.

What was it that made Husserl so blind to Heidegger's real propensities? Apart from personally relishing Heidegger's famulus-like servility and flattery – as late as 1925 he declared in a lecture that 'even today I still consider myself a learner in relation to Husserl'[29] – Husserl was seduced by the prospect that Heidegger held out of extending the phenomenological method to religion, history and even metaphysics, precisely those domains into which the scientifically trained Husserl had never ventured, but which carried such a high status-ranking in German academic philosophy. Heidegger raised the alluring project of a 'phenomenology of primal Christianity',[30] including a 'phenomenological elaboration of mystical, moral-theological and ascetic literature' focusing on 'Eckhardian mysticism'.[31] With that in mind, he tried to get Husserl interested in Rudolf Otto's *Das Heilige* (The Holy). At the same time 'he wanted to push phenomenology in the direction of a more radical historical philosophy of that question about being he had discovered in Aristotelian scholasticism, Brentano and Braig.'[32] All this was to be based on Dilthey's historicism and philosophy of Life, which was also not in keeping with Husserl's phenomenology. Thus 'Heidegger followed Dilthey's attempt to use the *Logische Untersuchungen* not, as Husserl had sought to do, for the sake of "pure logic", but rather for the sake of a "fundamental science of life".'[33] But Heidegger was no more true to Dilthey than he was true to Husserl. Dilthey's hermeneutic method of understanding, with its objective scientific orientation, he referred back to the theological sources in Schleiermacher, the Church Fathers, Protestant theologians and Bible scholars from whom Dilthey had derived it in the first place. What he ended up with was phenomenology in the guise of a kind of scholastic hermeneutics, one that treated, not phenomena of consciousness, but conceptual problems of historical understanding as matters of quasi-theological interpretation. Thus, for example, 'Heidegger reinscribed Husserl's discussion of the temporal character of intentionality from the standpoint of kairological time that he was discovering first in primal Christianity and Dilthey, then in Aristotle.'[34] Unfortunately, Husserl was too slow to see what all this was about, so dazzled was he by his putative son's verbal brilliance. When he finally saw the danger, it was too late to do anything about it, for Heidegger had become firmly installed and hailed as a German genius. Then it was Heidegger's turn to 'dare to become a father-killer'.

Gentile had less of the 'father-killer' instinct than any of the others. He did sincerely wish to get on amicably with Croce. The relation between them from the very start had been more of a collaboration than that between any of the others. Croce was clearly the senior partner in their intercourse, having already an established reputation as aesthetician, critic and historian when Gentile was barely starting his academic career and just beginning to think for himself. There is no question of Gentile's dependence on Croce in most respects. He writes from Palermo around 1905 to Croce in the following pathetic terms:

> Apart from my family, you are the whole world for me; and everything for me concludes in you . . . Who will give me the strength and joy to live that for the last six years your words, which I have so often sought, have given me.[35]

The most that can be said for Gentile at this stage is that he was already a more thoroughgoing metaphysician and already more committed to Hegelian Idealism than Croce ever became. Indeed, Guido de Ruggiero, when still a disciple of Gentile before the First World War, charges Croce with this as a failing: 'Croce has never been a Hegelian in the strict sense;

he never became a really close and earnest student of the philosopher of Stuttgard till after he already found himself.'[36]

From our present point of view it is to Croce's credit that he never succumbed to the siren song of Idealism and maintained at all times a critical distance from Hegel. For de Ruggiero, however, Croce is not enough of a Hegelian, for he harbours supposedly non-Hegelian tendencies, in fact, anti-Gentilian ones, such as a proneness to draw categorial distinctions in the seamless web of the unity of Spirit. And he dares even to evince dreaded 'traces of naturalism'.[37] Only Gentile, by contrast, is seen by de Ruggiero as capable of carrying out the 'task before philosophy', that is, 'to fuse into a fresh unity the distinctions of the Crocian system, without, however, ignoring the just demands which these distinctions are designed to satisfy. Above all, it is necessary to deepen the concept of reality as spiritual actuality, that is to say, concreteness, or to use an expression of Gentile's, of reality as philosophy.'[38] According to de Ruggiero, all that was merely implicit in Croce receives its full explicit realization in Gentile. Writing in 1912 at a time when the full text of Gentile's primary masterpiece was not yet available, but basing himself on an introductory sketch, the essay 'The Act of Thinking as Pure Act', de Ruggiero is already quite confident that it 'contains in this respect a complete programme'.[39] The 'new philosophy' is to be Gentile's 'theory of absolute immanence', that of 'the Pure Act as the act of self-creation'. We can be quite certain that this was also Gentile's own estimate of his achievement in relation to that of Croce, who was thereby to be set aside. And this is itself a kind of parricide, but without the hostile animus that usually accompanies this intellectual act.

In conclusion, it is apparent that the sons took over the work of the fathers and transformed it to serve their own ends, which were quite contrary to what the fathers intended. However, there were unfortunate features in the fathers' work that enabled the sons to do this and still give the appearance of maintaining continuity so convincingly that the fathers themselves were largely fooled at first. A comprehensive discussion of all four cases would require a thorough examination of four more major thinkers, which is clearly impossible in this context. So I shall content myself here with a somewhat longer treatment of Russell followed by just a few notes on each of the others.

Russell made most of the initial moves on logic and language which Wittgenstein converted into his main theses in the *Tractatus*. But as Hao Wang remarks, 'what is striking is Wittgenstein's tendency to select a position, often suggested tentatively as a partial measure by Russell, and push it to a radical extreme.'[40] What Wittgenstein took up with great alacrity was Russell's reductivist tendencies, or what Hao Wang calls 'Russell's ill-defined notion of Occam's razor', which he believes 'has done more harm than good in philosophy'.[41] Wittgenstein was particularly intent on exploiting the reductive potential inherent in Russell's 'theory of descriptions', for by this means he could eliminate all kinds of entities and classes. This is the reason that in the *Tractatus* he prefers Russell's critique of language to Mauthner's though later he went back to Mauthner once again. The 'theory of descriptions' pointed to the disjunction between the apparent logical form or 'grammar' of a sentence and its real 'logical grammar'. It also implied that it is possible to assert that there is a final analysis of any expression in language, at least in principle, though this might be inordinately difficult in practice, as Wittgenstein allows.

Russell's overall position just prior to the publication of the *Tractatus* is set out by Hao Wang as follows:

> According to Russell's view of the period, logic is universal and the central concepts are terms (or entities), propositions, and propositional functions. A proposition is a complex of entities (or terms) which are its constituents. The theory of descriptions serves to eliminate (some of) the fanciful entities (or 'nondenoting terms', if one equivocates a little about the term 'term'). The next step is to eliminate classes or sets.[42]

Wittgenstein took up these basic presuppositions, but extended the range of their reductive and simplifying powers much further. He seemed, thereby, to have provided 'solutions' to some of the basic problems raised by Russell, and these were for a time accepted by Russell himself. Wittgenstein believed them to be so definitive and final that nothing further could ever be said in philosophy. Hao Wang sets out how some of these 'solutions' follow Russell's tenets outlined above:

> Hence, we see here already something close to the frame of the *Tractatus*, which, as will be recalled, proposes to eliminate quantifiers by conjunctions and disjunctions (5.2), treats a number as the exponents of an operation (6.021), pronounces the theory of classes superfluous in mathematics (6.031) and takes care of mathematics by equations (6.2). When the *Tractatus* is viewed in this manner, we are less mystified by the fact that Russell and Wittgenstein seem to have viewed it as a solution, elegant and final, of Russell's important problem.[43]

Of course, it is very far from being that, as Wittgenstein came to realize soon after. But by this stage he came to believe that the problems Russell had raised were not real problems at all, not problems to be solved, rather pseudo-problems or confusions to be dissolved. In doing so he was willing to abandon most of mathematical logic – a drastic step which hardly any other logician since has been willing to follow.

As for the other fathers, Weber, Husserl and Croce, there are also major failings in their philosophies which provided the launching pads for their sons' flight into totality and eventual totalitarianism. Weber's decisionism of fundamental values, his subjective choice of value-oriented points of view and the nominalism of his ideal-type concept construction provided the opening that Lukács needed to decide for Marx and the proletariat and interpret that as evincing a perfect objectivity in touch with an essential reality. I have already shown how Weber's methodology of 'causal imputation' and 'objective possibility' lent itself to misuse for this purpose, but that is more of a problem of explication than a flawed methodology. Husserl's noetic understanding of pure phenomena, his intuition of essences (*Wesenschau*) and his transcendental reduction through a recourse to an *epoche* to bracket off everything contextual – thereby eliminating all linguistic, social, psychological, cultural and historical determining conditions – was just what Heidegger could seize on in promoting his own theologically inspired hermeneutic interpretations. Husserl's substitution of analysis for argumentation enabled Heidegger to dispense with the need for justification and rationality altogether. If the phenomenological 'essence of things' is what simply appears or 'shines forth', then Heidegger's irrationalist conception of truth as *alytheia* or that which reveals itself, a revelation beyond argument or dispute, is given considerable warrant. Finally, Croce's Idealist all-embracing historicism, which made everything a matter of historical unfolding or self-development towards a preconceived and in some sense predetermined end, and his denial of any autonomous objectivity capable of scientific explanation, namely, his emphasis on free Spirit alone, made it possible for Gentile to imagine that once he could interpret Spirit as pure act he had accounted for everything.

All these were the sins of the fathers visited upon the sons, with the sons' full connivance, nay, eager embrace. However, free of their faults, the philosophies of the fathers provide a better point of departure for philosophy even now than those of the sons. There are instances of other thinkers, apart from the sons, who also took off from the starting points provided by the fathers and developed these much more sensibly, even if more modestly. For example, Russell's early work can be seen as providing the decisive impetus for both Wittgenstein and Kurt Gödel, 'who had each absorbed Russell's influence in his own manner and gone beyond it in significant ways along different directions,' as Hao Wang maintains. But it is Gödel, not Wittgenstein, who is more true to Russell, his 'broad concept of logic corresponds more closely to Russell's early ideas than to those of the *Tractatus*'.[44] Hence, a better course for philosophical logic to follow is to retrace its steps back to Russell and then proceed along the way charted by Gödel, for 'Gödel's conception of logic may also be seen as pointing to another solution to the problem which the *Tractatus* was supposed to have solved.'[45]

In an analogous fashion it is possible to return to each one of the other fathers and then proceed forward through the work of one or another, usually lesser known, thinker who took off from the same starting point as a malign master but developed this in a sounder, less extreme, manner. In this way one might return to Weber and proceed through the work of Norbert Elias, rather than Lukács, towards a general sociology of philosophy. One might return to Husserl, especially the early work, and then proceed through the now completely neglected work of Herman Schmitz towards a different kind of phenomenology, one closer to Goethe than to Heidegger. Finally, one might return to Croce and then proceed through the work of his great admirer Robin Collingwood towards a more thoughtful and responsible Idealist exposition of a philosophy of Spirit, that is, of such topics as history, culture, art, morals and education, than that provided by Gentile. Obviously, all these are quite heterogenous and very different approaches, ones in dialectical conflict with each other, but each one has something to offer to the future course of philosophy that might avoid the impasse philosophers have been brought to by blindly following the malign masters. I shall have little more to say about this here for obviously it is the subject of another book.

Summing it all up, it is apparent that the relation between the sons and fathers was in each case an extremely complex one, both personally and intellectually. But there are close analogues in all four cases, and there is a similar pattern emerging from the way that each relation built up and broke down. The break usually began with the appearance of the primary masterwork, which made it apparent what kind of son the father had been nurturing. From that point on the hostility between them grew rapidly and led inevitably to a complete rupture at about the time of each son's *Kehre*. The political affiliation of each of the sons towards one or another of the burgeoning totalitarian movements, which the fathers abhorred, was the final breach in the degeneration of their relation that made all thought of any kind of reconciliation impossible. Gentile's Fascism made him anathema to Croce; Heidegger's Nazism was the last nail in the intellectual coffin of his mentor Husserl, officially considered a Jew by the new regime and with Heidegger's connivance consigned to academic perdition; Lukács' Stalinism made him the intellectual enemy of Weber's surviving legacy, he detested his brother Alfred Weber, and would have felt the same in respect of Max himself had he remained alive in the 1920s and 1930s; Wittgenstein's flirtation with Bolshevism aroused the ire of Russell, who was opposed to that regime almost from the start. The philosophical course that the sons followed after the *Kehre* was so at variance with that of the fathers that the latter could only look upon it with utter incredulity and complete contempt. This is more or less what Croce felt for Gentile's Fascist philosophy, Husserl for Heidegger's Nietzsche inspired Nazi departure, Russell for Wittgenstein's common language approach and Alfred Weber for Lukács' later Stalinist course.

Again, as I have stressed before, it should be amply apparent that this was no mere coincidence in personal relations among a few philosophers. It was a fundamental generational break that exemplified a decisive division in European culture. For just as the *anciens régimes* of antediluvian Europe were so decisively overthrown by the totalitarian movements led by the great dictators, so, too, were the philosophies of the old masters destroyed by the new intellectual movements led by the malign masters. Both the political and philosophical 'revolutions' were themselves parts of a more general upheaval in almost all aspects of European cultural life that brought the whole period of European modernity, one that had its beginnings in the Reformation, to a rapid, and perhaps, premature end, as I tried to show in my book *A New Science of Representation.*

The fathers were not, of course, the only formative influences moulding the philosophical character of the sons. As I shall show in what follows, the sons imbibed teachings from many diverse sources, though mainly from their extended background in the nineteenth century. Most notably, they recovered the by then abandoned thought of the great Idealists as well as that of a group of later followers of the Idealists. This I have already previously indicated and will go on to explore at greater length in the next chapter. But before moving back in time to that, it is first necessary to trace the more immediate influences, a group of turn-of-the-century figures who stood behind the fathers and who might be considered on that account grandfathers.

The fathers and grandfathers were closely in touch with each other both singly and as a group. Thus Gentile's first teacher, Donato Jaja, was in close communication with Croce. Lukács began his first serious studies in Berlin at the feet of Georg Simmel, a close friend of Weber. Wittgenstein first approached Gottlob Frege with his problems in logic and Frege sent him on to Russell with whom he had previously corresponded on the paradoxes. Heidegger completed his first dissertation on Duns Scotus under Heinrich Rickert, who was a neo-Kantian well known to Husserl who succeeded him in the chair at Freiburg. Max Müller, a pupil of Heidegger, reports that 'when he received his qualification to teach at the university his thinking was close to that of Rickert'.[46]

It is a clear indication of the changed intellectual situation after the First World War to note the contrast between the hostility or near indifference that obtained between the sons and the close knit relations, frequently amounting to friendly alliances, between all the fathers and grandfathers who almost constituted a community of thinkers in touch with each other. Thus Weber knew Rickert as well as Simmel intimately, he corresponded with Croce, whose work he discussed, and was cognisant of Husserl. Husserl discussed the work of Frege, with whom he was also in correspondence, and knew of the work of Russell and, of course, Rickert, and would have been aware of Croce. The combinations and permutations of these relationships are very numerous. By contrast, the sons never knew each other and almost never mention each other, unless it is to exchange abuse. Thus Lukács treats Heidegger with utmost contempt, and Heidegger reciprocates by never referring to Lukács at all. Gentile and Wittgenstein never even knew of each other. The main explanation for this is that ideological differences had made communication and normal scholarly intercourse impossible. A subsidiary explanation is that the megalomaniac egos of the malign masters did not allow them to recognize rivals, much less so peers. The situation was very different when they were students themselves, for then there was a European network of intellectuals and scholars. I shall briefly outline their student careers so as to show the kind of cultural world from which they emerged and to trace the influence on them of their grandfathers.

Gentile's very first major teacher was the literary critic Alessandro d'Ancona, but he soon abandoned this humanistic approach for the sake of Hegelian metaphysics under the instigation of Jaja, to whom he became personally utterly devoted. Through the attraction of Jaja he moved into the orbit of nineteenth-century Italian romantic Idealism in which he revolved for ever after. In particular, Jaja made him aware of Spaventa, the great nineteenth-century Neapolitan Hegelian, who also happened to have been Croce's uncle, which inevitably brought him in touch with the latter as well.

Jaja is not a thinker who is now remembered, nor worth remembering except as the formative influence behind Gentile. For it is clear that Jaja's philosophy – which synthesized all the currents of Italian nineteenth-century Idealism, such as those of Gioberti, Fiorentino and Spaventa – is the constitutive milieu of Gentile's education in which his thought remained permanently embedded. Hence it might be said that the influence of Jaja was perhaps more significant in his intellectual development than that of Croce. It was Jaja, with his striving for unity and systematicity, rather than Croce, with his many and varied interests and differentations, who provided Gentile with his model of philosophizing. As Manlio di Lalla explains:

> Jaja was wholly taken by a fundamental problem of speculative philosophy, that of the critical systematisation of the unity of the Real, of the rational mysticism of its speculative construction – a unity of rationality that sought to resolve itself in a mature and anguished identity of the world of thought and of being. Jaja immersed all the terms of his speculative philosophy in cognitive activity because the basis of all life is thought.[47]

This assertion of the primacy of thought led Jaja to an absolute spiritualism, in which course he was followed by Gentile. The main problem for both of them was how to reduce nature to thought, that is, to spiritualise it. As di Lalla puts it:

> The realist Idealism of Donato Jaja consists of an incessant search in the pursuit of a resolution of the concept of Nature in that of the activity of Spirit. The solution of this problem was not found. But, according to Gentile, no philosopher felt the importance of this problem of all problems like Jaja.[48]

If this is a problem, then it is one that makes sense only in Hegelian terms, and as such it was tackled by many in the Idealist tradition, including such thinkers as Collingwood.

Gentile followed the Right-Hegelian tradition; Lukács eventually took the Left-Hegelian one. But before he did so, he had a spell of neo-Kantianism under Simmel. Simmel's neo-Kantian philosophy, his sociology and aesthetics made a profound impression on Lukács, which is very evident in his early works and is still there, though partly effaced, in *History and Class Consciousness.* For political reasons Lukács dare not fully acknowledge his debt to the 'bourgeois' thinker Simmel, though he does mention him in passing, albeit with considerable condescension. Simmel's *Philosophy of Money* is 'a very interesting and perceptive work *in matters of detail*'.[49]

But it is precisely the *Philosophy of Money* that exerted a profound influence on Lukács' work. As Bryan Turner argues, 'not only was Lukács' analysis of reified consciousness in bourgeois society mediated by Simmel's analysis of money as reified social relationship, but Lukács' perspective depended in large measure upon Simmelian sociology.'[50] He concludes by asserting that 'Lukács' Marxism was parasitic upon neo-Kantian sociology.' Bottomore and Frisby make an analogous claim:

> It is, however, Lukács' *History and Class Consciousness*, which stands as the most decisive reception and reinterpretation of Marx's work in the 1920s, that is also significant for following up Simmel's influence on Lukács' work . . . In the *Philosophy of Money* Simmel outlines a theory of alienation based on the process of objectification, though one that is largely directed towards showing the alienation of culture and the inevitability of that process. Simmel frequently employs the concept of reification (*Verdinglichung*), a concept also employed by Nietzsche as well as Marx.[51]

But not only was Simmel's influence on Lukács pronounced, it was also to be felt in the other German exponents of a Hegelian Marxism, especially those of Jewish extraction such as the members of the Frankfurt School, Horkheimer and Adorno. The intellectual milieu from which they all emerged was a particularly close-knit one.

In fact, there were indirect links between Lukács and Heidegger in their formative years. Heidegger was a pupil of Rickert and Lukács had hopes of becoming one as well. Both were also closely connected to another pupil of Rickert, the enigmatic Emil Lask who died in the early years of the war. Lask was a friend of Lukács in the Weber circle at Heidelberg, and is remembered primarily for the jibe that there are four Evangelists: Matthew, Mark, Lukács and Bloch. He was also known by and influential on Heidegger. Thus John van Buren writes that 'in Rickert's seminars Heidegger also learned of the former's student Emil Lask, who, "mediating between Rickert and Husserl, attempted also to listen to the Greek thinkers",'[52] as Otto Pöggeler puts it. Thus Lask provided a direct link not only between Husserl and Rickert, but also between Lukács and Heidegger. The latter relied heavily on Husserl, Rickert and Lask for his doctoral dissertation 'The Doctrine of Judgement'. But even the later Heidegger was still 'particularly influenced by a fundamental distinction in the theory of concept-formation developed by Dilthey, Simmel and especially Rickert, namely, the distinction between "generalising science" and "individualising science", which Heidegger saw as corresponding to the "generalising" and "individualising" functions of meaning in Scotus,'[53] as John van Buren states. It is this distinction, and how it figures in *Being and Time*, that I shall now discuss in more detail.

In his account of History and the cultural or humane sciences in general in *Being and Time* Heidegger does not advert to his teacher Rickert, but instead to Wilhelm Dilthey and his friend, the far more conservative Count

Yorck von Wartenburg, whose views Heidegger upholds. Through the mouth of Yorck, Heidegger criticizes Dilthey's conception of a methodological hermeneutics in terms of which an objective scientific conception of History and the humane sciences is to be sought. However, the main issues he discusses are not so much those raised by Dilthey as those raised by Rickert, who remains unmentioned, such as, for example, the issue of the individualising versus the nomothetic approaches to History or what he calls historiology:

> The question of whether the object of historiology is just to put once-for-all 'individual' events into a series, or whether it also has 'laws' as its objects is one that is radically mistaken. The theme of historiology is neither that which has happened just once for all nor something universal that floats above it, but the possibility which has been factically existent.[54]

This is a characteristic Heidegger retort: he outlines a problem that has been broached by many methodologists, historians and sociologists; pronounces them all to be mistaken in somehow having confused or missed the real issue; then presents the issue in the technical terminology of his philosophy which but vaguely, if at all, relates to the original problem. What is 'the possibility that has been factically existent'? How does it meet the original problem or undo the basic distinction?

It is the same with his whole account of historiology, so-called, where he claims to go one better than Dilthey and presumably also Rickert, Weber and everyone else. What he claims to accomplish is the following: 'we may venture a projection of the ontological genesis of historiology as a science in terms of Dasein's historicality.'[55] The issue is thus one of 'science' and of the objectivity of science, and everything that pertains to the scientific methodology of History. Indeed, it is to this very problem of 'objectivity' that Heidegger claims to provide an answer: 'the historiological disclosure of the "past" is based on fateful repetition, and is so far from "subjective" that it alone guarantees that "objectivity" of historiology'.[56] The key to scientific objectivity thus seems to lie in 'fateful repetition'. This is spelled out in the following terms:

> Only by historicality which is factual and authentic can the history of what-has-been-there, as a resolute fate, be disclosed in such a manner that in repetition the 'force' of the possible gets stuck home into one's factical existence – in other words, that it comes towards that existence in its futural character . . . Even historiological disclosure temporalizes itself *in terms of the future.* The '*selection*' of what is to become a

> possible object for historiology has *already been met with* in the factical existential *choice* of Dasein's historicality, in which historiology first of all arises, and in which alone it is.[57]

Even a cursory glance at this quotation makes it patently obvious that it has little to do with objectivity or science or methodology in History and the cultural sciences. One need only compare it with Weber's treatment of the methodology of a *Verstehende* sociology, which also derives from Dilthey and Rickert, to see the difference between serious scientific discourse concerning method and this pretence to something deeper and more metaphysical. The terms that Heidegger resorts to, such as fate, repetition, authenticity, etc., are vaguely reminiscent of Spengler's notion of Destiny and his acausal typologies, which Heidegger does not mention, and even more so of Nietzsche's conception of 'monumental history', which he does. If *Dasein* is here interpreted as the Nation, since there is an obvious communitarian emphasis in the later part of *Being and Time*, then what Heidegger seems to be saying is that the Nation chooses its past in accordance with its goals for the future; or at least it chooses the historical objects with which its historians will be concerned. Thus, if the future goal of the German nation is the Third Reich, as it soon became, then the objects prescribed by this 'futural character' are only too obvious. Everything in Heidegger's account serves to justify such an ideologically biased 'selection of what is to become a possible object for historiology'.

Thus it is clear from this that Heidegger has taken the idea of hermeneutics from Rickert and Dilthey, but instead of utilizing it for any proper methodological purpose, as Weber did, he has reverted to the kinds of theological uses from which Dilthey and Rickert sought to rescue it in the first place. Heidegger's hermeneutic readings are always based on his own metaphysical presuppositions, which he simply assumes as somehow ontologically valid beyond any question or possibility of criticism. This is the reason that any text of which Heidegger gives a reading ends up sounding like Heidegger and every philosopher whom he favourably interprets ends up appearing as his precursor, who unfortunately got some things wrong, for otherwise he would be saying the same as Heidegger himself.

The importance of Rickert also made itself felt in Heidegger's metaphysics almost from the beginning to the end of his career in his conception of the unique event, the *Ereignis* of history. He speaks of Rickert's notion of the 'unsurveyable multiplicity' and 'heterogeneity' of 'actuality in its individuality', and calls the historical sciences '*Ereignis*-sciences'.[58] This ambiguous term *Ereignis* was to assume great importance in his philosophy almost throughout, and from the start he interpreted it metaphysically.

At first he did so in a neo-scholastic manner by identifying it with Duns Scotus' *haeccitas* or *thisness*. But then he extended it further for all of being for *thisness* calls for *otherness* or alterity, and he quotes Rickert to the effect that 'there is given [es gibt] no object if there is not given [es gibt nicht] the one and the other'.[59] Thus in this early effort at interpretation Rickert and Scotus are combined in this unusual manner in Heidegger's qualifying dissertation on 'Duns Scotus' Theory of Categories' which was dedicated to 'Heinrich Rickert in most grateful admiration'. This became his standard hermeneutic practice and led to the above predictable results.

Later in his work *Ereignis* is closely linked to this 'es gibt', translated as 'it worlds', to 'provide a temporalizing-sense of the being-question',[60] as van Buren puts it. As is his etymological wont, he soon split up the word into *Er-eignis* which made it easy for him to link it with his favourite word *Eigen*, meaning owning and ownmost. This gave it the subjectivist edge of a sense of personal experience. Thus, he states that 'lived experiences are *Er-eignisse* in so far as they live out what is own [*aus dem Eigentum*] and life only thus lives.'[61] However, later in his writings *Ereignis* becomes a quite impersonal event or happening, a cosmic coming (e-vent). In his posthumously published tractate of 1938, *Beiträge zur Philosophie (Von Ereignis)*, it is treated as almost synonomous with Being itself, and regarded as a self-presenting presence or self-giving present or gift (*es gibt*), playing on the literal meanings of words in the way that Heidegger is notoriously prone to do.

Thus Heidegger's notion of *Ereignis* as lived experience is from the start also linked to Dilthey's *Lebensphilosophie* a link that was never completely severed despite the later impersonality of *Er-eignis*. His interest in Dilthey is very pronounced. In 1925 he gave a series of ten lectures on 'Dilthey's Research Work and the Struggle for a Historical Worldview'. Borrowing the terms *Lebenswelt* and *Umwelt* from Husserl, he reinterpreted them in Dilthey's sense of lived experience or everyday practical reality. In this way he combined Phenomenology with *Lebensphilosophie* such that phenomena became temporalized, as he sought to endow a historical dimension to Husserlian terms; and, at the same time, history became phenomenalized as he sought to give a phenomenological twist to Diltheyan terms. Dilthey himself had already provided the opening to this, for late in his life he 'saw the significance of Husserl's *Logische Untersuchungen* for a descriptive psychology of historical consciousness',[62] as van Buren puts it.

Dilthey was also important for mediating another important source for the multiple meaning of *Ereignis*, that of religious mysticism, 'more specifically, the medieval mysticism and the Romantic mysticism of Schleiermacher's free Christianity'.[63] Dilthey's work on Schleiermacher gave Heidegger an access to Lutheran mysticism. This was in turn combined with the 'rediscovery of primal Christianity in Pascal and especially Kierkegaard'.[64] His interest in Kiekergaard was no doubt first aroused by the appearance in 1911 of Theodor Haecker's translation in *Der Brenner*, a conservative journal published in Innsbruck by Ludwig Ficker. This is where Wittgenstein, too, developed his life-long intense interest in Kierkegaard, being at the time closely connected to the journal and its editor through whom he financially subsidized a number of its regular contributors, including Haecker. At this early stage in their careers, Heidegger and Wittgenstein stood very close to each other on the common ground of logic and mysticism: the former having worked on logic (in 1912 he published an essay on 'Recent Research in Logic'), and the latter moving from logic towards mysticism. But they soon parted company. Heidegger, who in his essay on logic acknowledged the influence of Bolzano, Frege, Meinong and Russell, soon lost all interest in the subject. Wittgenstein, working under similar influences, began to unify his logic and mysticism under the doctrine of the unsayable, that which only shows itself. For a time he even managed to persuade his philosophical father, Russell, to share these logico-mystical preoccupations; but not his grandfather, Frege, who held himself aloof from what he believed to be irrational by-ways when he first encountered them in the *Tractatus*.

Wittgenstein was always highly approving of Frege, who took a personal interest in him and encouraged his work, even when he found it utterly antipathetic, as he did the *Tractatus*. In the Preface to that book Wittgenstein refers to the 'great work of Frege', which he by implication contrasts to the merely ordinary 'work of my friend Mr. Russell'. As late as his final notebook, just prior to his death, he still refers to Frege with respect, when his attitude to Russell had changed to the opposite. Throughout his life he drew much from Frege's work. As Michael Dummett comments, 'some of Wittgenstein's work builds on, elaborates or complements that of Frege: and then, I think, Wittgenstein is at his happiest . . . In other cases, Wittgenstein fought the power of Frege's thought: and in such cases, I believe, he was almost always at his worst.'[65]

As the only instance of a grandfather commenting on a son's work, we have the letters Frege wrote to Wittgenstein about the *Tractatus*. Over and over again, despite his best will, he confesses himself utterly baffled. He cannot get beyond the first few sentences. He vainly implores Wittgenstein for some explanation: 'from the beginning I find myself entangled in doubt as to what you want to say, and so make no proper headway.'[66] But explanation was precisely what Wittgenstein was unwilling to offer because it would have meant having to argue for and justify the theses he was propounding, and that he was unable to do. One either understood and accepted or one did not. Frege's cautious probing into the exact meaning of expressions and terms made Wittgenstein uneasy. Frege 'expected to see a question, to have a problem outlined . . . instead, one came across a bald assertion without being given the ground for it.'[67] Wittgenstein's procedure was to nail theses to the door of philosophy and hammer away at them in the confident expectation that a reformation would occur sweeping everything before it, and making it unnecessary for him to explain himself.

Almost unwittingly, but with much greater acumen than Russell or any of the Logical Positivists, Frege had detected just how strange and idiosyncratic was Wittgenstein's approach to logic, science, philosophy or almost anything else of philosophical interest to Frege. Without saying so openly, he was clearly appalled by the metaphysical, mystical and other irrationalist tendencies in the work. He was particularly shocked by Wittgenstein's reversion to Schopenhauerian solipsism and by his reference in a letter to the 'deep grounds of idealism'.[68] Even Monk concedes that 'in a sense Frege was right to find the metaphysics of this view unintelligible.'[69] Frege was also right in seeing the *Tractatus* as 'an artistic rather than a scientific achievement; what is said takes second place to the way in which it is said,'[70] as he put it in a letter to Wittgenstein. Indeed, it is the mode of expression that so captivates philosophical readers, precisely because it disguises what is being expressed. Consequently, they do not understand it though they are sure it must be something very profound, way beyond common understanding.

How much of this was actually intended by Wittgenstein is not clear. He was not a charlatan; but neither was he the genius he made himself out to be. Right from the very first words of his Preface to the book he endows it with the mystique of the romantic artist whom nobody but a soul-brother will understand. Frege was particularly irked by that pose.[71] Consequently, Frege was himself dismissed as someone who fails to understand. With great exasperation and in a haughty tone he writes to Russell: 'I'm in correspondence with Frege. He doesn't understand a single word of my work and I'm thoroughly exhausted from giving what are purely and simply explanations.'[72] A few years later the same disparaging judgement is meted out against Russell. He writes to Moore that after two days of conversation about his new philosophy, Russell only 'seemed to understand a *little* bit'.[73] It seems that both Frege and Russell were bad pupils as far as he was concerned.

What Frege had stumbled upon and almost instinctively divined in Wittgenstein was eventually discovered by all the fathers in the works of their sons: these were not 'scientific' but rather 'artistic', more a matter of art than knowledge. Each of these works stood in a hostile relation to the philosophies, beliefs and values of their fathers. They evinced a general oppositional attitude that might be expressed in a series of 'anti' terms: anti-science, anti-rationalism, anti-humanism, anti-modernism, anti-liberalism, and, to top it all off, frequently anti-Semitism as well. This was a hostility to and revolt against all the major trends of European modernity as these had developed over a period of four centuries from the early sixteenth to the early twentieth century, at least till the onset of the First World War. We are not dealing here with any straight-out philosophical differences, but with a wholesale reaction against modernity, or at least against all those developments which had come to be regarded as 'progressive' tendencies and politically associated with the bourgeois class. The anti-bourgeois movements in Europe could take either a right-wing or left-wing form, or somehow both at once as with someone like Sorel. All the malign masters considered themselves to be 'anti-bourgeois' thinkers irrespective of whether they stood for the extreme right or extreme left or both at once, as in the case of Wittgenstein. Invariably they condemned their fathers as bourgeois.

It is characteristic that none of the malign masters was in any sense a scientist or knew much of any science – not even Wittgenstein who was briefly trained as an engineer but later showed no further interest in science. By contrast, nearly all the fathers and grandfathers were either highly distinguished in one or another science or very familiar with scientific work in general – all, that is, with the possible exception of Croce and Jaja, who instead had strong humanistic, historicist and literary leanings. Thus it is not surprising to find a general depreciation of science and objective knowledge in the work of the sons, which generalizes itself into a pervasive anti-rationalism, even if not always a decisive irrationalism. This takes characteristically different forms in each of them in keeping with their philosophical differences. It is usually less pronounced and more disguised in the primary masterworks than it is in the secondary ones for reasons that I shall presently examine.

I shall deal first with the case that appears to run contrary to this view, that of Wittgenstein's *Tractatus*. On the surface, judged by its mode of expression, it seems as if this work is the very cynosure of rational scientific rigour, especially in respect of logic and mathematics. This is how the Logical Positivists of the Vienna Circle took it, and they were very surprised when Wittgenstein preferred the poetry of Tagore to scientific discussion. Yet the Preface to this work should have forewarned them, for there Wittgenstein writes, referring to logical and scientific problems in general, 'the second thing in which the value of this work consists is that it shows how little is achieved when these problems are solved.' Wittgenstein considered himself to have definitively solved all such problems, and he treated the questions of ethics, religion and all those matters that he regarded as ineffable, those which only show themselves, as immeasurably higher and more valuable. For all that is true in logic and science, all that is said in propositions 'can express nothing of what is higher'; alternatively, 'how things are in the world is a matter of complete indifference for what is higher.'[74] Partly this is a throwback to the old monkish attitude of contempt for the world and the denigration of all secular knowledge as irrelevant to the one thing that matters, the salvation of the soul. But it is much more than that.

Though scientific truth and logical validity are not denied in the *Tractatus*, yet there is a consistent and constant undertone of trivializing the results of science and logic. Thus we are told that no scientific theory has any bearing whatever on philosophy: 'Darwin's theory has no more to do with philosophy than any other hypothesis in the natural sciences.'[75] Worse still, science, apparently, explains nothing, for 'outside logic everything is accidental'.[76] To accept a scientific theory is merely to adopt a convention of description. Thus Newtonian mechanics is a purely arbitrary descriptive scaffolding for facts which could be described in many other ways. Science provides 'the illusion that the so-called laws of nature are an explanation of natural phenomena', but it explains no better than mythology: worse, in fact, for 'the view of the ancients is clearer in so far as they have a clear and acknowledged terminus, while the modern system tries to make it look as if everything were explained.'[77]

But it is not only that the *Tractatus* denigrades science and maths in an evaluative sense, it actually makes them impossible. Hao Wang argues that the basic assumptions of the *Tractatus*, if taken strictly, make any kind of scientific, mathematical or, indeed, rational thinking without any point or purpose. The three basic presuppositions on which the *Tractatus* system is constructed he calls respectively the principle of atomicity (T1), the principle of finiteness (T2) and the principle of extensionality (T3). Applying these principles to science produces the following results:

> It appears that T3 eliminates psychology, T2 trivializes or makes mathematics impossible, and T1 renders it impossible to understand how we could ever get physics as we know it or, indeed, how we can actually attain any knowledge to speak of.[78]

In other words, the *Tractatus* philosophy is one of the most reductive and demeaning philosophies of science ever devised. No wonder that Wittgenstein held that if scientific problems are solved, almost nothing is achieved.

He continued to maintain this attitude in his later philosophy as well. Thus when he declared that 'one might also give the name "philosophy" to what is possible *before* all new discoveries and inventions',[79] what he meant was that philosophy ought to be indifferent to all science, logic or mathematics. Elsewhere he stated that 'even 500 years ago a philosophy of mathematics was possible, a philosophy of what mathematics was then',[80] apparently meaning by this ambiguous statement that his philosophy of mathematics could just as well be carried out with fifteenth-century mathematics as with twentieth-century. Given his lack of advanced mathematical knowledge, it is understandable why he should say it, but it makes little sense from an historical or mathematical point of view. He even went so far as to make a virtue of his lack of scientific knowledge, declaring that 'at bottom I am indifferent to the solution of scientific problems'. And he considered his work to have no relevance to science or mathematics whatever: 'nothing seems to me less likely than that a scientist or mathematician who reads me should be seriously influenced in the way he works.'[81]

Before the Second World War he could still express such an insouciant indifference to science and scientists, saying 'it is all one to me whether or not the typical western scientist understands or appreciates my work, since he will not in any case understand the spirit in which I write.'[82] But after the war he gives vent to an antipathy to science that verges on the paranoid:

> It is not absurd e.g. to believe that the age of science and technology is the beginning of the end for humanity; that the idea of great progress is a delusion, along with the idea that the truth will ultimately be known; that there is nothing good or desirable about scientific knowledge and that mankind, in seeking it, is falling into a trap.[83]

It might be supposed that this outburst was provoked by fear of the bomb and nuclear catastrophe, but actually Wittgenstein went as far as to welcome the advent of the bomb in that it promised to rid the world of the despised science:

> I can't help thinking: if this [the bomb] didn't have something good about it the *philistines* wouldn't be making an outcry. But perhaps this too is a childish idea. Because really all I can mean is that the Bomb

> offers the prospect of an end, the destruction of an evil – our disgusting soapy water science. And certainly that is not an unpleasant thought; but who can say what would come *after* this destruction? The people now making speeches against producing the Bomb are undoubtedly the scum of the intellectuals.[84]

The evil of science is such for Wittgenstein that to be rid of it he condones the destruction of a large part of mankind. Those who decry the prospect of such appalling slaughter on moral or religious grounds are only the 'scum of the intellectuals'. He would not have been surprised to see the by now despised Russell leading them eventually.

Heidegger's attitude to science and technology is quite as paranoid as Wittgenstein's. Like the latter, he never differentiated between them, nor did he distinguish between the various kinds of modern technologies – it was all an undifferentiated whole and all equally bad as far as he was concerned. For, as he states over and over again, it is not the real machines and techniques that matter, not technology as a practical issue, but what he calls the 'essence' of technology. The problem of technology is a metaphysical question for him. It is a stage in the history of Being, in fact, the last stage. Beginning with Descartes, modern philosophy – which, he believes, is responsible for science and technology – has ever more insidiously 'concealed' the true essence of beings by treating them as objects standing in opposition to subjects. This scientific representationalist attitude to the world he regards as an occlusion of Being itself.

From that point onwards, science and technology proceed according to the stages of the eschatology of Being which are also the phases of the self-concealment of Being, concluding with the final one of the 'will to will', an expression he coins on the model of Nietzsche's 'will to power'

> The basic form of appearance in which the will to will arranges and calculates itself in the unhistorical element of the world of completed metaphysics can be stringently called 'technology'. This name includes all areas of being which equip the whole of beings: objectified nature, the business of culture, manufactured politics, and the gloss of ideals overlying everything. Thus 'technology' does not signify here the separate areas of the production and equipment of machines. [It] is understood here in such an essential way that its meaning coincides with the term 'consummated metaphysics'.[85]

In the name of technology all is condemned: in the name of technology all is condoned. Those who perpetrated the Holocaust are condoned as doing no worse than what modern farmers are doing in applying technical processes to nature. The whole of modern civilization is condemned, not on the basis of historical comparisons with other civilizations of the past, but absolutely as a manifestation of the final stage of metaphysics that is technology.

Heidegger's aversion to metaphysics followed his *Kehre* and his deepening involvement with Nietzsche and the Nazis. Prior to the *Kehre* he highly valorized metaphysics. Then his attack on science was based on the contrary charge, that it did not follow the guiding precepts of metaphysics. Heidegger reverted to the scholastic idea of metaphysics as queen of the sciences, urging all scientists to give heed to the metaphysics of Being and Nothing in their researches. He did not mean that they should return to past metaphysics, but rather pay attention to modern metaphysics, above all, of course, to his own philosophy. This is more or less the tenor of his notorious inaugural lecture 'What is Metaphysics?'. One can imagine how working scientists would take to this kind of recommendation, coming from a philosopher whose knowledge and appreciation of science was such that a few years later in his lectures on metaphysics he could glibly declare that nothing much had happened in science since the turn of the century: 'it has remained unchanged despite a certain amount of house cleaning.'[86]

Such mere bagatelles as Relativity and Quantum theory had little philosophical significance for Heidegger for whom the whole of modern science was no truer and no better than Greek or scholastic science:

> [We cannot] say that the Galilean doctrine of freely falling bodies is true and that Aristotle's teaching, that light bodies strive upward is false; for the Greek understanding of the essence of body and place and the relation between the two rests upon a different interpretation of entities and hence conditions a correspondingly different kind of seeing and questioning of natural events. No one would presume to maintain that Shakespeare's poetry is more advanced than that of Aeschylus, it is still more impossible to say that the modern understanding of whatever is, is more correct than that of the Greeks.[87]

According to Heidegger, the Greeks saw falling bodies move differently from the way modern scientists see them move; and presumably someone who does not know the laws of gravity even now sees them move differently from someone who does. What can 'seeing' mean in this context? Are better or worse ways of seeing even possible? On the highly dubious analogy of the absence of 'progress' in art, he is prepared to deny that comparisons of truth or rationality, or on any other such standards of objectivity, can be made between different kinds of theories of nature. On this basis, like Wittgenstein, he is prepared to maintain that Greek mythology should be considered just as true as science. In fact, following his eschatology of Being and the reconception of truth as unconcealment, the whole of modern science is false compared to the philosophy of the pre-Socratics and that of their contemporary avatar, Heidegger himself.

Heidegger's rejection of science and his espousal of mythology are correlative with each other. Thus, Tom Rockmore states, 'it is interesting to note Heidegger's antiscientific rejection of science, including mathematics, and his resurrection of the idea of blind fate.'[88] Fate, as this figures in *Being and Time* and elsewhere in his writings, stands for a conception of history that completely abandons all attempts at explanation as these might be ventured in the social and cultural sciences. Heidegger, as we know, particularly despised these sciences. Karl Löwith reports that 'he loathed sociology and psychoanalysis'.[89]

There is also an ideological reason for this bias, as Max Müller notes, 'his deep respect for the people [Volk] was also linked to certain academic prejudices, for example, the absolute rejection of sociology and psychology as big-city and decadent ways of thinking.'[90] Presumably, his folkish ideology would also have been averse to the fact that so many Jews were active in these sciences. It is apparent from this that his rejection of what he calls 'anthropology' and his separation of his so-called analytics of *Dasein* from any humanistic or scientific knowledge, on the basis of his ontological-ontic distinction, is really a self-protective devise to keep his philosophy insulated from any possibility of scientific critique or rejoinder.

Gentile is not as assertively arrogant about the superiority of his philosophy to science as Heidegger. But he too affirms a version of the old thesis that metaphysics is the queen of the sciences, yet he is more naive about it. Hence, to consider him anti-scientific would be something of an exaggeration, since he is not really interested in the sciences at all and shows scant knowledge of any one of them. Even his sympathetic commentator, Harris speaks of 'his own ignorance of science', and concedes that 'his philosophy acquired something of the character of a polemic against science.'[91] In his plans for the reform of the educational curriculum, the sciences figure only as a minor preliminary stage in the preparation for philosophy. In fact, his school reforms were wholly classical and humanistic, leading to a decline in scientific teaching, which later Fascist ministers, such as Bottai, had to repair urgently when the regime required a scientific and technical workforce for industry and war.

In his primary masterwork science plays no part at all. For example, his whole discussion of space and time refers itself exclusively to Kant and other philosophers and shows not the least trace of any awareness of the debate in the then contemporary physics on these issues. He can only conceive of atomism in philosophic terms going back to the Greeks; so that the idea of splitting the atom is seen as a philosophical error of those who 'must divide the atom even to infinity'.[92] Whenever he refers to a science, as when he discusses empirical psychology, it is only to relegate it to a subsidiary role. His discussion of the so-called 'dialectics of Nature' faithfully follows Hegel, being treated as a 'logical' problem of the relation of individuals to universals, with no reference to the natural sciences.

Later in his writings Gentile took some interest in the philosophy of science of Boutreux, which, inspired by Poincaré, was an attempt to elaborate an anti-modern conception of science. Perhaps he did this under the instigation of his pupil, Ugo Spirito, who did try to apply Actual Idealism to science. As far as I know, this has left no mark and is best considered a forgotten incident in the history of philosophy.

Lukács, like Gentile, is not overtly hostile to science, but he, too, is little influenced by it and, though he does not state this openly, he has little regard for it. As a Marxist he had to pay lip-service to the idea of scientific objective truth, but he shows in his writings that it meant little to him; that is, until his final stage when working on the *Ontology* he did try to come to terms with scientific knowledge, but only in a metaphysical spirit. In his early work he is ambivalent about science. For though the truth and objectivity of science and scientific method in relation to the natural world is not denied, yet the application of any such approach to the social world is regarded as 'bourgeois science' and condemned. This is clearly apparent from his very hostile review of the work of Bukharin, which he accuses of bourgeois deviationism, almost a capital crime in the Soviet Union of the time:

> The closeness of Bukharin's theory to bourgeois, natural-scientific materialism derives from his use of 'science' (in the French sense) as a model. In its concrete application to society and history it therefore frequently obscures the specific features of Marxism: that *all economic or 'sociological' phenomena derive from social relations of men to one another.* Emphasis on a false 'objectivity' in theory leads to fetishism . . . But, as a necessary consequence of his natural-scientific approach, sociology cannot be restricted to a pure method, but develops into an independent science with its own substantive goals. The dialectic can do without such independent achievements; its realm is that of the historical process as a whole, whose individual concrete, unrepeatable moments reveal its dialectical essence precisely in the qualitative differences between

> them and in the continuous transformation of their objective structure. The *totality* is the territory of the dialectic.[93]

The argument about 'unrepeatable moments' is vaguely reminiscent of Rickert, but it is used to affirm a 'dialectics of totality' as against sociology or any other autonomous science. Only a 'dialectical conception of totality . . . the only method capable of understanding and reproducing reality'[94] can give rise to a proper Marxist science. All other scientific approaches are incapable of entertaining 'contradiction' and are the products of a reified consciousness, for 'the methodological ideal of every fetishistic science and every kind of Revisionism rejects the idea of contradiction and antagonism in its subject matters.'[95] Such sciences are 'ideas necessarily held by agents of the capitalist system of production . . . the ideology of its ruling class'.[96] Thus Weber, Simmel and all of his other teachers are firmly disposed of at one stroke this early in his career.

Till near the end of his life Lukács never deviated from the official Party line on science. In his Stalinist phase he condemned, in chorus with all the faithful, the officially proscribed sciences, such as Mendelian genetics and Relativity theory, and showed considerable appreciation of Lysenkoism. He tried to make up for these errors of subservience in his final works, which he tried to infuse with as much scientific awareness as he was able at this late stage to muster. But it was too late, he could not acquire more than a smattering of scientific knowledge.

All the malign masters suffered grievously from a lack of or disinterest in scientific knowledge of the kind obviously relevant to their work. Thus Wittgenstein elaborated a philosophy of language with no knowledge of linguistics; Heidegger propounded a study of human being with no knowledge of psychology, anthropology or sociology, sciences he despised; Gentile wrote on politics, law, economics, morals and education with scant knowledge of any social science; and Lukács tried to develop a Marxist approach to literature that confused the sociology of literature with theoretical aesthetics and critical judgement. This hostility to a scientific approach leads not to a relativity of judgement, but its opposite, a narrow dogmatism that does not allow for debate, criticism or self-correction. Since no opposing theory, hypothesis or point of view is allowed to exist, it follows that the only one presented is the indisputable truth which cannot be questioned or criticised. Each malign master proceeds in a 'non-argumentative and evocative fashion',[97] as Ernst Tugendhat puts it in relation to Heidegger alone, but with equal bearing on all the others.

In all these respects the malign masters stand in absolute contrast to their fathers and grandfathers. In reacting against them, the malign masters were also rejecting all the manifestations of modernism that the former generally upheld. They were, in effect, rebelling against the modern world. This took diverse forms in them, but with close analogies from the one to the other. In all of them there is a condemnation of the liberal 'bourgeois' present and an affirmation of one or another pre-Enlightenment authoritarian attitude. Wittgenstein asserts an authoritarian standard in ethics and religion, insisting in the *Tractatus* that the ethical law must take the form of an absolute 'Thou shalt' with no regard for reasons or consequences.[98] Later he was to argue that religion is not only not subject to any rational considerations, but does not require speech at all (see the discussion in chapter 2). Heidegger, as Max Müller and others maintain, affirmed the values of peasant life, of Volk, blood and soil, over against those of degraded urban civilization. Lukács also condemned the present as 'an age of total sinfulness', but later concealed this eschatological rejection of modernity behind a Marxist façade of denunciation of bourgeois capitalism, the society of reification. Gentile was most opposed to modern 'intellectualism', under which rubric he placed everything in the present he disapproved of or with which he could not cope, such as science.

All of them adopt anti-modernist attitudes to art and culture in general, which become stronger and more pronounced as they venture further into totalitarianism. At the beginning of their careers, before the First World War, they show a youthful interest in modernist tendencies in the arts. But at some point after the war they soon abandon this as they invariably return to the classics of the early nineteenth century. Heidegger went back to Hölderlin, Hebel and the other German romantics; apart from the Greeks, he appreciated little from outside Germany. Wittgenstein was similarly drawn to minor German romantic poets and realist authors, as well as to some minor works of Dickens and Tolstoy; in music he abhorred the Jew Mahler and listened to nothing later than Bruckner and Labor, a household composer of his family. Lukács, who initially took a keen interest in modernist literature, also soon reverted back to the Weimar classics and the realist novel. Gentile, a pronounced nationalist, stuck to Leopardi and Manzoni all his life and never ventured outside Italy for literature or art.

This pervasive anti-modernism was accompanied by a more sporadic anti-humanism, anti-historicism, anti-liberalism and anti-Semitism, that is, a wholesale rejection of the principles and values of the Enlightenment. In later Heidegger anti-humanism assumes the dimension of a whole quasi-theology of the priority of Being and Language over Man. And, as I have previously shown, this joins up with his eschatology of Being which takes the place of real history. In Wittgenstein anti-humanism is never openly expressed, but it is implicit in his affirmation of basic 'forms of life' and 'language-games' as simply given and not subject to criticism, control or even historical alteration. Real history is nowhere in evidence, its place being taken by fictitious anthropology. Gentile explicitly abandons what he calls the 'humanism of culture' for the 'humanism of labour': the former is the whole humanist tradition since the Renaissance, the latter is the new culture to come under Fascism. To call this humanism in any sense is in fact tantamount to a denial of the term. Something similar might also be said of Lukács, who advocates the Marxist version of a 'humanism of labour'. History plays a role in Gentile and Lukács only in so far as it fits their opposed political ideologies.

The fundamental difference in outlook and procedure between the work of the sons and their fathers was not at first perceived. Except in the case of Lukács, who was not widely known as a pupil of Weber largely due to his own suppression of this fact, in all the other instances it was generally assumed that the work of the sons was a direct continuation of that of their fathers. None of these sons made any effort to disabuse the philosophical public of this misapprehension. Whether deliberate or not, this pretence of maintaining a direct continuity between the work of the sons and the fathers worked to the great advantage of the former and to the disadvantage of the latter, it was at least partly responsible for the extraordinary success of the sons primary masterworks which eclipsed the works of the fathers. The early readers of these works took it that the sons were addressing and solving the problems defined in the works of the fathers. But, while presenting themselves as the true heirs of their fathers, thereby inheriting their fame, the sons could at the same time present themselves as going beyond them and be frequently accepted as superior to them. It was generally given out that the philosophies of the sons were deeper, profounder, more encompassing continuations of what their fathers had only begun. Thus it was thought that Heidegger was a more fundamental phenomenologist than Husserl, Wittgenstein a more philosophically sophisticated logician than Russell, Gentile more of a philosopher than Croce, and Lukács more of a dialectician than Weber, who, after all, was only a mere sociologist. In this way, because they were read as superior to the works of their fathers, the primary masterworks were from the very beginning surrounded with misapprehensions and confusions from which they are still not free.

5 Forefathers and Other Ancestral Figures

The biggest outrage that the malign masters perpetrated against their fathers was to return surreptitiously to their philosophical enemies, the great Idealists. The fathers believed that they had fought a long and finally victorious battle against the influence of Idealism and that it would never resurface. Russell, Husserl and Weber thought that they had put paid to Idealism in their youth. And even Croce, who belatedly came to Hegel at a late stage, held that only some limited aspects of Hegelianism could be kept alive; the rest was 'dead'. Little did they suspect that their sons harboured hidden affinities for the Idealism which would become so patently apparent in their primary masterworks. Thus Wittgenstein revived Schopenhauer, Heidegger recovered Schelling and Lukács and Gentile reworked Left and Right Hegelianism respectively, together with relevant aspects of Fichte.

In becoming neo-Idealists some of the malign masters, particularly Lukács and Heidegger, were reacting against the neo-Kantianism of their fathers or grandfathers and that of their immediate background. Simmel, Weber and Rickert were the clearest exponents of neo-Kantianism, and Husserl, though not himself a neo-Kantian, was closely connected to it through his close Marburg relation to Cohen, Natorp and Cassirer. It was in that circle that he managed to place his pupil Heidegger. There was considerable neo-Kantianism in Wittgenstein's background as well, for though neither Frege nor Russell were neo-Kantians, they were strongly preoccupied with it. As Peter Hylton states, 'the lack of recognition of Kantian elements in Frege's thought is surely due, at least in part, to the fact that Frege never articulates in any systematic way the Kantian metaphysical and epistemological views he seems to assume.'[1] Of the fathers and grandfathers only Jaja and Croce, the two Italians, seem not to have been touched by neo-Kantianism, though they knew their Kant.

The significance of the move away from the neo-Kantianism of the fathers to the neo-Idealism of the sons must be assessed not in individual but in generational terms; and not as a mere change in the academic field of philosophy, but as a cultural change in the intellectual mentality of Europe. It is the transition from a pre-1914 mind-set to a post-1914 one, which was part of the whole social and cultural transformation I have already examined. The rationalism, respect for science, humanism, liberalism and even moralism of the older generation gave way to irrationalist trends, full of speculative enthusiasm and metaphysical visions of eschatological fulfilment, of the younger one. This change in outlook was by no means merely confined to the malign masters. Many of their peers and contemporaries shared in the rediscovery of the Idealists, especially of Hegel. There were many Left neo-Hegelians, such as Korsch and Gramsci, who kept company with Lukács; and later there was Kojève and the other Hegelians of whom Merleau-Ponty, Sartre and Lefebvre are only the best known. And there were equally many, though not as famous, Right neo-Hegelians who kept company with Gentile. The revival of Schelling was more sporadic, but, as well as Heidegger, there were Jaspers, Rosenzweig, Huessi and many theologians, especially in the South German Catholic circles from which Heidegger originated, who also took a great interest in this mystical philosopher. In this period Schopenhauer seems not to have attracted philosophers, apart from Nietzscheans, but he did appeal to almost all major writers, including Mann, Proust and Lawrence, as well as Freud and other psychoanalysts.

The shift from neo-Kantianism to neo-Idealism in many ways parallels that from Kant himself and his followers to the great Idealists. In both cases revolution and war brought to a close the older movement and inaugurated the newer one. As Thomas Willey states, 'the war, and then Cohen's death in 1918, brought the Marburg movement to an end, though its overall influence lingered on until it was eclipsed by the philosophies of his two former Marburg students, Husserl's phenomenology and Heidegger's *Existenz*.'[2] It was in the same way that Kant's philosophy was displaced by that of the Idealists, starting with Fichte, at the time of the Napoleonic Wars and the reactionary aftermath in Germany. In both periods a stable social order was disrupted by what seemed like revolutionary chaos, to be followed by the sterner order of strong states and great leaders. The Caesarist state Napoleon sought to establish was the initial precursor of the totalitarian states of the great dictators. The adulation surrounding the former was a distant premonition in the past of the hero-worshipping glorification of the latter in the present. Indeed, Hegel's expostulation that he had seen the 'World Spirit on horseback' after the battle of Jena was a presentiment of how the malign masters would view their political leaders. Of course, I am not claiming that what happened in philosophy from 1914 to 1945 was simply a repetition of what had happened from 1789 to 1830; or if it is seen as a repetition, then this must be taken in the sense of Marx's rendering of the Eighteenth Brumaire: 'the first time as tragedy, the second as farce.'

Idealism was not only a German movement, for it spread from its German sources all over the Western world to countries as far apart as Russia and the United States. There were strong Idealist schools in France, England and Italy. The same fusion of metaphysical philosophy conceived of as Science, sublimated Christianity and either radical or conservative politics produced a predisposition to Idealism among certain kinds of intellectuals. While these foreign versions of Idealism were burgeoning, in Germany itself it almost died out after 1848 as Positivism, Empiricism and Materialism, philosophies much better attuned to the new scientific, technological and industrial temper of the times, began to predominate. In the 1860s even Marx was driven to complain that Hegel was being treated like a 'dead dog' and sought to recover something of his dialectical spirit for Marxism. This was perhaps the first of many such sporadic attempts which did not fully succeed until the onset of neo-Idealism after the First World War. In the meantime, in philosophy neo-Kantianism began slowly to proliferate in German academia through the work of Lange and Cohen.

Idealism began to revive, though only very fitfully, in the years just before the war. The publication of Dilthey's *Young Hegel* in 1908 and the edition of his early writings by Nohl sparked off a small revival. Schelling had been kept alive by Catholic theologians like Carl Braig who influenced the young Heidegger. Schopenhauer was perhaps more prominent than the others, but mainly among littérateurs. What helped swell the rising Idealist tide was the growing success of their secondary, nineteenth-century, followers such as Kierkegaard, Spaventa and Weininger, as well a rediscovery of the Young Marx, all of which I shall examine later in relation to the malign masters. But before the war there was little to indicate that Idealism would return with such force after it.

The war and its revolutionary aftermath brought this about through the reaction against all the pre-war rationalistic, scientistic, humanist and liberal philosophies. This led to a rejection of neo-Kantianism and a general distaste for Positivism and Empiricism, except among circles of scientists. What Weber in his great post-war speech, 'Science as Vocation', referred to as a 'modern intellectualist form of romantic irrationalism',[3] accompanied by a yearning for what he called pseudo-religious 'experience', was very favourably disposed to neo-Idealism. The same mixture of speculative philosophy masquerading as science, of eschatological religious hopes and of revolutionary political aspirations, recurred, as after the French Revolution, but this time with much greater explosive potential. It proved an intoxicating brew to the young generation Weber called 'youth', among whom the more philosophically minded became followers of the malign masters.

In this turbulent milieu neo-Idealism was closely linked to the nascent totalitarian movements. This is particularly clear with respect to Bolshevism and Fascism, both of which espoused variant forms of neo-Hegelianism largely through the agency of Lukács and Gentile respectively, though many others were involved as well. The Bolsheviks reacted against the orthodox scientific Marxism of the Second International, as represented by Karl Kautsky and the so-called Revisionists, by emphasizing the dialectical Hegelian side of Marx. Even before Lukács, Lenin had already shown the same bias, as Alan Wood notes:

> Russian Marxism always retained a more Hegelian cast, and this was especially true of the Bolsheviks. Lenin already criticized Marxists of the Second International on similar grounds, and his *Philosophical Notebooks* (written during World War I, published posthumously in 1929) contain lavish praise for Hegel's system of speculative logic, together with meditations on how to effect the materialist transformation of the Hegelian dialectic.[4]

Lukács and the other Bolshevik Marxists, such as Korsch and Gramsci, followed a parallel course. Later in France, Bolshevik Marxists or fellow-travellers flocked to the lectures on Hegel's *Phenomenology* given by Kojève, a Russian émigré, yet staunch admirer of Stalin. Among his auditors were the great names of twentieth-century French literature and thought: Queneau, Lacan, Bataille, Klossowski, Koyré, Weil, Merleau-Ponty, Aron, Fessard, Gurwitsch, Corbin, Desanti and Breton. Even those who later opposed Hegelian Marxism, such as Althusser and Foucault, were still initially influenced by it, as Tom Rockmore shows.[5] Of course, not all Hegelian Marxists were Bolsheviks or Stalinists, there were those, such as the Frankfurt School thinkers in Germany or Hyppolite in France, who were neither. Nevertheless, neo-Hegelianism and Stalinism fitted well together in this interwar period.

This was less so the case with the right-wing variant of neo-Hegelianism in its relation to Italian Fascism and German Nazism. But, nevertheless, there, too, there were close linkages. In Italy Gentile carried with him most of his neo-Hegelian students into Fascism. In Germany many of the conservative revolutionary and proto-Nazi intellectuals were inspired by Hegel, especially by Hegel's historical and political theories, among these were Moeller van den Bruck, the author of *The Third Reich* (1923), Ernst Kriek, the author of *The Idea of the German State* (1917) and Hans Freyer, the author of *The State* (1925). The Nazis also made good use of the other Idealists. Fichte was a particular favourite because of his nationalism; the philosophical society formed in his name was very active in support of

Nazism. Schelling's conservativism and tendency towards mystic religiosity and mythology was absorbed into the general miasma of Teutonic romanticism, which the Nazis fostered. Even Schopenhauer, despite his individualist indifference to politics and history, was honoured as the teacher of Wagner and Nietzsche, the ancestral deities in the Nazi pantheon.

The turning towards totalitarianism (*Kehre*) effected by the malign masters was wholly in keeping with their tendency towards neo-Idealism. That move was also in keeping with their sense of themselves as the heirs of an illustrious ancestry which even surpassed their fathers and grandfathers. Which of the Idealists they favoured and what they took from them, I have already partly explored in Chapter 1. Here I shall merely extend this a little further, beginning with Schopenhauer's influence on Wittgenstein.

It is generally recognized that Schopenhauer is a major presence in the *Tractatus* and possibly in his later philosophy as well, even though Wittgenstein never adverts to Schopenhauer in his work. But his disciples were told in private that this is the case. Thus Anscombe speaks of 'his solipsism, his conception of the limit and his ideas on value'[6] as deriving from Schopenhauer. Monk adds more to this: 'Wittgenstein's remarks on the will and the self are, in many ways, simply a restatement of Schopenhauer's Transcendental Idealism, with its dichotomy between the "world as idea", the world of space and time, and the "world as will", the noumenal, timeless world of self.'[7] In the light of all this it is something of a psychological puzzle why Wittgenstein never acknowledged publicly the influence of Schopenhauer. David Weiner raises that issue at the start of his book, which catalogues in detail all that Wittgenstein owes to Schopenhauer – a great deal, indeed.[8] Remarking on Wittgenstein's later boast, 'it's a good thing I don't allow myself to be influenced',[9] Weiner puts it rather cuttingly that 'of all modern philosophers Wittgenstein is probably the most negligent in acknowledging his intellectual debt', and that 'he seemed almost at pains to conceal his connection to other sources.'[10] The answer to this puzzle does not seem to me to require the deep psychologizing Weiner engages in to explain it, but is more simply accounted for, in Weiner's own words, by Wittgenstein's need to 'project the misleading image of a supergenius whose philosophy emerged *ex nihilo*'[11] and whom nobody was capable of understanding.

Weiner shows quite convincingly how Wittgenstein 'constructed entire sections of the *Tractatus* by revising Schopenhauer's ideas'.[12] The whole structure of his book follows that of Schopenhauer: 'these two books share a common organizational principle; both are structured as progressive arguments that lead the reader from ontology, logic and science to higher realms of aesthetics, ethics and mysticism.'[13] There is hardly an idea or image that does not have its antecedents in Schopenhauer. Thus the metaphors of 'eye', 'ladder' and 'limit' come straight from his work. All in all, Weiner shows that 'Wittgenstein offers us a sterilized version of Schopenhauer's first book, Wittgenstein's "I" is thin and his "world" is impoverished.'[14] Much of what Wittgenstein has to say on language, logic and science also originates from Schopenhauer, but in a highly simplified and distorted way, for 'through his selective appropriation of Schopenhauer, Wittgenstein arrives at a stilted, restrictive view of meaningful discourse.'[15]

I cannot elaborate here in all the detail that Weiner provides how the later sections of the *Tractatus* are either restatements of Schopenhauer or modifications arising from Wittgenstein's divergence from him. In short, it can be concluded that Wittgenstein engaged in an intense internal debate with Schopenhauer on all issues to do with ethics, aesthetics and religion: on the subjects of life, death, the eternal present, happiness, man as microcosm, will and will-lessness, quietistic impassivity and almost on everything else towards the end of the book. However, not only there, Schopenhauer's influence makes itself felt at all points throughout the *Tractatus.* Thus Weiner argues that 'Schopenhauer's distinction of saying and showing emerges as a central thesis of Wittgenstein's *Tractatus*'[16] – Schopenhauer's, not Wittgenstein's, distinction, since it is firmly rooted in Schopenhauer's separation of percepts and concepts or intuition and language. Wittgenstein simply adapted it for his own purposes.

Weiner does not seem to realize that Wittgenstein overlaid the saying showing distinction with Schopenhauer's other fundamental separation of idea and will. Thus what can be said belongs to the world as ideas or representations, taken by Wittgenstein as the world of propositions and facts, a logical version of the phenomenal world. By contrast, that which only shows itself belongs, as it were, to the world as will; this is the noumenal world of Self and values, that is, of good and bad will and all else that is outside space and time. The parallel is not exact, for logical form, which in Wittgenstein belongs to the noumenal realm of showing, is in Schopenhauer part of the phenomenal world of ideas. Nevertheless, the spirit of the Schopenhauerian distinction infuses itself into Wittgenstein's dichotomy.

Furthermore, the shadow of the Schopenhauerian split also falls on the so-called logical distinction in later Wittgenstein between first person and third person uses of mental verbs, such as I feel/you feel, I see/he sees, I know/they know, etc. Thus 'he feels pain', asserted on the basis of behavioural criteria, is, as it were, in the phenomenal world of representations. On the other hand, 'I feel pain' is a pure expression or exclamation for something 'inner', the feeling of pain, as it were, in the inner noumenal world that is otherwise ineffable. Hence, according to Wittgenstein, I can be wrong whether 'he feels pain' but not whether 'I feel pain', the latter is supposedly a purely incorrigible avowal. But this goes totally against the phenomenology of pain, for it is certainly possible to be in pain yet not be aware of it owing to other mind-distracting preoccupations, as when soldiers in a battle who are shot sometimes act as if they felt nothing. Unfortunately Wittgenstein is not interested in the phenomenology of pain or that of any other mental state. To him it is all a matter of a so-called 'logical grammar' of the meaning of words. However, this logical grammar, such as that which he presents in his famous private-language argument, loses its supposed conceptual purity and becomes tendentiously metaphysical once it is realized that it is modelled on the fundamental Schopenhauerian distinction.

Morris Engel claims that the influence of Schopenahuer is also at work in other ways in late Wittgenstein, especially so Schopenhauer's 'contributions to logic and language . . . which have their remarkable parallels in Wittgenstein's late work'.[17] He instances such things as Schopenhauer's conception of 'dialectics' as the 'art of controversy' which, he believes, influenced Wittgenstein in his notion of 'conceptual confusion' and his idea of 'misconceptions of language' in general. He states that Schopenhauer's philosophy of language 'seems to have anticipated several of the key points of Wittgenstein's philosophy of language'.[18] Hence, there can be little doubt that Schopenhauer had an impact on Wittgenstein's treatment of language. However, Wittgenstein had numerous other sources from which to derive his critique of language, most crucially from the work of Mauthner, who might have himself been influenced by Schopenhauer. Thus in respect of language it is not clear whether this is a direct or indirect influence at work.

Heidegger also never referred to the influence Schelling had on him in his published work. The full extent of this has only recently become apparent after his death when the texts of his lecture courses and private correspondence were released. From this we know that in the winter of 1927–8 he lectured on 'Schelling, On the Essence of Human Freedom'. Later in 1929, during his lecture course on 'German Idealism and the Present Situation of Philosophical Problems', he wrote to Jaspers: 'I am lecturing for the first time on Fichte, Hegel, Schelling – and a world is dawning for me again.'[19] Of the three, he held Schelling in highest regard. Following Schelling he increasingly turned to myth. Echoing Schelling he wrote that 'myth [is] the destiny of a people'.[20] And in a review of Cassirer's work he insisted that Cassirer is 'taking up Schelling's insight that "myth", "the mythical understanding of being", is a unique possibility of human

Dasein which has its own kind of truth',[21] as John van Buren writes. These insights into myth he later applied to the poetry of Hölderlin, to Nietzsche and to the pre-Socratics. He also went on to elaborate his own mythology.

Hegel also played a considerable part in Heidegger's neo-Idealism, but not to the extent that he figured in Gentile and Lukács. The opposition of Lukács to Heidegger in the twentieth century is prefigured in that of Hegel to Schelling in the nineteenth. Hegel accused Schelling's philosophy of tendencies to irrationalist mysticism. According to John Toews, Hegel claimed that Schelling's 'absolute ultimately remained in the "beyond" as an unmediated otherness that could be encountered only in the subjective experiences of intellectual intuition, aesthetic contemplation or religious feeling and thus communicated only in private, esoteric "edifying" discourse of metaphor and symbol or the authoritarian discourse of dogma and catechism.'[22] Put into the more vituperative and ideologically loaded terms of twentieth-century Marxist discourse, these are very much the charges that Lukács lays at Heidegger's door. The earlier opposition between Schelling and Hegel, as the later one between Heidegger and Lukács, is one manifestation of the struggle between the romantic and classic tendencies in German culture in general. Schelling sided with German romanticism in art, law and theology, with Schlegel, Savigny and Schleiermacher. Hegel sided with the enlightened classicism of the Prussian bureaucratic reformers continuing the work of von Humboldt.

The whole debate between Schelling and Hegel was carried out in quasi-religious terms, for each of them maintained a *filosofia teologizzante*. Hegel's philosophy, especially in its late stages, was closely linked to a sublimated form of Protestant Christianity. Hegel's followers experienced their adhesion to his philosophy as a kind of conversion. As John Toews notes:

> To become a Hegelian, to experience and think the world from the perspective of the identity of logic and metaphysics, involved a philosophical 'rebirth'. The language that individual Hegelians used to describe the shedding of their old merely finite, 'egoistic' selves, and the attainment of the 'blessedness' of the identity with the infinite spirit through the 'labor of the concept', indicated the extent to which Hegelians experienced the appropriation of the Hegelian perspective and language as an existential transformation equivalent to 'redemption' or 'salvation'.[23]

It was in this kind of spirit that the secondary Idealists took up these issues.

Out of the debates between Schelling and Hegel and those within the inner factions of the Hegelian movement itself there arose a number of young radical philosophers among whom Kierkegaard, the Young Marx and Spaventa are of primary interest here because they had an enormous influence on Heidegger, Lukács and Gentile respectively, in some respects exceeding the influence of the great Idealists themselves. Weininger, a minor follower of Schopenhauer, who similarly decisively influenced Wittgenstein, will for the moment be set aside for he emerged later from a different tradition. The two most important of the secondary Idealists are undoubtedly Kierkegaard and the Young Marx. Both engaged in extensive critiques of Hegel. Kierkegaard was launched on his philosophical course by old Schelling's lectures against Hegel, and in that sense he might be considered a follower of Schelling, some of whose philosophical and religious insights he developed in a more radically subjectivist manner. Young Marx took off from Feuerbach's critique of Hegel, but later returned to Hegel himself, as Lukács insists. Their two books coincidentally written in 1846, *Concluding Unscientific Postscript* and the *German Ideology*, were the high points of the critique of Hegel delivered from quite different quarters. But both took a strongly individualist stand focused on the sheer contingency of existence in solitude or in society. These were the positions that Heidegger and Lukács rediscovered after the First World War.

In what follows I shall examine the appropriation of the secondary Idealists by the malign masters, starting with Heidegger's adaptation of Kiekegaard in *Being and Time*. I shall then consider the religious and mythological features to be found in the primary masterworks and trace their sources.

Kierkegaard's influence on early Heidegger is very strong, particularly so as it is largely unacknowledged. Division II of *Being and Time* is frequently a kind of paraphrase of Kierkegaard. In their sympathetic study of this part of Heidegger's work Hubert Dreyfus and Jane Rubin begin their account with the statement that 'Heidegger takes over from Kierkegaard much more than he acknowledges.'[24] This remark runs like a refrain throughout their whole piece. Thus we are told repeatedly that such and such a part of the Heideggerian machinery of 'existence' is borrowed, adapted or purloined from Kierkegaard. In this regard they remark that 'although no footnote acknowledges Heidegger's source, one cannot help recognizing in the existential pairs thrown/projecting, facticity/transcendence – that which sets boundaries to possibilities and the possibilities themselves – versions of Kierkegaard's factors: necessity and possibility.'[25] Again we are told that 'not only does Heidegger take over from Kierkegaard the idea that the self is the stand a set of factors takes on itself, [he] also accepts that some stands define the factors so as to do justice to the structure of the self and some do not.'[26] And again, that 'he accepts Kierkegaard's account of the present age as an anxiety-motivated cover-up of the basic structure of the self.'[27] Again and again they reiterate the same note, as when they state that 'his account of anxiety is a secular version of an explicitly Christian analysis developed by Kierkegaard.'[28] All in all, it is clear from Dreyfus' and Rubin's account that Heidegger owes to Kierkegaard the following ideas: his conception of the nihilism of the present age as a state of levelling in contemporary society; his structuration of the self; his notion of anxiety; his interpretation of death and guilt; his versions of falling, fleeing and fallenness; his view of resoluteness as relating to the Moment; his whole view of Authenticity; and considerable portions of his view of historicality as repetition or retrieval (*Wiederholen*). Thus in the case of fallenness, we are told explicitly that 'Heidegger . . . can be read as again secularizing Kierkegaard, in this case Kierkegaard's interpretation of the Christian doctrine of the fall';[29] 'that Heidegger is secularizing original sin is clear when he treats lostness in the one [usually translated as the They] not as a structural tendency but as a psychological temptation.'[30] Again we are told that 'Heidegger then secularizes and formalizes Kierkegaard's concept of the Moment.'[31]

But not only does Heidegger take so copiously from Kierkegaard, he makes strenuous efforts to cover his traces and pretends he owes him little if anything. As Dreyfus and Rubin note with regard to fallenness and the Fall, 'not only does Heidegger fail to thank Kierkegaard in *Being and Time*, in his lectures he protests with strange vehemence against any idea that what he says about fallenness has religious or psychological associations.'[32] Heidegger states that 'it should be noted here that the explication of these structures of Dasein has nothing to do with any . . . theory of original sin.'[33] Where Heidegger does acknowledge Kierkegaard, in three footnotes in *Being and Time*, it is invariably to make backhand compliments by stressing where Kierkegaard is inadequate and deficient as compared to Heidegger himself. Thus we are told by Heidegger that 'Kierkegaard is probably the one who has seen the *existentiell* phenomenon of the *Augenblick* with the most penetration; but this does not signify that he has been correspondingly successful in interpreting it existentially.' And again, 'but the existential problematic was so alien to him that, as regards his ontology, he remained completely dominated by Hegel and by ancient philosophy as Hegel saw it.'[34] Heidegger is always putting himself in the superior existential position and placing Kierkegaard in the inferior *existentiell* one. Similarly, he castigates all theology, above all the Christian one, as merely *existentiell* compared to his own ontology.

However, as Dreyfus and Rubin note perspicaciously, 'in spite of his denial and against his will, Heidegger seems to have taken over from Kierkegaard a dogmatic-Christian conception of society and of sinfulness.'[35]

But what Dreyfus and Rubin fail to note is that in doing so Heidegger has made nonsense of it. For in Kierkegaard the dogmatic-Christian theology is grounded in faith and cannot be established in any other way, it cannot be 'justified or grounded in any way, be it transcendental, empirical or phenomenological,'[36] as Dreyfus and Rubin remark. But this is precisely what Heidegger tries to do, he removes the dogmatic-Christian conception from any basis in faith, as well as from Revelation, Church and the whole of the Christian tradition, and instead seeks to ground it in phenomenology and ontology, which is precisely what Kierkegaard is most adamant should not and cannot be done. As Dreyfus and Rubin put it, 'Heidegger, on the other hand, seeks a phenomenological *demonstration* of these structures that are constitutive of human being in general.'[37] But they are only so constitutive on a dogmatic-Christian conception, which is precisely what Heidegger seeks to repudiate and from which he vainly tries to separate himself thereby cutting off the very support on which he stands. Dreyfus and Rubin, however, believe that this is a justifiable move, and consider it a defensible 'secularization and formalization': 'this repudiation of the Christian-dogmatic side of Kierkegaard's thought we call Heidegger's secularization of Kierkegaard.'[38] They believe it needs to be accomplished. Thus they hold that 'authenticity seems to be a successful secularized version of [Kierkegaard's] Religiousness A with all its benefits and none of its contradictions.'[39] If only it were that simple.

Whether or not it is free of contradictions, which I shall not consider here, just how beneficial is such a secularized authenticity? Perhaps its benefits can be judged from the fact that it led Heidegger straight into the arms of Nazism. The concepts that pertain to it, such as resolve, repetition, heritage, Destiny and historicity, prepared the ground for Heidegger's acceptance of the Party card. This is apparent from sentences such as this from *Being and Time*: 'Dasein's fateful destiny in and with its "generation" goes to make up the full *authentic* historicizing of Dasein.'[40] Heidegger's striving for historical authenticity led him to accept the 'fateful destiny' that seemed to present itself to his 'generation' to follow its chosen hero. All this is well known, but seems to have escaped Dreyfus and Rubin.

This 'secularizing and formalizing' of Christian theology – usually carried out through the mediation of Kierkegaard – had a particularly pernicious effect on many other thinkers apart from Heidegger. Without Christ and his Church, without faith, doctrine or dogma, such a perversion of theology tended frequently to end up in one or another totalitarian 'religion'. This was also the path that Lukács took; and Wittgenstein, too, followed it for a certain distance. Both were also influenced by Kierkegaard and developed on this basis a kind of secularized religiosity. In Lukács it led to an absolute ethical commitment to Revolution and Bolshevism, through which a Revolutionary Party of avant-garde intellectuals would lead the masses to secular salvation. This is not all that dissimilar to Heidegger's aristocratic-conservative conception of an elite of authentic elect rising far above the crowd of fallen *They* to create a national State as the supreme work of art. This partly accounts for the perceived similarity in the work of the two thinkers which has been brought out by Lucien Goldmann. Wittgenstein's secular theology went in a less political direction, for basing itself on Tolstoy's idealization of ordinary life and ordinary people (peasants in Tolstoy's Russia), it produced a desire for the authentic individual to seek salvation in an immersion in the common life of the people, to lose the Self in the They, in Heidegger's terms. But the sole authentic individual is the 'genius' as Wittgenstein understood this in accordance with the secularized theology of Weininger.

Unlike Heidegger, who at least refers to Kierkegaard, Wittgenstein never publicly acknowledges Weininger at all. But he was strongly influenced by him throughout his life and did not hesitate to recommend him to his closest friends and disciples. Perhaps this omission can be explained as the privilege of genius; Wittgenstein, as we have already seen with regard to Schopenhauer, was exceedingly lax in acknowledging his sources. Or perhaps it was a tactical choice to remove the odium of a believed to be nefarious writer, as Weininger would not fail to be considered in England, from his writings. For whatever reason, Wittgenstein fails to mention Weininger even once. He mentions Mauthner once in the *Tractatus*, only to disagree with and reject him. But he also fails to acknowledge how much he owes him as well in that and in his later writings, as a number of scholars have since pointed out.[41] Mauthner does not even merit a private recommendation or mention to his close friends and disciples.

That the *Tractatus* owes much to Weininger has also been noted by scholars. Allan Janik has written on this, as have Ray Monk in his biography of Wittgenstein and Jacques Le Rider in his book on Weininger. What they remark on in particular is that the *Tractatus* derives from Weininger its peculiar conception of the relation between logic and ethics. Weininger stated that 'logic and ethics are fundamentally the same, they are no more than duty to oneself . . . All ethics is possible only by the laws of logic, all logic is also ethical law.'[42] Weininger arrived at this view through a misconception of Kant and Schopenhauer whose successor he believed himself to be, 'carrying through a program initiated by the great pessimist', as Janik notes.[43] Le Rider points out that 'il confond la raison théorique et la raison pratique: il éthecise la logique au point de parler d'un "logisches Gewissen" (chez Kant Gewissen signifie conscience morale).'[44] There is hardly any need to discuss Weininger's sublime sounding phrase any further here, Le Rider's verdict on it is obvious enough.

However, Wittgenstein found it very enticing and structured much of the *Tractatus* argument on it. Logic and ethic are one in the sense that both logical form and ethical law cannot be stated, they only show themselves. Both thereby inhere in the mystical. For by 'ethics' Wittgenstein, following Weininger, meant also much that could be considered religion, especially in its mystical aspects. Since logic and ethics were the same, Wittgenstein could present his religious conclusions as emerging, as it were, from purely logical premisses – though at the same time he denied any such deductive relation. Logic and mysticism were one: the opening of the *Tractatus* dealing with *Principia Mathematica* matters and the ending touching on *Geschlecht und Charakter* matters were essentially at one with each other. It was this combination of logic and mysticism that so surprised and confounded Russell and Frege. Wittgenstein, of course, never referred to Weininger in trying to explain it to them.

He owed to Weininger even more than these scholars have so far discovered. I believe that his view of the identity of solipsism and realism, the view that 'I am my world', also has a Weiningerian source. Wittgenstein explicitly refers to it in terms of the relation of the microcosm to the macrocosm, and it is in these same terms that Weininger discusses the relation between genius and the world. According to Weininger, the genius is the microcosm who is identical with the macrocosm. As Le Rider paraphrases it, 'le grand home porte en lui le monde entier et le génie est un microcosme vivante. Il est le tout . . . en lui le monde et le moi sont devenue un seul même chose.'[45] Weininger derived this from Fichtean premisses of the identity of the identity formula 'A = A' with Descartes' *Cogito,* premisses which Wittgenstein would not have accepted, but he did accept the conclusion that the 'I' and the world are one and the same without restricting this to the genius alone.

The problems of secularized and formalized theology, which I noted in the relation of Heidegger to Kierkegaard, are even worse confounded in the relation of Wittgenstein to Weininger. As a thinker, Weininger cannot be compared to Kierkegaard, but he did a little, and very badly at that, of what Kierkegaard had done to theology – he restated it couched in the philosophical terminology of Idealism. Just as Kierkegaard drew on Schelling and Hegel for this purpose, so Weininger drew on Schopenhauer and Kant. Despite its philosophical trappings, it is a religious view that Weininger is presenting, a kind of Manicheanism of spirit and purity battling against flesh and sin. Wittgenstein took this over tacitly without ever expressing it in so many words or trying to justify it. But it infused itself into much of his philosophizing. All this serves to show how theology philosophized comes back to philosophy in a disguised form to produce all kinds of strangely anomalous effects in thought and idea.

Marxism is a particularly rich field of such effects. As has often been observed, there are features of a theology philosophized in the Young Marx, precisely the ones to which Lukács returned: the conception of alienation as separation from reality and severance from unity; the view of the proletariat as the new Israel of humanity – those who are now nothing but will in the immediate future become everything; the idea of the Revolution as an apocalyptic event transforming all of reality; greed for money as the root of all evil, and the worshippers of money – both Jews and capitalists alike, for he identified them – as those against whom the final Armageddon must be fought; and, finally, the view of himself as the prophet offering a new gospel of human liberation. All of these and many more features of Marxism arise from theology secularized and politicized. The philosophy in terms of which they are couched is that of Hegel and his followers, the Left-Hegelians, who were simultaneously preoccupied with the problems of religion and revolution, seeking to develop on a Hegelian basis what might be called a theology of liberation. This is the intellectual milieu out of which Marx arose and which remains infused in his writings no matter how much he later tried to distance himself from it.

It is ironic to note that perhaps the earliest scholar to elicit the Hegelian sources of Marx and to view Marxism as a Hegelian philosophy was Gentile, in a book, *La filosofia di Marx*, published in 1899 and subsequently widely reviewed. None other than Lenin himself praised this work and recommended it to Marxists: 'the author points out some important aspects of Marx's materialist dialectic which ordinarily escapes the attention of the Kantians, positivists, etc.'[46] – namely, all those Marxists of the time, by far the greatest majority, who wanted to see Marx as anything but a Hegelian. Gentile, in opposition to the prevailing Marxism, pointed out how Marx had elaborated a dialectical philosophy of history and argued that his so-called materialism had nothing to do with scientific or positivist conceptions of matter, that is, with dead matter, and everything to do with living activity, praxis, a notion which Marx drew not only from Feuerbach but all the more so from Hegel himself. In short, the resurrection of the Young Marx, from the grave to which he had been consigned by the Old Marx, Engels and their successors – something that had supposedly been first accomplished by Lukács and the Marxist Hegelians of the 1920s – was in fact carried out by Gentile decades earlier. There is no book on Marxism that even mentions that fact.

It would be interesting to know whether Lukács had read Gentile. In view of the fact that he visited Italy frequently in his young years, that he wrote on Italian politics in 1920, and in view of Lenin's recommendation, one must suppose that he did. What makes it even more probable is that his close friend at the time, Lajos Fülep, together with whom he visited Italy and edited the journal *A Szellem*, was an intimate of many Italian philosophers. As Kadarkay reports, 'Fülep was an active member of the *Circolo di Filosofia*, which was chaired by Calderoni, and contributed to *La Biblioteca Filosofica*, which was edited by Giovanni Gentile.'[47] But by the time he wrote and published *History and Class Consciousness* it was no longer politically possible for him to have admitted any inspiration from Gentile, the hated Fascist. Years later in the early 1930s he saw and helped decipher the manuscripts of Marx's *Economic and Philosophical Notebooks* and the *German Ideology* at the Marx-Engels Institute in Moscow and had his earlier view of the centrality of alienation confirmed. Much later in his introduction of 1967 to *History and Class Consciousness* he congratulates himself on his prescience, but without mentioning Gentile's even earlier anticipation which would have been known to him.

Under the strong influence of Ernst Bloch, his intellectual friend, the young Lukács arrived at Marxism from a decidedly theological direction. He did not express this as openly and directly as Bloch, who in his *The Spirit of Utopia* of 1918 could uphold 'primal religious desire' and insist that 'throughout all the movements and goals of worldly transformation, this has been a desire to make room for life, for the attainment of divine essence, for men to integrate themselves at last, in a millennium, with human kindness, freedom, and the light of the *telos*.'[48] Lukács would never sound like that or use this kind of imagery; on the whole, he stuck to the jargon of orthodox Marxism. Stylistically he was not as gifted as Bloch. However, every now and then a religious undertone can be heard sounding beneath what otherwise might be taken as the hackneyed themes of the Marxian dialectic, as in the following passage from an essay of 1919:

> It was in the class-consciousness created by Marxism that the spirit, indeed, the very meaning of social development, emerged from its previously unconscious state . . . Hence we Marxists not only believe that the development of society is directed by the so-often disparaged Spirit, but we also know that it was only in Marx's work that this spirit became consciousness and assumed the mission of leadership. But this mission cannot be the privilege of any 'intellectual class' or the product of any form of 'supra-class' thinking. The salvation of society is a mission

> which only the proletariat, by virtue of its world-historical role, can achieve. And only through the *class-consciousness of the proletarians* is it possible to achieve the knowledge and understanding of this path of humanity that is essential to 'intellectual leadership'.[49]

The Spirit becoming conscious in Marxism and assuming the mission of leadership for the salvation of society by the proletariat – this vision is not so far removed from that of the Spirit becoming incarnate for the sake of the salvation of mankind. In other words, a basically Christian theological hymn is there as the ground for Lukács' variations. It is true that what Adorno called 'die grosse Blochmusik' cannot be heard in Lukács, but those who are religiously attuned can detect a no less insistent religious music.

Like Lukács, Gentile too went back to Hegel, but not so much through the mediating agency of Marx as of Spaventa, a native Italian source. 'Gentile held that a return to the teaching of Spaventa was the key to future progress,'[50] Harris maintains. Bertrando Spaventa was a Neapolitan philosopher of the *Risorgimento* who taught in Turin. He put forward the view that the nation is the realization of the Idea: 'the meaning of the history of the nation as the history of Ideas. And the history of Ideas is seen by Spaventa as the history of philosophy.'[51] The fatal combination of Idealism and Nationalism, which was to take such a grotesque expression in Gentile, is already nascently in evidence in Spaventa. Spaventa assured himself and his fellow Italians that it was no national disgrace to be a Hegelian, since in acquiring the philosophy of the German Hegel they were only taking back what belonged to the philosophical heritage of Italy anyway. 'The greatest speculative philosophy emerged from Italy during the Renaissance, expressed in other terms, and returned to the country of origin in the Nineteenth century through the Hegelian tradition in Italy,' as di Lalla puts it.[52] Hegel and Idealism in general are only the culmination of the 'circulation of Italian thought in that of Europe'. Starting with Giordano Bruno and continuing with Vico, Italian philosophy had not only historically made possible Idealism in Germany, but also developed it to the same level in the philosophy of Gioberti, the Italian Hegel: 'with Vincenzo Gioberti the Italian speculative thought of the nineteenth century attained to the height of the German,' as de Ruggiero boasts. Hence its return to Italy was only a kind of homecoming at the conclusion of its tour through Europe.

Nevertheless, in his Italian fashion, Spaventa 'remained all his life a loyal Hegelian'; although, as Harris adds, 'in his continual efforts to rethink the whole course of the idealist tradition, he was more or less unconsciously offering a novel interpretation of the Hegelian dialectic.'[53] One can judge how much of a departure from Hegel it is by this representative quotation:

> In defining being I do not *distinguish* myself, as thought, from being: I *extinguish* myself, as thought, in being; I *am* being. Now this extinction of thought in being is the contradiction of being; and this contradiction is the first ray of the dialectic. Being contradicts itself because this extinction of thought in being (and only by this is being possible) is really a negation of extinction: it is distinction, it is life.'[54]

The couplets being–thought, distinguish–extinguish, contradiction–negation all dance around each other forwards and backwards in a kind of dialectical ballet of concepts. This kind of free-play of language was not only taken up by Gentile, but in a peculiar way it seems to anticipate Heidegger's manner of writing as well. Heidegger's disciples, especially the Deconstructivists under Derrida, have made a fetish of this kind of language play, carrying it to absurd lengths of alliterative punning across different languages.

Gentile took over from Spaventa the general idea that thought is totality; as Spaventa puts it, 'thought is a dialectical act, a world, a totality, a system.'[55] Here we find the origin of the concept of totality which will eventually, by odd twists and turns, generate that of totalitarianism. It took Gentile's genius to make that possible, to complete the move from totality to totalitarianism. For though his primary masterwork, *The Theory of Spirit as Pure Act*, appeared a little before the rise of Fascism, yet there is something to be said for Herbert Marcuse's view that 'it shows most clearly the affinity between Italian neo-Idealism and this authoritarian system and provides a lesson as to what happens to a philosophy that fosters such affinity.'[56] This affinity between neo-Idealism and Fascism realised in Gentile was anticipated by the relation between neo-Idealism and Nationalism developed in Spaventa.

In their recovery of the secondary Idealists, the malign masters were not alone, they were simply following well-charted irrationalist trends of the pre-1914 period. Kiekegaard had already been rediscovered and translated before Heidegger heard of him. Weininger's book *Geschlecht und Charakter* was a best-seller going through many editions. Spaventa was well known in Italy, though not outside. And the Left-Hegelian Young Marx was not forgotten by Marxists, though most followed Engels' lead in regarding this phase of his work as best left to the 'gnawing criticism of the mice' who had nearly chewed up the *German Ideology*. In following in the footsteps of these secondary Idealists, the malign masters were pursuing other well-demarcated paths of irrationalist thought in the period. Most of these were of a quasi-religious or mystical nature, and left their indelible marks on the primary masterworks.

Each of these is in effect a *filosofia teologizzante*, in Vico's phrase. Each contains an occult theology, which, as I have stated, is invariably a species of Christian heresy reflecting the idiosyncratic religious preoccupations of its author. The malign masters were well attuned to the advanced trends of religious thinking of the pre-1914 era. In this respect, too, they were utterly unlike their fathers, who, in Weber's phrase, were 'religiously unmusical'. By contrast, the sons dabbled in all the cults of occult mysticism, which became popular among small circles of intellectuals just prior to the First World War. They read early Christian theology, neo-Platonism and Hermeticism, the medieval German mystics, above all Meister Eckhart, and subsequent German traditions of religious thought, such as Jakob Böhme, and some even ventured into Jewish mysticism from the Cabbalah to Hassidism.

All this traditional religious literature was supplemented with the discovery of the new Russian literature, then recently translated into other languages, above all the novels of Tolstoy and Dostoevsky, especially the latter, who was regarded as a profound religious thinker. And added to it was the revival of early romantic literature, such as the poetry of Hölderlin, Novalis and various other till then obscure writers. The modernist literary trends at the time, especially the symbolist and expressionist poetry of George, Rilke and Trakl, led in the same direction. To explore in detail the profound effect that the Russian novelists alone had on the German-speaking masters – for Gentile seems not to have known them – would require a work of its own. Remains it to be recalled in brief that Heidegger quotes from Tolstoy's *The Death of Ivan Illych* in *Being and Time*, that Wittgenstein was intensely preoccupied with Tolstoy's stories throughout his life, and that Lukács wrote extensively on his novels. The ethical-religious views of Dostoevsky, especially as presented in the Grand Inquisitor parable from *The Brothers Karamazov*, had a no less intense impact on all three philosophers. Lukács in particular drew Dostoevskian conclusions regarding the Russian Revolution and revolutionary action in general which, of course, were quite contrary to Dostoevsky himself. Similarly, it is mostly the case that the philosophers used these literary sources in ways that went quite counter to the meaning of the works themselves.

The primary masterworks reflect all these intoxicating influences in all sorts of ways. There are not only theological themes in them, but also mythological, poetic-metaphoric and rhetorical ones as well, to such a degree that some of them might be seen as engaging in what is tantamount to word magic. This can occur in the most unlikeliest of contexts. I will confine myself to a few brief examples, but there are very many others as well.

Thus, underpinning the supposedly logical structure of the *Tractatus* there is the mythology and number magic of Genesis. As in God's creation of the world, the *Tractatus* begins with the chaos of atomic facts in no logical order or sequence; it proceeds to order these into molecular complexes in a 'logical space', so-called, over the course of six major stages, which echoes the days of creation; characteristically, the creation of Adam, the 'human' stage of will and ethics, is left last to the sixth day; and, finally, on the seventh day it rests, like God, in sabbatical silence. However, unlike the Judaic transcendent Creator God, the author of the *Tractatus* world, like an immanent demiurge, withdraws into his own creation by merging with the world he has formed and consigning the creative act to oblivion in the ineffable wordless-mysticism of the unspeakable. The author thereby declares himself at once to be omnipotent and impotent. He performs an Indian rope-trick act of constructing a logical ladder which he climbs till he disappears from sight pulling the ladder behind him. One does not need to engage in any deep psychoanalytic speculations to appreciate what inner compulsions this philosophical epiphany of self-revelation and self-annihilation satisfies.

Heidegger's *Being and Time* reveals analogous mythological and magical features. It continually practises a word magic in supposedly tracing the etymology of certain key words back to their original roots so as to reveal the 'hidden' essence of things. Of course, it is always the root-meanings of words in Greek and German, the two Aryan 'holy tongues' of philosophy, that count; no others are considered. As many authors have since shown, most of this so-called etymology is fake, a mere pretence at linguistic research, which is no better than common misconception and prejudice.[57] In any case, irrespective of whether these word derivations are true or false, the very idea that etymological beginnings are somehow definitive of the 'essence' of things is itself a residue of the belief in the magic of words such as is often to be found in medieval and Renaissance writings on the Adamic 'theory' of language. The Cabbalah is full of it; but, of course, there it is Hebrew that is the original tongue, whereas Heidegger never abandoned his belief in the innate virtue of the Germanic languages. He comes up with these ideas in his last interview for *Der Spiegel* of 1966.

However, despite such lapses into what one can only consider a species of philosophical superstition, there are also much sounder and more interesting theological themes in all the primary masterworks. For the most part these are not obvious for they have been distorted and disguised in various ways. Indeed, as I have already noted, this made for the strong appeal of these works for the generation of intellectuals immediately after the First World War. They both yearned for a religious message of hope and salvation, but were inhibited in seeking it in the traditional churches and theologies, for they were no longer believers in the old ways. Many had departed completely from the religion of their birth and considered themselves atheists. For such people a hidden and unacknowledged religious agenda, dressed in the trappings of a secularized philosophy, was most appealing. They could both have their religion and deny it at the same time. This was a kind of early version of double-think that the malign masters introduced, and thereby accustomed themselves and their readers to the cruder versions that they were encouraged to practice under totalitarianism later.

The hidden religious provenance of nearly all the concepts of *Being and Time* has long been noticed and explored by commentators. Thus the Protestant theologian Rudolf Bultmann, with whom Heidegger worked it Marburg, already noted in the late 1940s that the 'existentialist analysis of the ontological structure of [*Dasein*] would seem to be no more than a secularized philosophical version of the New Testament view of human life.'[58] Löwith observed likewise concerning 'the hidden history of his concepts' that 'all of them originated in the Christian tradition, however much death, conscience, guilt, care, anxiety, and corruption are formalized ontologically and neutralized as concepts of the Dasein.'[59] Even his concept of time has a wholly traditional Christian source, as Thomas Sheehan notes:

> There was the discovery of what he called 'kairological time' in the writings of Paul, especially in the fifth chapter of Thessalonians. The eschatological thrust of early Christianity, the expectation of the *Parousia*, opens up an absolutely unique understanding of time, wherein all questions of 'when' are transposed from the chronology (*chronos*) into 'the moment of insight' (*kairos, Augenblick*). The question of when the *Parousia* will occur is not answered by reference to objective time but is referred back to factical lived experience and becomes a matter of the way a man leads his life . . . Out of such experience, Heidegger asserts, authentic temporality is generated.[60]

Thus, for Heidegger, time is really Christian time, for he has inscribed Christian theology into the very nature of time.

The precise theological sources of Heidegger's concepts have all been unearthed by now and are well known. They range across the whole

Christian tradition from the Gospels and St Paul onwards. Of particular importance in *Being and Time* are the Protestant Reformers, Luther and Calvin, for this was the period in his life when he converted from his native Catholicism to a mystical Protestantism of his own devising. To select just two theologians, one early and another late, who were most crucial to him one might choose Augustine as the former and Barth as the latter. Unfortunately, I do not have the space here to explore what these meant for him and what he derived from them, but it is known that both preoccupied him throughout the 1920s, the period of composition of his primary masterwork. They receded only when he simultaneously moved towards Nazism and Nietzscheanism, both of which impelled him into a version of a 'religious atheism' for a time. Later he withdrew into the quietistic mysticism of his own devised mythological religion of the Event and the four-fold. The Event (*Ereignis*), a term derived from Rickert and Dilthey, which 'Heidegger regarded as untranslatable', as Tom Rockmore notes, 'included meanings associated with Greek poetry, the birth of Greek philosophy as a separate entity, and the history of philosophy since this moment until the point at which it was surpassed through modern technology'.[61] Clearly, since this is a complex mytho-poetic symbol, rather than an idea or concept, it cannot be rationally discussed.

Compared to Heidegger, Wittgenstein was in theological matters a naive amateur. But he too had read and been impressed by the Gospels, St Paul and St Augustine, an impression that never left him for the rest of his life. As all the others did, he dabbled in the medieval German mystics. However, the most important religious influence on him was undoubtedly the *Gospels in Brief*, Tolstoy's rendering of the Christian message in somewhat heretical terms. For a while during the war he became in effect a lay preacher and was known as 'the man of the Gospels'. Tolstoy's simplified version of Christianity with its emphasis on this-worldly activity, life in the present as eternal and the common life of men as beyond the Ego suited Wittgenstein's anti-transcendent orientation and self-denying immersion in the world. Doestoevsky also played a key role in his religious conception, especially the asceticism and message of love of *The Brothers Karamazov*, which he reread countless times throughout his life. He also read Kiekegaard, though how he understood him and what he derived from him is harder to fathom.

All this undoubtedly had a strong impact on the composition of the *Tractatus*, 'transforming it from an analysis of logical symbolism in the spirit of Frege and Russell into the curiously hybrid work which we know today, combining as it does logical theory with religious mysticism',[62] as Ray Monk puts it. Hence, all his comments concerning 'ethics' in this work have little to do with this subject as it is usually understood in philosophy. As Weiner shows, what he says has to be filtered through and read in terms of Schopenhauer's discussion of the genius and the saint, that is, of art and ethics as ways to salvation.[63] Both involved 'the mystical', and both led to the same end, which is the reason that he declares that 'ethics and aesthetics are one and the same.'[64]

However, Wittgenstein's conception of eternal life in the present that affords salvation is far closer to Christianity than Schopenhauer's Buddhistic *Erlösung*. His terms line up with those of orthodox theology. Thus his statements concerning the good and bad will are secularized versions of grace and sin, and those concerning happiness and unhappiness are similarly versions of salvation and damnation. But, of course, it is this-worldly states that he is concerned with, not other-worldly ones. Statements to the effect that the world of the unhappy Self is different from that of the happy must be given a religious reading; namely, meaning that the saved soul-world is different from the damned soul-world, given his solipsistic identification of Self and world. This very closely parallel's Heidegger's distinction between authentic and inauthentic existence, for this, too, 'corresponds to Bultmann's distinction between faithfulness and sinfulness,' as Michael Zimmerman notes.[65]

There are also analogies between Wittgenstein's and Heidegger's conceptions of death as a kind of limit or boundary of life, not to be encountered as an event in life itself, as I have previously shown. Both attempt to render the religious concept of eternal life in non-transcendent terms. According to Wittgenstein, there is no death for one who lives fully in the present; and according to Heidegger, since death is present in every living moment, it does not mean any kind of an end or finish. Both of them consider death in solipsistic terms always and only as 'my death', and never as the death of other people. Death thus becomes a purely formal notion unrelated to the real facts of dying and being dead as these are experienced in life in relation to others and oneself at once.

Before he became a Bolshevik Lukács too pursued a strongly religious predisposition towards mysticism. Like the others, he read Augustine and Eckhart, and was well versed in Kierkegaard. Even more than they, he was steeped in the Russian novel and regarded Dostoevsky almost as his personal evangelist. He made every possible attempt to lead his life in a Dostoevskian spirit, even to the point of marrying a Russian anarchist who might have emerged as a character from the pages of one of the novels. However, unlike the others, he also imbibed a considerable amount of Jewish Cabbalistic and Hassidic mysticism through the influence of his friend Martin Buber who later became an existentialist philosopher.

Some of this, though highly distorted, is reflected in his primary masterwork. The strongest religious influence there reveals itself as what he was much later to call disparagingly 'the messianic, utopian aspirations [of the] sectarianism of the twenties'.[66] Much of this undoubtedly came to him through his friendship with the religiously inspired revolutionary, Bloch. Bloch undertook the translation of Marxism away from the scientific socialism of the Second International and back to its original chiliastic aspiration as a total revolutionary transformation of a fallen world. Lukács accepted this vision of the bourgeois world as totally sinful and by itself incapable of salvation, which could only come from outside through the agency of a new chosen people, the proletariat. In his primary masterwork Lukács takes exception on minor points with Bloch's writings, but essentially, as he later admitted, he had accepted and absorbed their messianic and chiliastic spirit.

Bloch deliberately brought Marxism back to its unacknowledged religious sources. He aligned it with the apocalyptic movements of the Middle Ages and Reformation period, especially to the ideas animating the various peasant insurrections, the radical sects of the Reformation, such as the Anabaptists, and the subsequent sectarian groups, such as the Millennarians of the English Civil War. All of their chiliastic ideas can be traced back to the early medieval heresy of Joachim of Flora with its doctrine of the three ages, that of the Father, Son and Holy Ghost, which was taken over by the radical Franciscans and broadcast throughout Europe as the basic creed of all subsequent revolutionary groups. This view of Marxism as a secularized version of this whole religious tradition was clearly anathema to orthodox Marxists, especially so after the Revolution. Lukács was never able to live down the traces of this religiously inspired apocalypticism in his primary masterwork, no matter how hard he tried to disguise them. He ran afoul first of Lenin himself, then of Zinoviev at the Third International, and of many subsequent Party theoreticians. He responded by totally rejecting his own work. Bloch, however, went on in this same vein till his death.

Gentile did not share the same religious traditions as the other Central European masters. His was a more parochial Italian milieu where traditional Catholicism was the only religion to be considered. In particular, he had little sense of or sympathy for Protestantism, not to speak of any other sect or faith. All his life he defined himself as a Catholic – albeit in his own peculiar designation – even when he was strongly opposed to the Church. As he declared, 'I am a Christian. I am a Christian because I believe in the religion of the Spirit. But I would like to add, without any equivocation, I am a Catholic.'[67] But no sooner did he utter this credo than he began to equivocate, for obviously his conception of Catholicism and the orthodox one were worlds apart.

In this respect he followed the lead of Gioberti, the early Italian Idealist, who also professed a purely private Catholicism, arguing that there are as many Catholicisms as there are Catholics. But in essence, his religion was his philosophy, Actual Idealism; he simply saw Catholicism as the nearest approximation to it among the established religions. He had constituted this philosophy in his primary masterwork by incorporating into it as many features of an abstract and idealized Catholicism, bereft of Christ and his Church, as could be made compatible with Idealism. For this purpose he relied strongly on the neo-Platonic strands in Christianity as derived from Plotinus and incorporated into the Church tradition by Augustine. Together with that, he also absorbed elements of traditional Christian mysticism from Eckhart to St John of the Cross. As he declared, 'mysticism is the essence of religion.'[68]

Later he came to identify his creed with Fascism, seen as a religion of the Nation and State. But unlike Panunzio and other philosophical Fascists, he did not wish to have it doctrinally defined and institutionally established. At the Bologna Congress of March 1925 he fought hard against them in order to keep the religious character of Fascism relatively open, arguing that it was a 'totalitarian religious spirit rather than a religious or philosophical creed',[69] and his view was officially accepted. For a short while, that is, for soon all that became a distinction without much difference. During the Second World War he resorted to a kind of Fascist mysticism, 'a sane mysticism, which in the austere conception that we ought to have of the war, as likewise of the whole of life, will give us the patience to wait with quiet confidence.'[70] Presumably he was waiting not for God, but for the victory of Fascism over its enemies.

There is a strong element of perverted and repressed Catholicism not only in Gentile but in the other malign masters as well, a kind of religious unconscious to which they could not own up. It is there in the never to be completely erased influence of his Jesuit schooling on Heidegger, who held Suárez to be one of the greatest metaphysicians; in Wittgenstein's submission to tradition and authority and rejection of rationalism and science; and also in Lukács' view of the Communist Party as the City of God in History and, therefore, as infallible, just like the Church. All this must be given much more exposition than I have space for here, but it can at least be mentioned for it is part of the explanation of the extraordinary initial impression made by the malign masters on so many followers who became true believers. Their philosophies offered a kind of secular salvation to philosophically inclined intellectuals by providing a gnostic vision of totality that seemed to have all the answers to the problems that troubled them in such difficult times. At the same time, they satisfied the hatred that such intellectuals had come to feel for the very processes of intellectualisation and disenchantment of which they were themselves the modern products. Thus they catered to the very self-hatred that, following a political course, set these intellectuals on the road to totalitarianism.

6 Friends and Followers

The success of the malign masters can be explained sociologically, but only in general terms, for that kind of explanation does not really account for the specific career path that each followed and how out of this arose the groupings of supporters who would eventually constitute his following. The human factors that play such a large part in winning over people to a cause, especially in its early stages, are also operative in philosophy. Sometimes one single friendship might be of crucial importance in establishing a reputation and gaining supporters. On its own a single relationship cannot create a philosophical movement, but in the right social setting one influential friendship can multiply itself many times over, whereas under unfavourable conditions it remains isolated and withers in the bud. The interweaving between the personal and the social is of great complexity and can only be analysed by unravelling and untangling the numerous separate threads which make up the web of the cultural fabric. I shall concentrate in the first place on personal relations, following these like a kind of red thread throughout all the varied career patterns of the malign masters. After that I shall consider more general social factors.

Before the malign masters could recruit followers, they first had to win over friends. This each of them managed to do with an unerring instinct for impressing others. Early in their careers they appeared to be exemplary pupils to their teachers and loyal colleagues of their peers. Throughout their lives they cultivated a winning style that made them constantly friends and supporters. But invariably they broke with these friends, usually in acrimonious circumstances, for hardly ever did their relations endure and not finish in personal antagonism and irrevocable rupture. But prior to that inevitable break, their friends ensured them a reputation before they even published their primary masterworks. When their works first appeared they already had an expectant public prepared to receive them rapturously, for their friends had built them up in anticipation as works of genius. This partly explains the extraordinary instantaneous success of these works.

Of the many friends they made, I shall concentrate on the one or two who were in each case most nearly their equals: Jaspers in relation to Heidegger, Bloch in relation to Lukács, Moore and Schlick in relation to Wittgenstein and Lombardo-Radice in relation to Gentile. Apart from the last case, these friends were frequently intellectual precursors, St John the Baptist figures, preceding the masters themselves in preaching the new gospels of philosophy. This was clearly the case with Jaspers and Bloch in relation to Heidegger and Lukács, and in some respects partly so with Moore in relation to Wittgenstein. All the major themes that I have located in the primary masterworks were mostly already there in some of the works of the friends. One can find there a predisposition towards a metaphysics of totality, towards a non-egoistic solipsism, towards a secularized mysticism, and, in general, a revolt against rationalism, science, modernism and liberalism, though not always in quite the extreme form that the malign masters were to evince. Despite their originality in these respects, the friends were never as well regarded or successful as the malign masters. The reasons for this are puzzling and require explanation beyond the question-begging judgement that the masters were geniuses and the friends merely talented thinkers.

As personalities, the friends seem morally, if not intellectually as well, more appealing than the masters. Their work is more coherent and consistent. They did not undergo the intellectual turnabout and radical break of a *Kehre*, for none of them was seriously involved with any of the totalitarian movements. On the contrary, they mostly stood up against totalitarianism. The only possible exception was Bloch, who remained a sentimental Stalinist, but mainly from the safety of capitalist America; he never allowed himself to become a Party propagandist, as Lukács did. Of the others, Jaspers went into an 'inner emigration' after the Nazis came to power; Lombardo-Radice opposed Mussolini from the start and was abandoned by Gentile, just as Heidegger ceased to have any truck with Jaspers; Moore and Schlick were never tempted by the blandishments of totalitarianism which so appealed to their friend Wittgenstein. All in all, the friends were morally the better human beings, and intellectually they were not far inferior – some of their works stand comparison with those of the malign masters. I do not have the scope here for close comparative studies of *Being and Time* and *Philosophie, History and Class Consciousness* and *Geist der Utopie*, or the *Tractatus* and some of the early writings of Moore or Schlick. But it is of some interest to note that, according to Herbert Feigl, 'Wittgenstein studies owes a tremendous debt to Schlick . . . [for] . . . Schlick forced Wittgenstein to clarify themes that were to become central to his development during the 1930s.'[1] Furthermore, Feigl goes on to add, 'to my chagrin Schlick ascribed to Wittgenstein philosophical ideas that he [Schlick] had already expounded much more lucidly in his 1918 book on epistemology.'[2] Wittgenstein studies are called for that will cast more light on these brief remarks and further explore Wittgenstein's relation to his friends. Such research is also called for in elucidating the relation between Gentile and his educationalist friend Giuseppe Lombardo-Radice, the editor of the journal *Nuovi Doveri*.

So why is it that the works of the malign masters are now so well regarded whereas those of their friends are almost forgotten? Leszek Kolakowski asks himself this very question in relation to Jaspers and Heidegger:

> Jaspers has not entered – or, perhaps, not yet entered – the circulation of ideas in the Anglo-Saxon world. This is especially striking if we compare his position to Heidegger's . . . Why that is, I do not know. Perhaps – and that is only an impression – the reason for it rests less in the content of his philosophy than in his style and manner of self-presentation. Heidegger's lexical aggressiveness and prophetic inflexibility made him a highly successful ravisher of minds: irritating and fascinating at the same time, like Nietzsche, he appeared to be a true pioneer, a bearer of the great promise, with whose help we might expect to open by force the door to lost Being. Compared to him Jaspers appeared to be cautious, moralizing, and much more bound to the conventional language of European philosophy – in spite of his easily recognizable, characteristic and very individual style and vocabulary – fitting better into the mainstream of Western thinking and thus less visible in his uniqueness. Ultimately, the difference between them was perhaps that between a prophet and a teacher.[3]

It is perhaps not surprising that our age should prefer false prophets to true teachers. As Kolakowski shows, the very factors that make Heidegger malign and Jaspers benign caused the one to seem superior to the other in the eyes of their contemporaries and still continue to do so even now. For the recent revelations concerning Heidegger's morally abhorrent behaviour and his conceited political self-righteousness, which made him refuse to admit that he had been wrong or to expressly abjure his Nazism, have given him a bonus of publicity and exposure and made him all the more famous. Unfortunately, these days in philosophy, as in advertising, all publicity is good publicity. The ethos of a market culture pervades the higher reaches of academia as elsewhere in society.

Could Jaspers or any of the other friends have become malign masters if they had wanted to? Were they, so to speak, malign masters *manqués*? It is doubtful whether someone with Jaspers' personality or that of the other friends had the drawing power on students or the urge to dominate them that the masters displayed. If there were malign masters *manqués* they must be sought elsewhere. In France there were two potential candidates who might have succeeded to this role: Kojève and Sartre. Both were seriously handicapped in not having academic positions of power. Sartre was personally far too erratic to be able to hold such a position or use it to groom disciples. Kojève seems the more promising candidate, for at one time he had nearly all the major French intellectuals and philosophers at his feet. He introduced into France the German practice of reading one's own ideas into the texts one chooses to interpret. Possibly he learned this from Heidegger, whose works he knew, or perhaps from Jaspers, under whom he got his doctorate. Thus he gave readings of Hegel's *Phenomenology* to argue his own pet theory that history came to an end with Stalin. Francis Fukuyama has recently repeated this 'end of history' thesis, but altered the ending to fit American preconceptions. Kojève's Hegelian Marxism proved more influential than Lukács' and could possibly have made him a malign master had he chosen to become one. Instead, he gave up philosophy for unknown reasons and became a French civil servant.

It would have been very difficult for Bloch to challenge Lukács for malign master status, quite irrespective of the relative quality of their writings. For Lukács commanded world-wide attention as a political activist from the Kun *coup d'état* in 1919 onwards till after the Hungarian revolution of 1956 and even through to his death. From the late 1920s he was considered one of the leading Soviet literary critics, feared by Brecht and other communist writers and littérateurs, some of whom he hounded mercilessly. After the Second World War he was the officially designated Soviet philosopher at a number of international conferences, debating against all-comers and inveighing against 'decadent' Western tendencies, at that time, above all, Sartre's Existentialism. By contrast, Bloch, who refused to accept the Party dictate, remained a private scholar in exile in America and later in East and West Germany. Lukács tried to justify his own submission to the Party with the excuse that had he not done so, then like Bloch and other communist nonconformists, he would have been unable to take part in the anti-Fascist struggle. But there is no evidence that in 1928, or even 1929 when he made his total surrender to the will of the Party, the anti-Fascist struggle was of any great moment to him, or to Stalin for that matter. Stalin believed that a Nazi accession to power was to be welcomed for it would be the prelude to a communist revolution, and there is no reason to believe that Lukács thought otherwise.

For analogous political reasons Lombardo-Radice or any other Italian thinker could not possibly compete with Gentile for fame and influence. Gentile rose with the rise of Fascism and fell with its fall. He did not succeed in achieving an independent presence, except in small circles of neo-Idealists in England, and even that faded after the Second World War. In Italy itself his students converted almost *en masse* to a Gramscian mode of Marxism. For in a very peculiar way Gramsci's Hegelian Marxism, which had been influenced by Gentile's Actual Idealism, continued it in a disguised form and in the name of the opposite ideology. Gentile's neo-Idealism itself was repressed in the so-called anti-Fascist censorship that gripped Italian culture after the Second World War. Even Croce's work was rejected as part of this anti-Idealist sweep. Italian philosophers turned instead to the international scene, to French and Anglo-Saxon philosophy comprising mainly Phenomenology and Positivism, together with variants of Heidegger and Wittgenstein. Only now are Italian philosophers trying to return to their neo-Idealist heritage of Croce and Gentile. Thus Giovanna Borradori writes that because 'Fascism, which in order to pursue its nationalist politics, put a strong emphasis in every field on the "national" element, this is why, still today, many authors hesitate to acknowledge the national roots of their discourses, in which, very often, their originality lies.'[4] But obviously a return to the father, Croce, holds much more promise than a revival of the son, Gentile; and, if it were to take place, would be in keeping with the back to the fathers movement advocated in this work.

Neither Schlick nor Moore could rival Wittgenstein, and neither even wanted to. On the contrary, each did all he could to help establish his reputation and to win him disciples. Schlick brought the whole Vienna Circle to sit at his feet and was himself swept off his own feet in wonder and adoration. Moore attended his classes as if he were himself a disciple, thereby giving a lead to many others. In the academic politics of Cambridge, the leading centre of philosophy in the English-speaking world till after the Second World War, Wittgenstein's position as a source of influence was thus very strong. It was made supreme when Moore handed over his Chair to him, rather than to Russell, who was out of work at the time and soliciting Moore for a position. Wittgenstein also lobbied very effectively through his friend Keynes. Thus he became the leading official professional philosopher that he kept on protesting he did not wish to be and that he dissuaded his disciples from becoming. His hold on these disciples was almost total at times, ensuring not only their philosophical obedience, but even in many cases submission in the conduct of their private lives. His mannerisms of speech and gesture were imitated throughout philosophical Cambridge, and from there they spread to the furthest outlying reaches of the English-speaking world, as far as Melbourne in distant Australia where I encountered them in the mid-1950s.

Ultimately, what distinguished the malign masters from their often no less able friends was a charismatic personality that made so many generations of friends, followers and students stand in awe of them. Almost everyone who encountered a malign master felt in the presence of genius. They had this capacity to impress from the start of their careers. Among the first people to succumb to them were their own fathers, who must in this respect be counted as their first followers. And this power they retained throughout their lives. Not only philosophers, but many in other disciplines recognized them as 'great thinkers' and accorded them all the deference that the name philosopher has traditionally commanded. But it is hard to think of any great philosopher in the past who was so revered in his own time as the malign masters were in theirs.

As I have already indicated, the followings that formed around each of the malign masters have some of the features of the narrower and wider circles of any charismatic movement. Each of them was surrounded by esoteric and exoteric circles of friends and followers. Close to the master himself was a group of close disciples or companions; further removed were the sympathetic fellow-travellers; and surrounding this core was the mass of students and interested readers. Throughout the long career of each master the composition of these layers of followers changed repeatedly, especially so as the masters themselves went in and out of their *Kehre*. Hence, generally, around each of them there formed themselves two schools, one of pre-*Kehre* and one of post-*Kehre* followers. For just as each has an early and late philosophy, so they also have groups of early and late followers, each of whom lays claim to being the authentic exponent of the master's philosophy. The differences between these schools sometimes resulted in embittered battles even during the masters' lifetimes; and after their death there took place disputes over their legacy. All this continuing controversy concerning their work greatly augmented their reputations and consolidated their fame.

In twentieth-century intellectual matters in general reputation and fame is largely bound up with the generation of controversy. That alone can hold the attention of the large groups of people who make or unmake outstanding careers. In philosophy, as elsewhere, only a few 'stars' can emerge and shine; everyone else merges into the dark anonymous background. The malign masters had this 'star' quality through their capacity to generate controversy. Their claims were large, almost to the point of megalomania, but at the same time they could not be ignored. Hence, even those most opposed to them, if they sought to counter them in public, were, despite themselves, contributing to their reputations. To attack a malign master has always meant to help him thrive, and the masters were adept at provoking attacks. It is ironic, and bitter for me to contemplate, that this very work itself is likely to contribute to the same end.

This crucial capacity of being provocative and generating controversy is particularly true of Heidegger. Thus Karl Löwith writes of him in these terms:

> Like Fichte, only one half of him was an academic. The other – and probably greater – half was a militant preacher who knew how to interest people by antagonising them, and whose discontent with the epoch and himself was driving him on . . . The enormous success of his lectures and the extraordinary influence of his work, despite its difficulty, pushed Heidegger beyond the originally desired limits and made his thought fashionable. While this was indeed not intended by him, it was at the same time a natural consequence of his role as displaced preacher.[5]

His lecturing, or really preaching, style was artfully crafted at once to dazzle and to over-awe his listeners. Löwith states that 'his lecturing method consisted in constructing an edifice of ideas, which he himself then dismantled again so as to baffle fascinated listeners, only to leave them up in the air.'[6] One of the effects of what Löwith calls 'this art of enchantment' was that it 'attracted more or less psychopathic personalities'; but the combination of indoctrination and intimidation also made for very loyal disciples. The other malign masters had very different personalities and lecturing styles, but the effect on students was very similar. They built up by these means large and devoted followings.

But there is a great discrepancy in the size and endurance of the following of the different malign masters, and this also requires some explanation. In general the main reason is political. The failure of Gentile's philosophy to survive the defeat of Fascism is largely due to his open and publicly proclaimed loyalty to Mussolini and the German-dominated Salo Republic, which led directly to his death. Had he joined the other side, even at the last moment, and lived to take his place besides de Ruggiero, his old disciple, who became Minister of Education after the liberation, a very different story might now have to be told. Even so, the fate of Idealism was bound to remain tenuous after the Second World War. In England Collingwood's stock sank very low in the ensuing years; and even a successful academic like Michael Oakeshott (who, by the way, always considered Wittgenstein a charlatan) could only thrive in a limited personal way; what he stood for was generally disregarded. In America hardly any Idealists remained in distinguished positions apart from some followers of Whitehead. In Europe the situation was more complicated, but there, too, Idealism was considered *passé*. Hence, even if Gentile had lived, his philosophy could not have flourished all that much. It lacked a base of support from which disciples might be drawn.

Lukács had such a reserve base of followers among all the various kinds of intellectual communists and fellow-travellers. But his fidelity to Stalin and the Party stood him in poor stead, at least till he broke away and declared his independence as a free-thinking Marxist after the Hungarian uprising. But even then his success was limited by a number of political factors. In his native Hungary he remained a marginal figure, scarcely tolerated by the Kádár regime. Only the most loyal disciples, members of the so-called Budapest School, stood by him. In the other satellite countries of Eastern Europe his chances of attracting intelligent dissident followers were scotched by the fact that he was discredited because of his past subservience to Stalinism. Later, his refusal to be consistently critical of official communism, due to his persistence in a Leninist line, also redounded against him among dissidents. In the West these factors made it impossible for him to make much headway during the Cold War period. Only the rediscovery of his early work by the independent Marxists in France in the 1950s and later by the New Left movements of student radicalism of the 1960s kept his name alive. The subsequent exile of the members of the Budapest School and their acquisition of positions in Western universities also helped in giving his writings an institutional presence. But it was all too little and too late – Lukács could not possibly challenge the hold the already established master philosophers had in academia. Institutional politics was against him. Now his influence has almost completely waned.

The great period of Lukács' influence was undoubtedly the 1920s. Then he inspired the movements of Hegelian Marxism which took so many forms and involved other independent thinkers, such as Korsch and Gramsci, as well. This is what Mearleau-Ponty, who rediscovered *History and Class Consciousness* in the 1950s, called Western Marxism. Western Marxism comprised very many different schools, of whom perhaps the most interesting was the Frankfurt School. This school took off directly from Lukács' early writings, and like him it proceeded to elaborate a philosophic form of Hegelian Marxism, which Horkheimer and Adorno later called negative dialectics. The relation between their pessimistic negative dialectics and Lukács' always optimistic 'positive' dialectics has been extensively explored and requires no elaboration here. But no matter how critical the Frankfurt School later became of Lukács, they never forgot him and kept his name in view of the philosophical public they jointly addressed, the Leftist intellectuals of the radical 1960s and 1970s. Since the fall of communism Lukács' star has receded ever further. Today almost no one would call himself or herself a Lukácsian, *tout court.*

Both Gentile and Lukács were destroyed by their totalitarian entanglements, but somehow, almost miraculously, Heidegger survived his with his fame ultimately much enhanced. How did he manage to do it? For a while after 1945, during the de-Nazification ban on his teaching, it looked as if it would be all over with his career and reputation. But he persevered, eventually returned to the lecture rostrum and continued to make followers. Ultimately he emerged as a world figure due to the translation of all his works into English in America and the institutionalization of his philo sophy in many departments, not only those of philosophy, but also of theology, literature and some others as well. At present he is perhaps the most discussed of philosophers, and the various scandals that surface periodically concerning him and his writings have certainly helped his fame grow. Somehow he managed not only to live down his Nazi past, but to capitalize on it as well. As I shall show, his clever tactical use of his Jewish disciples helped him to achieve these goals. Sad to say, many of them, such as Wilhelm Szilasi who was also Lukács' friend, were only too glad to be so used, despite his anti-Semitism, which could hardly have been unknown to them.

Since the end of the Second World War, as Tom Rockmore maintains, Heidegger 'has assumed a dominant role in French philosophy. If one overlooks Heidegger's impact on contemporary French philosophical discussion one cannot hope to understand its main problems and main approaches to them. There is a measure of truth in Heidegger's boast that when the French begin to think, they think in German.'[7] As with Hegel's followers, it is possible to distinguish two groups, a Right and a Left group of Heideggerians, in France, who differ markedly in ideology, social composition and style. The Right Heideggerians are a group of older disciples who were close to the master himself, such as Beaufret and his disciples. The Left Heideggerians are a new coterie of somewhat heterodox followers under the general leadership of Derrida who are known as Deconstructionists. This has become a joint Franco-American movement among whom Jews play a considerable part. By contrast, the old guard in France evinces strong strains of anti-Semitism, extending as far as denial of the Holocaust, as revealed by Beaufret's support for Faurisson. Both of these anti-Semites were probably acting under Heidegger's instigation, for there is a tendency towards Holocaust revisionism in him almost from the end of the war onwards, as his letters to Marcuse reveal.

Heidegger's present pre-eminence was slowly attained. Immediately after the Second World War, only the Existentialist movement, then rapidly coming to world attention, kept his name alive. He was considered one of its founding fathers; and Sartre himself, despite their political differences, paid homage to him as such. Sartre – to whom he apealed in a moment of need in a flattering letter of October 1945 ('your work is dominated by an immediate understanding of my philosophy the like of which I have not previously encountered') – was only a year later denounced as a mere littérateur and not a real philosopher and attacked in his Beaufret-inspired *Letter on Humanism*, a typical provocation which brought him to international notice.[8] This was eventually followed by his acclaimed appearance at the Cérisy Colloquium in 1955, when he was loudly applauded by the elite of French philosophers, including Marxists as well. All this ensured that he would remain a strong presence in France from that time till now. The Ecole Normale in particular became a breeding ground of future Heideggerians; and even those who went through it and did not come out outright followers were, nevertheless, strongly marked by Heidegger's mode of thought, as was the case with Althusser, Foucault and many other Normaliens.

Just as Heidegger's writ came to prevail throughout the Continent after the Second World War, so Wittgenstein's name came to rule over philosophy departments in the Anglo-Saxon world of liberal democracies and regions allied to these, such as the Scandinavian countries. It was an ironic outcome, given how much he disliked such societies. Under the name of Linguistic philosophy, or more generally Analytic philosophy, Wittgenstein's influence is still to this day predominant in these philosophy departments. After the Second World War his teaching emanated not so much from Cambridge as from Oxford, where, much to Wittgenstein's consternation, a group of philosophers, led by Ryle, Austin and Strawson, propagated some of his key ideas and practices, though not quite in the way he approved of and with not as much personal deference to him as that displayed by his close disciples at Cambridge. The latter were an esoteric circle who formed a sort of cabal around him, which he dominated not only intellectually but personally as well. Thus in England there arose two schools of Wittgensteinians: a High Church of mere conformists and a low church of 'true believers'. In America, where his influence spread soon after through the agency of Norman Malcolm, Max Black and many other disciples, such differences were less important. There the newer Linguistic philosophy merged imperceptibly with the older Logical Positivism carried by the exiled members of the Vienna Circle, who exemplified an earlier phase of Wittgenstein's influence, that of the *Tractatus*. Out of this confluence there emerged the Analytic approach, which is still prevalent as its exponents occupy the key institutional positions in leading American universities.

Thus Heidegger and Wittgenstein between them came to dominate academic philosophy in the West. The struggles for intellectual eminence and academic power fought out in their names, that is, the battles between Continental and Analytic philosophy, constitute much of the history of philosophy after the Second World War. The various inner divisions within each camp and the personalities involved also need to be studied. Here, however, I cannot undertake any such detailed investigations. But I shall return to the question why these particular philosophies were so successful in this period. At present the differences between their followers are not so marked as these were originally. In these postmodernist times, eclectic philosophers are emerging who move smoothly between both camps and even seek to synthesize them. In the confusing 'anything goes' climate of contemporary culture, it is easy to pretend to an amalgamation of both approaches. Whether this is an improvement on the original more purist work of the masters themselves or their earlier disciples remains to be seen.

Among these there were some independent thinkers who followed in the footsteps of the malign masters but who sooner or later went off on their own. I shall merely mention a few of the major ones. Harris states that 'the most important philosopher influenced by actual idealism was Robin George Collingwood';[9] Merle Brown, too, shows in some detail what Collingwood derived from Gentile's aesthetics.[10] But Collingwood went back to Croce and was highly critical of Gentile, even if he did learn a little from him. However, a clear-cut case of a Gentile student who later attained complete independence was Collingwood's friend Guido de Ruggiero, whose relation to his master was at first particularly close and later became painfully distant. A similar case was the historian Adolfo Omodeo, who also broke with Gentile over the issue of Fascism.

Lukács too had many distinguished followers deriving from the Sunday Circle in Budapest, as I have already mentioned, but none of these remained Lukácsians for long. Later, after the Second World War, the most outstanding independent Lukácsian was no doubt Lucien Goldmann. He went back to the early Lukács of *History and Class Consciousness* and was strongly critical of the later Lukács. Goldmann has attempted an interesting preliminary study of the similarities between early Lukács and early Heidegger, in which he brings out some of the common features I have discussed in the previous chapters.

Heidegger influenced many outstanding thinkers who did not become full-fledged Heideggerians. This is true of some French philosophers, such as the Jewish theologian Emmanuel Levinas, the Catholic theologian Gabriel Marcel and the Protestant thinker Paul Ricoeur. Heidegger's impact on theologians of all religions was particularly strong for reasons that have much to do with the pseudo-religious character of his work. For other reasons, he also influenced some psychoanalysts such as Binswanger, Boss and Lacan. The major case of someone who began as a disciple and remained such, but did develop his own quite different approach, is Hans-Georg Gadamer. He never actually criticizes the master himself, yet he departs from his philosophy in many respects. He reaches out tentatively to the contrary scientific and even Positivistic movements that the master detested. He also seeks to make common cause with traditional English conservativism and the more recent common-sense and common-language tendencies, which the master also found abhorrent.

Among Wittgenstein's followers there were many who maintained their independence. Early on both Frank Ramsay, who tragically died young, and Friedrich Waismann, whom the master later drove away, managed to pursue their own work in parallel to that of the master without being absorbed by him. This was also the case later with the Oxford Linguistic philosophers, Ryle, Austin and Strawson. Of these only Ryle had come close to Wittgenstein personally and absorbed some of his ideas at first hand. When he later published these ideas, in a slightly modified form, without even mentioning Wittgenstein in his book, *Concept of Mind*, the latter was understandably furious. He placed the whole Oxford School under an interdict, declaring Oxford to be an 'influenza area' of philosophy.

It is perhaps a curious oddity, which in this case might be merely coincidental, that the chief executors of two of the masters' wills were women disciples: Elizabeth Anscombe and Agnes Heller. These then became the heiresses of their respective father figures. In the third case, that of Heidegger, this was almost so, as Hannah Arendt more or less appointed herself as the chief exponent of his philosophy outside Germany and France, a kind of world ambassador at large promoting his cause, especially so in America where she saw to the translation of his work. Only Gentile did not have a woman disciple to inherit his philosophical estate; a man, Ugo Spirito, became the chief beneficiary. Perhaps this reflects the restrictive condition for women in Italian universities and the inferior role they were allotted by Fascism. In other countries, where women had made greater inroads into universities, it was possible for some to become philosophers and enter a hitherto all-male preserve. Were they less threatening and more devoted to their masters than even their most faithful male disciples, ideal daughter figures, as it were? Is this perhaps the explanation of the coincidence?

Of their devotion there is no doubt. They have managed their inherited legacies with exceptional skill. They have done all in their power to maintain the reputations of their masters' intact. In some cases they have even acted to prevent any damaging information from leaking out. Thus, as he himself has made known, Friedrich von Hayek the great economist, and a distant cousin of Wittgenstein, was prevented by the executors of Wittgenstein's estate from proceeding with his planned biography of the master soon after his death. Elizabeth Anscombe expressed herself in no uncertain terms when she wrote to Paul Engelmann, an early friend of Wittgenstein, that 'if by pressing a button it could have been secured that people would not concern themselves with his personal life, I should have pressed the button.'[11] Obviously, had she succeeded in pressing this button of oblivion a work such as this would have been made impossible and Wittgenstein would have remained the incomprehensibly fascinating enigma that he was to his contemporaries.

Hannah Arendt, too, would have wished to press such a button for the sake of Heidegger. Now that she is dead, and her own personal life more fully revealed, her role in trying to insulate his philosophy from any damage wrought by his 'personal life' can be at last fully documented. Not only did she forgive him his personal betrayal of her before the war, but after it she overlooked his contempt for her own work. In the words of her biographer, Elizabeth Young-Bruehl, she 'chose to indulge Heidegger by behaving like a none-too-bright female.'[12] Submission to a master and self-abnegation for his cause can hardly go further than that. She campaigned assiduously in public and behind the scenes to defend him and his work and to promote his reputation. Thus she played a key role in his post-war efforts at rehabilitation and willingly made herself available to be used for this purpose, as, unfortunately, most of his other Jewish disciples did as well. It was a carefully calculated campaign, for, as Hugo Ott maintains, 'much could be said about the method of apologia for Heidegger; it is masterful and has strategic features.'[13] Young-Bruehl reports that she was largely instrumental in introducing Heidegger to the English-speaking world through her influence on J. Glenn Gray, whom she 'urged to the editorship of Harper and Row's series of Heidegger's work in English'.[14] At the same time she dissuaded Gray from probing into his political past or even asking him any questions about it. Her recently released correspondence with her other mentor, Jaspers, reveals a persistent effort to reconcile him to Heidegger and win him over to his philosophical cause; in the process she tried as far as possible to exonerate Heidegger, making sure to remove any lasting taints of Nazism. She went so far as to try to enlist Jaspers' support for a moratorium on further probing of Heidegger's political indiscretions. 'People ought to leave him alone,'[15] she wrote to Jaspers. Jaspers, who knew Heidegger all too well, wisely refused to be drawn. But Arendt did not stop at that; to secure wher ends she calumniated for Jaspers' eyes one of the first, very mild, studies of Heidegger's politics, Alexander Schwan's book *Politische Philosophie im Denken Heideggers*, calling it an anti-Heidegger tract instigated by the 'detestable' Adorno and his Jewish clique of the Frankfurt School – a Jewish plot no less:

> I have the feeling that the whole thing was staged and organized by the Adorno camp . . . You said yourself that anti-Semitism was not an issue. But the attacks on him are coming only from that quarter and no other . . . then, too, I can't prove it, but I'm quite convinced that the real people behind the scenes are the Wiesengrund–Adorno crowd in Frankfurt . . . For years now he and Horkheimer have accused or threatened to accuse anyone in Germany who was against them of being anti-Semitic. A really disgusting bunch . . .[16]

It is not to my purpose here to probe into the inner recesses of Arendt's mind so as to discover the unconscious motives for her perversely devoted and utterly blind attachment to Heidegger. But the effects of it are still to be felt to this day precisely in disguising the anti-Semitism that Heidegger evinced most of his life. His personal relations with Arendt and other Jewish disciples, followers, friends and teachers do not argue to the contrary. For as virulent modern anti-Semites since Richard Wagner have known and practised it, and as Heidegger no doubt knew, it pays to take from Jews since one need not pay them back, the more they give the less they are owed, for they are not, after all, people like others to whom moral scruples apply.

So far I have concentrated on personal relations in accounting for the success of the malign masters. However, not even such extraordinary devotion as displayed by some of their disciples can altogether explain their prominence. Much more robust and far-ranging sociological and historical factors will also have to be brought in to provide the background conditions which enabled these charismatic movements in philosophy to flourish. What was there in the post-Second World War situation that enabled Heidegger to sweep the Continental and Wittgenstein the Anglo-Saxon world of philosophy? Conditions were different in these two spheres, and these differences also help to show why each triumphed in a particular one. However, there was one common element in both, namely, the role of elite institutions in appropriating and monopolizing the study of philosophy.

After the Second World War philosophy ceased almost completely to attract an unattached intelligentsia of free-thinkers, that is, intellectuals without firm institutional, academic or clerical affiliations, as philosophy had done before. In fact, such intellectuals had almost ceased to exist. The only intellectuals remaining outside academic institutions were the odd political ideologue, the rare journalist or some kinds of religious thinkers, few of whom were any longer interested in philosophy. All others who were still intent on philosophy had to seek academic positions in the universities, that is, to become teachers of philosophy, which only some of the major philosophers and only one of the fathers, Husserl, had been in the past. Only in France did something of the role of philosophers as intellectuals survive, but solely for those resident in Paris on the Left Bank. Sartre and de Beauvoir were among the few notable examples of philosophers who were not academics.

In the university departments, in which nearly all philosophers settled, they had to confront the challenge of the sciences. This was a challenge which philosophy had been facing already for some centuries, but never with as much acuity as in this century. I have previously described in *The Ends of Philosophy* the long process of gradual secession of the sciences from philosophy which began at the time of the Scientific Revolution when natural philosophy first established itself as a distinct and autonomous mode of knowledge. It continued with the rise of physics, chemistry and biology as separate sciences in the eighteenth and nineteenth centuries. The emergence of the social and cultural sciences, largely during the nineteenth century, carried the process further, with economics, psychology, politics, philology and, finally, sociology gradually removing themselves from the ambit of philosophy. As a result of all these secessions, which continued well into the twentieth century, philosophy eventually found itself evacuated of all substantive knowledge content.

In response to these pressures from the sciences, philosophy has been carrying out a rearguard holding action, demarcating spheres of exclusivity and elaborating conceptual segregations that would make it immune to scientific challenge. No philosophies did this better than those of the malign masters for they were hostile to science and determined to promote philosophy as superior to it. Each of them advocates a view of philosophy as distinct from science and untouched by anything that might happen in the sciences; with the result that no new theoretical insights or discoveries in the sciences any longer matter to philosophy. Each of them expounds a fundamental bifurcation that places philosophy on the side of a higher knowledge and the sciences on that of a lesser knowledge. In Heidegger it is the distinction between the ontological and ontic; in Wittgenstein that between the conceptual and the empirical; in Lukács that between the dialectical and the merely factual; and in Gentile between thinking thought (*pensiero pensante*) and already thought thought (*pensiero pensato*).

Thus in Western universities the philosophies of Wittgenstein and Heidegger in particular served a useful purpose for disciplinary philosophy in keeping the sciences at bay. On their basis philosophy could segregate itself as a profession or *Fach* that was distinct from every other, subject to its own norms of knowledge research, criteria for publication and modes of discussion. And so external critiques could no longer touch it for no outside knowledge was any longer relevant to it. In the security and isolation of their departmental fastness, philosophers could cultivate a kind of puristic *l'art pour l'art* manner of philosophizing, for which the main lead was given by Wittgenstein and Heidegger, who promoted the necessary self-justification of philosophy as an end in itself. Thus, ironically, the very professionalization of philosophy demanded philosophies that made a fetish of claiming to be the least professional.

Such puristic professional philosophies tended to gravitate to the elite universities because in the struggle for academic power elite status matters most in attracting disciples and launching movements of influence. From these positions of high status it was easy to oversee and dominate all the lower placed universities. In the elite schools of leading countries, such as the Ecole Normale in France, the old-established universities in Germany, Oxbridge in England and the Ivy League in America, philosophy could be cultivated as a mystique for the privileged and initiated. Only those inducted into these institutions and passing through them as students or teachers had any chance of acquiring the 'proper' philosophical knowledge and being considered qualified in it. By these means a few universities were able to monopolize the teaching of philosophy and use this power to colonize the whole academic system in their particular countries. A typical colonialist centre – periphery relation obtained between the elite and the rest; thereby the elite universities were enabled to perpetuate and consolidate their exclusivity and superior status.

Philosophies that served this function of preserving professional monopoly had to be ones that could not be learned from books alone. In other words, they had to be philosophies that no one outside the privileged institutional setting could acquire, pass on or practice. They could be learned only if they were obtained through the right channels and received from the proper hands. Such, indeed, were the philosophies which the malign masters themselves and then, by right of succession, their disciples came to dispense from the elite schools where they had gained positions of power. No one who did not pass through their hands could practise or teach or even discuss their philosophies.

Philosophies suitable for this purpose had to be ones which could insulate themselves from attack both from other philosophies within the discipline as well as from other disciplines outside. Heidegger's and Wittgenstein's philosophies were precisely ones immune to any inside or outside challenges. Criticisms from other philosophies could be dismissed as incomprehensions or misunderstandings in all the ways that the malign masters taught their disciples to do. Criticisms from the outside, from other disciplines, could also be set aside as not being really 'philosophical' and so not counting, for no general theory, empirical findings or evaluative norms were held to be relevant. Since science was out and all humanistic scholarship was beside the point, there was nothing left that could disturb philosophers. Such a 'purist' philosophy, practised as a mystique among groups of initiates, was hermetically sealed against any challenge.

However, the two types of puristic philosophies, the Wittgensteinian and Heideggerian, are very different and satisfy quite opposed requirements. Those to whom the one appeals are rarely also those to whom the other appeals. They are almost mutually exclusive. In the condition of post-Second World War philosophy, the one appealed almost wholly to Anglo-Saxons the other to Continentals. Since racial, national or linguistic affinities are not in question, what is it that explains this difference? In offering a sociological explanation, I shall refer to a number of underlying background factors, both cultural and political. But to begin with, the most obvious explanation is to be found in the different courses of development and rates of expansion that higher education underwent in these separate spheres of world learning. This in turn led to much greater growth, organization and professionalization of disciplines in some countries than in others.

Professionalization in philosophy ensued much faster and earlier in America than elsewhere. England and the British Commonwealth countries followed a little later and at a slower pace. The Continental countries were in the ruck of these developments, which in some still have not fully taken place. C. Wright Mills had already undertaken a study of the professionalization of philosophy in America in the 1950s.[17] He showed how the earlier generation of philosophers, who were an odd assortment of lawyers, librarians and scientists, were displaced by the academic professors who organized themselves into a professional guild with its conferences, journals, promotion ladders and all the other trappings of academic disciplines. In these conditions, philosophers could no longer be considered free-thinkers or intellectuals, as Russell Jacoby argues in a more recent study.[18] For such academic professionals, a philosophy best suited to their requirements was one that did not depend on theories, ideas or any extensive background knowledge in science or the humanities, and that did not engage with contentious question of social or political life. What they wanted was a mode of philosophizing that could be practised as a technical skill to be learned pragmatically through an on-the-job training by discussion, somewhat like that of lawyers. At the other extreme of professional development, the Continentals were still tradition-bound to the view of the philosopher as sage and philosophy as a mystique dealing ponderously with all the most serious issues most seriously. There the master–disciple relation and the ensuing practices of patronage were still the prevalent authority forms.[19]

Such background factors of organization and professionalization serve to explain why Wittgenstein became the philosophical apostle to the Anglo-Saxons and Heidegger to the Continentals. Linguistic philosophy was more suited to an impersonal organization with hundreds if not thousands of members. On the other hand, the more traditional setting of seminars with masters and disciples sitting at tables could be better served by the hermeneutic philosophy. The former specialized in papers delivered to large audiences, to be followed by verbal jousts among a few chosen champions concerning fine points of linguistic usage. The latter specialized in the close reading and commenting on classical texts, for in the hermeneutic approach philosophy had become synonymous with the history of philosophy.

There were also other factors that predisposed British and American academics to the seemingly unpolitical, anti-theoretical, common-sense, non-technical and untraditional philosophy of Wittgenstein, whereas Continentals favoured the more traditionally oriented, metaphysically abstruse, jargon-ridden and conceptually jaw-breaking, yet apparently existentially 'engaged', philosophy of Heidegger. It was differences of the two background cultures that mattered in this respect; differences which went back deep into history and might be referred to as cultural mentalities. These shaped the kinds of education systems and their curricula in Anglo-Saxon as opposed to Continental countries in which philosophy was embedded. Philosophy has always carried greater symbolic prestige and connoted deeper seriousness in the latter than the former. Hence, it would have been difficult for the Anglo-Saxons to treat Heidegger's vatic pomposities with the gravity they demanded; and impossible for Continentals to accord that much respect to Wittgenstein's linguistic trivialities.

Political conditions also favoured Wittgenstein among the old-established democracies and Heidegger in the countries that were disrupted by totalitarian upheavals. In the former, especially during the period of the Cold War, any ideological tendencies in philosophy were shunned. A cold, aseptic, unhistorical approach, a seemingly pure analysis of objective factors, untainted by values or commitments, was the safest course to pursue when any other could bring unpleasant political consequences. In the latter, especially in France, political differences were strong, ideological divides very sharp, and those affected philosophers as much as others. A way of sublimating them for the purposes of mutual academic work and discussion had to be found, such that the political differences need not be denied but could be relativized and at least temporarily set aside. Heidegger's sublime language of Being and his jargon of authenticity permitted these divisions in the political arena to be transcended. Marxists and Conservatives, Christians and Atheists, Gentiles and Jews, all could write their own distinctive versions of the Heideggerian speech and use it to talk to each other. Hence all such different varieties of Heideggerianism came into being.

All in all, there is no single or simple explanation as to why Wittgenstein and Heidegger won out as philosophers, or why one succeeded in one sphere of the world and the other in another. Apart from their own unusual abilities – not least their capacity to impress other philosophers, make friends and win and keep the devoted loyalty of disciples and followers – there were all the other background sociological factors that favoured them. The personal and the social were not dissociated. Wittgenstein's role in England as an exotic Continental genius, but who, nevertheless, presented an approach wholly in keeping with British common-sense attitudes made it possible for him both to fascinate and to satisfy – he presented the expected in an unusual guise. The accidental fact that he found himself at the prestigious English university of Cambridge during and after the war helped him make an impression across the Atlantic in the United States, especially among Anglophiles in the Ivy League universities, who still looked to Britain for philosophical initiatives. Similarly, the accidental fact that Heidegger found himself in the French zone of occupation as the war concluded helped him to receive French visitors and establish a bridgehead in France for his philosophy when it looked as if it might disappear in the rest of the world, including his own Germany. In his case, too, his personality as a philosophical preacher and sage suited the expectations of his potential public. To the French and other Continentals he appeared as the quintessential German thinker, both deep and incomprehensible. The effort he demanded seemed to reward those who were prepared to make it with a glimmering of understanding. The French in particular were keen to try to understand anything German as a result of their wartime occupation and postwar cooperation with Germany in building a united Europe. Heidegger played up to this French predisposition with his own personal initiatives, which proved all too successful.

Finally, what made both Heidegger and Wittgenstein so suitable for academic philosophers in all countries was the very fragmentary and disorganized nature of their later work. The slow rate of publication of the numerous sets of lecture courses that Heidegger delivered throughout his career and the stacks of diary-like notes that Wittgenstein made all his life meant that books by both authors have kept appearing at a steady rate from the early 1950s till now. Norman Malcolm estimates that from between 1929 and 1951 alone Wittgenstein's *Nachlass* consists of 'roughly

30,000 pages of philosophical material, in notebooks, manuscripts, and typescripts'.[20] And this is not counting the sets of lecture notes made by his students, which have been published since. Heidegger's *Nachlass* from this period alone is likely to be comparable in size, if not even larger. Each new appearance of another text from this vast corpus, each new book translated, or re-edited, calls for revisions, adjustments and general comments from dozens of disciples and scores of other philosophers, not to speak of the hundreds of theses by students. There was work there aplenty for many for over half a century or more. Hence, whole sub-branches of the publishing industry arose, with hundreds of books and thousands of papers on each philosopher. Numerous successful academic careers could be launched and substained on this basis.

Nevertheless, there was one beneficial side-effect of all this over-production of paper – it finally released a mass of biographical material that had for so long been kept under wraps. It was not until the late 1980s that official biographies were finally authorized by the executors of the estates of the malign masters. Even more to the point, unauthorized biographies and reminiscences also appeared. By piecing together details from all of these, as in a kind of giant jigsaw puzzle, a clearer picture of each malign master could finally begin to be assembled. This is why a work such as this would have been impossible until a few years ago.

At the end of this work it is now possible to understand both why the works of the malign masters are so utterly different from each other and also why they are somehow alike. They are very different in content, about as diverse as any philosophies can be, yet they are also analogous in the pattern of development that each describes. Each of the malign masters begins at a different starting point deriving from the work of his specific father and grandfather figures in his formative background. Each produces his primary masterwork out of the confluence of quite separate influences. Each enters his *Kehre* at the same time, but turns in a quite different direction owing to his involvement with a different totalitarian movement and its great leader. The secondary masterworks that result from this have even less in common than the primary ones had, but the process that went into their production is similar in each case. Hence, though their works are very different, the overall pattern of development is similar.

One of the reasons for that fact is that the malign masters were all responding to the same events in twentieth-century European history. This is not to say that they were products of these events, for no philosophy is ever simply the outcome of political history. However, in the first half of the twentieth century, philosophy was more under the sway of political pressures than perhaps ever before. Thus despite its disciplinary segregation, it has not been able to maintain its autonomy and keep itself independent as a mode of thought that is not at the behest of the powers of the world. The apocryphal story of Diogenes – who on being asked by Alexander what he might do for him, replied, from out of his tub, 'get out of my light' – points to the traditional moral of philosophical indifference to worldly power. The malign masters allowed themselves to be overshadowed by the great dictators, they gave up light and enlightenment as they became involved with the dark diabolic forces that promised them so much. Reeling under the trauma of their early experience of war and revolution, they succumbed to the lure of totalitarianism and the blandishments of the would-be Alexanders of our time. They thereby collaborated in the spiritual, cultural and moral destruction of Europe. They evinced in themselves the very darkness of the times and the nihilism that they so vociferously bewailed and denounced in all others. Their thought is itself symptomatic of the problems of our time.

We now live in the aftermath of that destruction. Unavoidably, we must learn to bear with the consequences that have been bequeathed to us. At present, fortunately, the fires of totalitarian passions are no longer burning to confuse the issue, they have dissipated with the smoke of history. There is time now for a calm recollective pause in philosophy as in other dimensions of culture. We can now look back and see where and when things went wrong, when the fatal turnings occurred that led to our present predicament. The first of these was when the malign masters departed from the ways of their fathers. It is not possible now to undo that, but it is possible to return to the fathers so as to discover how the sons went astray. This is the key proposal that this book has to make towards a future renewal of philosophy.

To summarize something of what I have discovered about the malign masters and to reveal in a graphic way their common pattern of development, I have tabulated my key results in the form of a matrix array. Obviously, this is a simplifying device which eliminates finer shades of difference. Yet it seems to fit surprisingly well, for only two of the boxes cannot be easily filled, and that can be accounted for without much difficulty: Wittgenstein had no direct relation to a great dictator (discounting a possible meeting with the young Hitler at the Realschule in Linz) since he was politically a recluse; Gentile had no late school of followers because his influence collapsed with the fall of Fascism.

For mnemonic purposes, which might also appeal to students, one could present the table in the form of the familiar Gospel story, that is, if one were forgiven the unavoidable blasphemy inherent in this whimsical analogy. Thus there is a trinitarian structure inherent in each philosophy consisting of a Son, Father and Holy Spirit, where the malign master and his mentor fill the first two roles and his Idealist forebears stand in for the *Geist* of the third. Each of the sons is prefigured by a John the Baptist, his close friend who acts as precursor. Around the Son a group of disciples gathers, among whom there is a St Peter, who does not necessarily inherit the keys of the Church, which most frequently go to a Mary Magdalene instead. Subsequently there emerges a St Paul figure, a disciple who develops a more independent approach. Eventually, in the name of the Son, numerous Churches arise and dispute the issues of orthodoxy and heresy. Given the charismatic nature of the malign masters and the movements that formed around them, the Gospel parallel is perhaps not altogether the joke it seems to be at first sight.

However, jokes aside, if the table is taken seriously then it can be read as the briefest possible epitome of the argument of the book. The fact that it can be produced at all is indicative of some key correlations in the career patterns of the malign masters which reflect their common general predispositions and tendencies. As such, it is a graphic representation of the socio-logic of the main trends and movements of twentieth-century philosophy, in so far as such a representation is at all possible. The historical course of philosophy, considered at once logically and sociologically, is schematically conveyed in the table by the relations it depicts between pretexts, texts and contexts in each case. Each malign master begins with the pretexts of his father's work and produces his own text in the context of all the other influences whose confluence informs and shapes the form and content of his own work. A particularly important part of this context were the nascent irrationalist tendencies of the period of the First World War, such as the revival of Idealism and the predisposition to mystical religiosity. This explains the similarity in the socio-logic of the primary masterworks and their common tendency to a metaphysics of totality, non-egoistic solipsism and inactive activism.

The further, more fatal, course the malign masters pursued from totality through totalitarianism to some kind of totalistic *Weltanschauung* can be similarly explained. It can be followed on the table by noting the entries on either side of the *Kehre*, the crucial dividing line which is to be historically located in the period of the ascendency of the totalitarian regimes and their leaders, the great dictators, to whom the malign masters were drawn.

Thus the *Kehre* can be seen both logically and sociologically as the moment of turning: logically, it mediates the transformation of the leading themes and ideas from the primary to the secondary masterworks; sociologically, it is the movement into totalitarianism and the partial withdrawal from it, at least to the extent of an attempt to idealise it and so distinguish it from what it became in reality. Both aspects of the moment enter into and infuse the constitution of the secondary masterworks, which are thereby overdetermined from the logical and sociological directions at once. In response to such multiple pressures, each of the malign masters elaborated his own totalistic world-view schema: Heidegger concocted his eschatology of Being, Wittgenstein imagined a cultural Utopia of a grammatically perspicuous and communitarian language, Lukács faithfully followed a Stalinist version of a Hegelian-Marxist history of Reason, and Gentile devised an ideal Fascist amalgam of the Ego, Society and State.

The extraordinary success of the malign masters in twentieth-century philosophy needs also to be sociologically accounted for both in personal and organizational terms. The entries with the salient names of individuals, schools and movements which figure in any such account are to be found at the bottom of the table. With that the table gives out, for it more or less brings things up to the present.

Malign Masters	Gentile	Lukács	Heidegger	Wittgenstein
Intellectual orientation and teachers	History of Philosophy & Philosophical History	Aesthetics and Sociology	Hermeneutics and Phenomenology	Formal Logic and Foundations of Maths
early (grandfather)	Jaja	Simmel	Rickert	Frege
late (father)	Croce	Weber	Husserl	Russell
Idealist influences				
early	Fichte–Hegel	Fichte–Hegel	Schelling	Schopenhauer
late	Spaventa	Young-Marx	Kierkegaard	Weininger
Religion and its main sources	Religion of the Nation	Apocalypticism	Mystical Protestantism	Primitive Christianity
early	Plotinus	Eckhart	Augustine	Gospels
late	Gioberti	Buber	Barth	Tolstoy
Best friend	Lombardo-Radice	Bloch	Jaspers	Moore and Schlick
Primary masterwork	*General Theory of Spirit as Pure Act*	*History and Class Consciousness*	*Being and Time*	*Tractatus Logico-Philosophicus*
Kehre, 1928–34				
Secondary masterwork	*Genesis and Structure of Society*	*Destruction of Reason*	*Nietzsche Vols. I–IV*	*Philosophical Investigations*
Totalitarian predilection	Fascism	Bolshevism	Nazism	Bolshevik fellow-traveller
and dictator	Mussolini	Stalin	Hitler	–
Heiress or heir and	Spirito	Heller	Arendt	Anscombe
leading follower	de Ruggiero	Goldmann	Gadamer	Ryle
Movements and schools				
early	Fascist Idealism	Western Marxism (Frankfurt School)	Existentialism (School of Paris)	Logical Positivism (Vienna Circle)
late	–	New Left (Budapest School)	Deconstruction (Yale School)	Linguistic Analysis (Oxford School)

Notes

INTRODUCTION

1. Leszek Kolakowski, *Metaphysical Horror* (Blackwell, Oxford, 1981), p. 1.
2. Ludwig Wittgenstein, *Culture and Value*, ed. G.H. von Wright, trans. P. Winch (Blackwell, Oxford, 1986), p. 67.
3. Martin Heidegger, *An Introduction to Metaphysics*, trans. Ralph Manheim (Yale, University Press, New Haven, 1959), p. 199.
4. John van Buren, *The Young Heidegger: Rumour of the Hidden King* (Indiana, University Press, Bloomington, 1994), p. 385.
5. Ibid.
6. Martin Heidegger, *Der Spiegel*, May 1976 (interview of 1966).
7. See C.G. Luckhard (ed.), *Wittgenstein: Sources and Perspectives* (Harvester Press, Brighton, 1979), p. 54.
8. Ludwig Wittgenstein, *Letters to Russell, Keynes and Moore*, ed. G.H. von Wright (Cornell University Press, Ithaca, NY, 1974), p. 136.
9. J.M. Findlay, *Wittgenstein: A Critique* (Routledge and Kegan Paul, London, 1984), p. 21.
10. Lucien Goldmann, *Lukács and Heidegger: Towards a New Philosophy*, trans. W.Q. Boelhower (Routledge and Kegan Paul, London, 1977), pp. 16–17.
11. Giovanni Gentile, *La Religione: Discorsi di religione* (Sansoni, Firenze, 1965), p. 431.
12. Ferenc Feher and Agnes Heller, *The Grandeur and Twilight of Radical Universalism* (Transactions Publisher, New Brunswick, 1991), p. 554.
13. G. Neske and E. Kettering (eds.), *Martin Heidegger and National Socialism* (Paragon House, New York, 1990), p. 143.
14. Ibid., p. 142.
15. Brian McGuiness (ed.), *Wittgenstein and his Times* (Blackwell, Oxford, 1982), p. 41.
16. Jader Jacobelli, *Croce: Gentile, Dal solidazio al dramma* (Rizzoli, Milano, 1989), pp. 203–4.
17. Quoted in Richard Wolin (ed.), *The Heidegger Controversy* (Columbia University Press, New York, 1991), p. 178.
18. Primo Siena (ed.), *Gentile* (Volpe Editore, Roma, 1966), p. 86.
19. van Buren, *Young Heidegger*, p. 144.
20. Charles Guignon (ed.), *The Cambridge Companion to Heidegger* (Cambridge University Press, New York, 1993), p. 76.
21. Ibid., p. 71.
22. Árpad Kadarkay, *Georg Lukács* (Blackwell, Oxford, 1991), p. 121.
23. Karl Jaspers, *Notizen zu Heidegger*, ed. Hans Saner (R. Piper Verlag, Zürich, 1978), p. 213.

24. Michael Löwy, *Georg Lukács – From Romanticism to Bolshevism* (NLB, London, 1979), p. 55.
25. Martin Heidegger, quoted by Theodor Kisiel, 'Heidegger's Apology', in T. Rockmore and J. Margolis (eds.), *The Heidegger Case: On Philosophy and Politics* (Temple University Press, Philadelphia, 1991), p. 134.
26. Quoted in Charles L. Creegan, *Wittgenstein and Kierkegaard* (Routledge, London, 1989), p. 15.
27. Quoted in Löwy, *Georg Lukács*, p. 96.
28. Ibid.
29. Karl Löwith, *Nature, History and Existentialism* (Northwestern University Press, Evanston, Ill. 1966), p. 55.
30. Ibid., p. 52.
31. Hannah Arendt, 'Martin Heidegger at Eighty', *The New York Review of Books* (October, 1971).
32. Findlay, *Wittgenstein*, p. 20.
33. Giovanni Gentile, *Theory of Mind as Pure Act*, trans. H. Wildon Carr (Macmillan, London, 1923), p. xi.
34. Neske and Kettering, *Martin Heidegger*, p. 198.
35. Friedrich Waismann, *Wittgenstein and the Vienna Circle*, ed. Brian McGuiness (Blackwell, Oxford, 1979).
36. Karl Löwith, *My Life in Germany, before and after 1933*, 'Curriculum Vitae' (1959), trans. E. King (University of Illinois Press, Urbana and Chicago, 1994), p. 150.
37. Max Weber, 'Science as a Vocation', in *From Max Weber*, ed. H.H. Gerth and C.W. Mills (Oxford University Press, Oxford, 1951), p. 129.
38. Ibid., p. 153.
39. Ibid.
40. Quoted in Otto Pöggeler, 'Heidegger, Nietzsche and Politics', in Rockmore and Margolis, *The Heidegger Case*, p. 120.
41. H.S. Harris, *The Social Philosophy of Giovanni Gentile* (University of Illinois Press, Urbana, 1960), p. 284.
42. Ibid., p. 244.
43. Richard Wolin, *The Politics of Being* (Columbia University Press, New York, 1990), pp. 71–2.
44. W.J. Richardson, *Heidegger: Through Phenomenology to Thought* (Martinus Nijhoff, The Hague, 1967) p. xvi.
45. Ibid., p. xviii.
46. Tom Rockmore, 'Heidegger's French Connection', in Rockmore and Margolis, *The Heidegger Case*, p. 378.
47. Quoted in George Pitcher (ed.), *The Philosophy of Wittgenstein* (Macmillan, London, 1964), p. 8.
48. Ray Monk, *Ludwig Wittgenstein: The Duty of Genius* (Vintage, London, 1990), p. 295.
49. Ludwig Wittgenstein, *Philosophical Investigations*, trans. G.E.M. Anscombe (Blackwell, Oxford, 1953), p. x.
50. I have dealt with this in my *A New Science of Representation* (Westview Press, Boulder, Col., 1994), ch. 1.
51. Wittgenstein, *Culture and Value*, p. 61.

CHAPTER 1 THE PRIMARY MASTERWORKS

1. Ludwig Wittgenstein, *Tractatus Logico-Philosophicus*, trans. D.F. Pears and B.F. McGuiness (Routledge and Kegan Paul, London, 1961), sec. 6·53.
2. Wittgenstein, *Tractatus Logico-Philosophicus*, sec. 5·26.
3. Tom Rockmore, *Irrationalism: Lukács and the Marxist View of Reason* (Temple University Press, Philadelphia, 1992), pp. 131–2.
4. Ibid., pp. 134–5.
5. Gentile, *The Theory of Mind as Pure Act*, pp. 254–5.
6. Ibid., p. 256.
7. David D. Roberts, *Benedetto Croce and the Uses of Historicism* (University of California Press, Berkeley, 1987), p. 112.
8. Martin Heidegger, *Being and Time*, trans. J. Macquarrie and E. Robinson (Harper and Row, New York, 1962), p. 44.
9. See Harry Redner, *The Ends of Philosophy* (Croom-Helm, London, 1986).
10. Quoted in John Gunnell, 'Strauss before Straussianism', in K.L. Deutsch and W. Nicgorski (eds.), *Leo Strauss: Political Philosopher and Jewish Thinker* (Rowman and Littlefield, Lanham/Maryland 1994), p. 111.
11. Georg Lukács, *History and Class Consciousness*, trans. R. Livingstone (Merlin Press, London, 1971), p. 10.
12. Ibid.
13. Ibid., p. 175.
14. Kadarkay, *Georg Lukács*, p. 272.
15. Ibid., p. 172.
16. Gentile, *The Theory of Mind as Pure Act*, p. 265.
17. Quoted in Roberts, *Bendedotto Croce*, p. 110.
18. Ibid., p. 112.
19. This is discussed in my earlier book, *The Ends of Philosophy*, pp. 125–8.
20. Michael Murray (ed.), *Heidegger and Modern Philosophy* (Yale University Press, New Haven, 1978), p. 230.
21. Ibid., p. 230.
22. Ibid., p. 235.
23. van Buren, *The Young Heidegger*, p. 61.
24. Wittgenstein, *Tractatus Logico-Philosophicus*, sec. 6·45.
25. Brian McGuiness, *Wittgenstein: A Life* (Duckworth, London, 1988), p. 221.
26. Ibid., p. 303.
27. Quoted in ibid., p. 245.
28. Wittgenstein, *Tractatus Logico-Philosophicus*, sec. 1.
29. Ibid., sec. 2·04.
30. See Monk, *Ludwig Wittgenstein*, p. 163.
31. Wittgenstein, *Tractatus Logico-Philosophicus*, 4·001.
32. Ibid., 4·11.
33. Ibid., 3·01.
34. Ibid., 5·61.
35. Ibid., 5·6.
36. Ibid., 4·113.
37. Immanual Kant, *Prologomena to Any Future Metaphysics*, trans. L.W. Beek (The Library of Liberal Arts, Indianapolis, 1950), p. 352.
38. Ibid.

39. Ludwig Wittgenstein, *Notebooks 1914–1916*, ed. G.E.M. Anscombe and G.H. von Wright (Blackwell, Oxford, 1961), p. 73.
40. Ibid., p. 84.
41. Jürgen Habermas, *Philosophical-Political Profiles*, trans. F.G. Lawrence (The MIT Press, Cambridge, Mass., 1983), p. 23.
42. Löwith, *Nature, History and Existentialism*, p. 57.
43. Michael Zimmerman, *Eclipse of Self* (Ohio University Press, and Allens, London, 1981), p. 149.
44. Lukács, *History and Class Consciousness*, p. xxxiv.
45. Roger W. Holmes, *The Idealism of Giovanni Gentile* (Macmillan, New York, 1937), pp. 16–17.
46. Goldmann, *Lukács and Heidegger*, pp. 67–8.
47. op. cit., p. 40.
48. Neske and Kettering, *Martin Heidegger*, p. 180.
49. Quoted in Allan Janik, *Essays on Wittgenstein and Weininger* (Rodopi, Amsterdam, 1984), p. 72.
50. McGuiness, *Wittgenstein: A Life*, p. 144.
51. Monk, *Ludgwig Wittgenstein*, p. 144.
52. McGuiness, *Wittgenstein: A Life*, p. 315.
53. Holmes, *The Idedlism of Gioranni Gentile*, pp. 112–13.
54. Gentile, *The Theory of Mind as Pure Act*, p. 258.
55. Thomas Sheehan, *Heidegger: The Man and the Thinker* (Precedent Publishers, Chicago, 1981), p. 14.
56. Ibid.
57. Martin Heidegger, *Basic Problems of Phenomenology* (Indiana University Press, Bloomington, 1982), p. 262.
58. Heidegger, *Introduction to Metaphysics*, p. 71.
59. See Harry Redner, *In the Beginning was the Deed* (University of California Press, Berkeley, 1982).
60. Georg Lukács, 'Tactics and Ethics', in R. Livingstone (ed.), *Political Essays, 1919–1929* (Harper and Row, New York, 1972), p. 17.
61. Ibid.
62. Ibid.
63. Gentile, *The Theory of Mind as Pure Act*, p. 15.
64. Lukács, *History and Class Consciousness*, p. 178.
65. Wittgenstein, *Notebooks 1914–1916*, p. 82.
66. Ibid., p. 85.
67. Wittgenstein, *Tractatus Logico-Philosophicus*, secs., 6·373 and 6·43.
68. Wittgenstein, *Notebooks 1914–1916*, p. 73.
69. Janik, *Essays on Wittgenstein and Weininger*, p. 85.
70. Ibid.
71. Ibid.
72. Quoted in ibid., p. 85.
73. Wittgenstein, *Notebooks 1914–1916*, p. 79.
74. Karl Löwith, 'The Political Implications of Heidegger's Existentialism', in R. Wolin (ed.), *The Heidegger Controversy* (Columbia University Press, New York, 1991), p. 172.
75. Ibid., p. 173.
76. Gentile, *A Theory of Mind as Pure Act*, p. 245.

77. Ibid.
78. Ibid.
79. Ibid., p. 244.
80. Lukács, *'Tactics and Ethics', Political Essays 1919–1929*, pp. 26–7.
81. Lukács, *History and Class Consciousness*, pp. xiv and xviii.
82. Wittgenstein, *Notebooks 1914–1916*, p. 73.
83. Ibid., p. 76.
84. Waismann, *Wittgenstein and the Vienna Circle*, p. 115.
85. Ibid., p. 118.
86. Ibid., p. 117.
87. Harris, *Social Philosophy*, p. 182.
88. Lee Congdon, *The Young Lukács* (University of North Carolina Press, Chapel Hill, 1983), p. 186.

CHAPTER 2 THE TURNING (*KEHRE*)

1. See Redner, *A New Science of Representation*, ch. 5.
2. Harris, *Social Philosophy*, p. 270.
3. Ibid., p. 264.
4. Benedetto Croce, *Philosophy, Poetry, History*, trans. Cecil Sprigge (Oxford University Press, New York, 1966), p. 653.
5. Harris, *Social Philosophy*, p. 273.
6. Leszek Kolakowski, *Modernity on Endless Trial* (Chicago University Press, Chicago, 1990), p. 236.
7. Rockmore, *Irrationalism*, p. 159.
8. Georg Lukács, *New Left Review* (No. 68, 1971), p. 58.
9. Kadarkay, *Georg Lukács*, p. 326.
10. Ibid., p. 261.
11. Löwy, *Georg Lukács*, p. 167.
12. Congdon, *Young Lukács*, p. 139.
13. Lukács, *History and Class Consciousness*, p. xxx.
14. Lukács, *New Left Review*, p. 18.
15. Georg Lukács, *Record of a Life: An Autobiographical Sketch*, trans. R. Livingstone (Verso, London, 1983), p. 83.
16. Louis Althusser, *For Marx: Contradiction and Overdetermination* (Penguin Books, Harmondsworth, 1969).
17. John Fuegi, *Brecht & Co: Sex, Politics and the Making of Modern Drama* (Grove Press, New York, 1994), p. 277.
18. Quoted in Michael Zimmerman, *Heidegger's Confrontation with Modernity* (Indiana University Press, Bloomington, 1990), p. 40.
19. Quoted in Wolin, *The Politics of Being*, p. 74.
20. Heidegger, *Introduction to Metaphysics*, p. 74.
21. Ibid., p. 69.
22. Ibid.
23. Ibid., p. 71.
24. Ibid., p. 72.
25. Martin Heidegger, *Poetry, Language, Thought*, 'What are Poets For', trans. Albert Hofstadter (Harper and Row, New York, 1971), p. 132.

26. Martin Heidegger, *On the Way to Language*, 'The Nature of Language', trans. Peter D. Hertz (Harper and Row, New York, 1971), p. 63.
27. Ibid., p. 82.
28. Ibid., p. 60.
29. Martin Heidegger, *Existence and Being*, 'What is Metaphysics', trans. Werner Brock (Henry Regnery, Chicago, 1949), p. 358.
30. Ibid.
31. Ibid.
32. Heidegger, *An Introduction to Metaphysics*, p. 83.
33. Ibid., p. 59.
34. Ibid., p. 77.
35. Brian McGuiness (ed.), *Wittgenstein and his Time* (Blackwell, Oxford, 1982), p. 54.
36. Monk, *Ludwig Wittgenstein*, pp. 313–14.
37. McGuiness, *Wittgenstein and his Time*, p. 50.
38. Quoted in Hao Wang, *Beyond Analytic Philosophy* (MIT Press, Cambridge, Mass., 1986), p. 248.
39. Quoted in Monk, *Ludwig Wittgenstein*, p. 353.
40. Ibid., p. 354.
41. Ludwig Wittgenstein, *The Foundations of Mathematics*, trans. G.E.M. Anscombe (Blackwell, Oxford, 1959), p. 57.
42. Wittgenstein, *Culture and Value*, p. 61.
43. Wittgenstein, *Tractatus Logico-Philosophicus*, sec. 4·0031.
44. Allan Janik and Stephen Toulmin, *Wittgenstein's Vienna* (Weidenfeld and Nicolson, London, 1973), p. 232.
45. See Redner, *The Ends of Philosophy*, ch. 2.
46. Quoted in Michael Murray (ed.), *Heidegger and Modern Philosophy*, (Yale University Press, New Haven, Conn., 1978), p. 314.
47. Karsten Harries, 'Heidegger as Political Thinker', in Murray, ibid., p. 215.
48. Quoted in ibid., p. 315.
49. Ibid., p. 316.
50. Ibid., p. 317.
51. Ibid., p. 318.
52. Harris, *Social Philosophy*, p. 108.
53. Ibid., pp. 108–9.
54. Giovanni Gentile, *The Genesis and Structure of Society*, trans. S.H. Harris (Universify of Illinois Press, Urbana, 1960), p. 82.
55. Ibid., p. 171.
56. Ibid.
57. Rockmore, *Irrationalism*, p. 157.
58. Ibid.
59. Waismann, *Wittgenstein and the Vienna Circle*, pp. 116–17.
60. Wittgenstein, *Philosophical Investigations*, sec. 122.
61. Quoted in K.T. Fann (ed.), *Ludwig Wittgenstein: The Man and his Philosophy* (Dell, New York, 1967), p. 68.
62. R. Rhees (ed.), *Ludwig Wittgenstein: Personal Recollections* (Blackwell, Oxford, 1981), p. 172.
63. Wittgenstein, *Philosophical Investigations*, sec. 118, p. 48.
64. Heidegger, *Being and Time*, p. 44.

65. Wittgenstein, *Culture and Value*, p. 17.
66. Murray, *Heidegger and Modern Philosophy*, p. 327.
67. Quoted in Löwy, *Georg Lukács*, p. 202.
68. Quoted in Harris, *Social Philosophy*, p. 168.
69. Agnes Heller (ed.), *Lukács Revalued* (Blackwell, Oxford, 1983), p. 77.
70. Harris, *Social Philosophy*, pp. 187–8.

CHAPTER 3 THE SECONDARY MASTERWORKS

1. Richard Deacon, *The Cambridge Apostles* (Robert Royce, London, 1985), p. 91.
2. Harris, *Social Philosophy*, p. 216.
3. Gentile, *Genesis and Structure of Society*, p. x.
4. Lukács, *History and Class Consciousness*, p. xxxvi.
5. Georg Lukács, *The Destruction of Reason*, trans. Peter Palmer (Humanities Press, Atlantic Highlands, NJ, 1981), pp. 16–17.
6. Domenico Losurdo, 'Heidegger and Hitler's War', in Rockmore and Margolis, *The Heidegger Case*, p. 155.
7. Ibid.
8. Ibid., p. 154.
9. Ibid.
10. Wolin, *The Politics of Being*, p. 152.
11. Quoted in Monk, *Ludwig Wittgenstein*, p. 418.
12. Ibid., p. 484.
13. Wittgenstein, *Culture and Value*, p. 49.
14. Quoted in Monk, *Ludwig Wittgenstein*, p. 486.
15. Redner, *The Ends of Philosophy* ch. 3.
16. Friedrich Nietzsche, *The Will to Power*, ed. Walter Kaufmann (Vintage, New York, 1968), sec. 584.
17. Karl Löwith, *Martin Heidegger and European Nihilism*, ed. Richard Wolin (Columbia University Press, New York, 1995), p. 110.
18. Martin Heidegger, *Holzwege* (Klostermann, Frankfurt, 1957), p. 301.
19. Martin Heidegger, *Nietzsche* (Vol. IV), ed. D.F. Krell (Harper and Row, New York, 1979), p. 205.
20. Ibid., p. 243.
21. Ibid., pp. 238 and 244.
22. Heidegger, *An Introduction to Metaphysics*, p. 30.
23. See Richardson, *Heidegger*, p. 638.
24. van Buren, *Young Heidegger*, p. 384.
25. Ibid., pp. 383–4.
26. Rainer Marten, 'Heidegger and the Greeks', in Rockmore and Margolis, *The Heidegger Case*, p. 184.
27. Wittgenstein, *Philosophical Investigations*, sec. 122.
28. Ibid., sec. 371.
29. Ernest Gellner, *Reason and Culture* (Blackwell, Oxford, 1992), p. 123.
30. Ibid.

31. Lukács, *History and Class Consciousness*, p. 10.
32. Jean-Paul Sartre, *Critique de la Raison Dialectique*, Vol. I (Gallimard, Paris, 1960), p. 40.
33. Kadarkay, *Geory Lukács*, p. 338.
34. Harris, *Social Philosophy*, p. 62.
35. Ibid.
36. Ibid., p. 65.
37. Wolin, *The Politics of Being*, p. 102.
38. Quoted in Kadarkay, *Georg Lukács*, pp. 337–8.
39. Gentile, *Genesis and Structure of Society*, p. 82.
40. Harris, *Social Philosophy*, p. 244.
41. Wang, *Beyond Analytic Philosophy*, p. 83.
42. *Culture and Value*, p. 102.
43. Heller, *Lukács Revalued*, p. 100.
44. Ernst Joos, *Lukács' Last Autocriticism: The Ontology* (Humanities Press, Atlantic Highlands, NJ, 1983), p. 4.
45. Rockmore, *Irrationalism*, p. 218.
46. Ibid., p. 244.
47. George Lichtheim, *Lukács* (Fontana Modern Masters, Collins, London, 1970), p. 116.
48. Ibid., p. 100.
49. Guignon, *Cambridge Companion to Heidegger*, p. 284.
50. Gerald Bruns, *Heidegger Estrangements: Language, Truth, Poetry* (Yale University Press, New Haven, 1989), p. 150.
51. Allan Janik, *Style, Politics, and the Future of Philosophy* (Kluwer Academic Publishers, Dordrecht, 1989), p. 1.

CHAPTER 4 FATHERS AND SONS

1. van Buren, *Young Heidegger*, p. 395.
2. W.J. Mommsen and J. Osterhammel (eds.), *Max Weber and his Contemporaries* (Unwin, London, 1987), p. 504.
3. Keneth Blackwell, 'Early Wittgenstein and Middle Russell', I. Block (ed.), *Perspectives in the Philosophy of Wittgenstein* (Blackwell, Oxford, 1981), p. 16.
4. Roberts, *Benedetto Croce*, p. 113.
5. Croce, *Philosophy, Poetry, History*, pp. 97–8.
6. Harris, *Social Philosophy*, p. 22.
7. J. Marcus and Z. Tar (eds.), *George Lukács: Selected Correspondence* (Columbia University Press, New York, 1986), p. 281.
8. Quoted in Kadarkay, *Georg Lukács*, pp. 251–2.
9. Ibid., p. 253.
10. Ibid., p. 345.
11. Murray, *Heidegger and Modern Philosophy*, p. 232.
12. Sheehan, *Heidegger*, p. 8.
13. Wolin, *The Heidegger Controversy*, p. 143.

14. In a letter to C.W.K. Mundle of 10 December 1968, quoted in Ronald W. Clark, *The Life of Bertrand Russell* (Penguin Books, Harmondsworth, 1975), p. 685.
15. Benedetto Croce, *An Autobiography*, trans. R.G. Collingwood (Freeport, New York, 1927), p. 93.
16. Jürgen Habermas, *Philosophical-Political Profiles*, trans. F.G. Lawrence (MIT Press, Cambridge, Mass., 1984), p. 32.
17. Quoted in Jacobelli, *Croce*, p. 293.
18. Wang, *Beyond Analytic Philosophy*, p. 82.
19. Ibid., p. 3.
20. McGuiness, *Wittgenstein: A Life*, p. 76.
21. Wang, *Beyond Analytic Philosophy*, p. 3.
22. See Kadarkay, *Georg Lukács*, p. 281.
23. Lukács, *History and Class Consciousness*, p. x.
24. Goldmann, *Lukács and Heidegger*, pp. 52 and 62.
25. Hubert L. Dreyfus, *Being-in-the-World: A Commentary on Heidegger's Being and Time* (The MIT Press, Cambridge, Mass., 1991), p. 30.
26. See Heidegger, *Being and Time*, p. 50.
27. van Buren, *Young Heidegger*, p. 205.
28. Quoted in ibid., p. 204.
29. Ibid., p. 205.
30. Ibid., p. 204.
31. Ibid., p. 145.
32. Ibid., p. 204.
33. Ibid., p. 208.
34. Ibid., p. 218.
35. Quoted in Jacobelli, *Croce*, p. 29.
36. Guido de Ruggiero, *Modern Philosophy*, trans. A.H. Hannay and R.G. Collingwood (Allen and Unwin, London, 1921), p. 346.
37. Ibid., p. 397.
38. Ibid., p. 357.
39. Ibid., p. 300.
40. Wang, *Beyond Analytic Philosophy*, p. 78.
41. Ibid., p. 69.
42. Ibid.
43. Ibid.
44. Ibid., p. 5.
45. Ibid., p. 73.
46. Neske and Kettering, *Martin Heidegger*, p. 179.
47. Manlio di Lalla, *Vita di Giovanni Gentile* (Sansoni, Firenze, 1975), p. 25.
48. Ibid., p. 222.
49. Lukács, *History and Class Consciousness*, p. 95.
50. Bryan S. Turner, 'Simmel, Rationalization and the Sociology of Money', *The Sociological Review*, Vol. 34, No. 1, Feb ruary1986.
51. In Georg Simmel, *The Philosophy of Money*, from the introduction by Tom Bottomore and David Frisby (Routledge and Kegan Paul, London, 1978), p. 20.
52. van Buren, *Young Heidegger*, p. 60.
53. Ibid., p. 111.

54. Heidegger, *Being and Time*, p. 447.
55. Ibid., p. 444.
56. Ibid., p. 447.
57. Ibid., p. 447.
58. van Buren, *Young Heidegger*, p. 279.
59. Ibid., p. 106.
60. Ibid., p. 270.
61. Ibid., p. 286.
62. Ibid., p. 279.
63. Ibid., p. 295.
64. Ibid., p. 150.
65. Michael Dummett, in Block, *Perspectives in the Philosophy of Wittgenstein*, pp. 31 and 33.
66. Monk, *Ludwig Wittgenstein*, p. 163.
67. Ibid., p. 176.
68. Ibid., p. 190.
69. Ibid., pp. 190–1.
70. Ibid., p. 174.
71. Ibid.
72. Wittgenstein, *Letters to Russell, Keynes, and Moore*, p. 77.
73. Ibid., letter of March-April, 1930.
74. Wittgenstein, *Tractatus Logico-Philosophicus*, sec. 6·42 and 6·423.
75. Ibid., sec. 4·1122, p. 49.
76. Ibid., 6·3, p. 137.
77. Ibid., 6·371, p. 143.
78. Wang, *Beyond Analytic Philosophy*, p. 100.
79. Wittgenstein, *Philosophical Investigations*, sec. 126.
80. Wittgenstein, *Remarks on the Foundations of Mathematics*, p. 157.
81. Wittgenstein, *Culture and Value*, pp. 79 and 62.
82. Ibid., p. 7.
83. Ibid., p. 56.
84. Ibid., p. 49.
85. Martin Heidegger, *The End of Philosophy*, trans. Joan Stambough (Harper and Row, New York, 1973), p. 93.
86. Heidegger, *An Introduction to Metaphysics*, p. 39.
87. Martin Heidegger, *The Question Concerning Technology of Other Essays* (Harper and Row, New York, 1977), p. 117.
88. Rockmore, *Irrationalism: Lukács and the Marxist view of Reason*, p. 283.
89. Löwith, *My Life in Germany*, p. 46.
90. Neske and Kettering, *Martin Heidegger*, p. 178.
91. Giovanni Gentile, *Genesis and Structure of Society*, from the introduction by Harris, p. 42.
92. Gentile, *The Theory of Mind as Pure Act*, pp. 112–14.
93. Lukács, *Political Writings 1919–1929*, pp. 136 and 140.
94. Lukács, *History and Class Consciousness*, p. 10.
95. Ibid.
96. Ibid., p. 4.
97. Quoted in Wolin, *The Politics of Being*, p. 19.
98. Wittgenstein, *Tractatus Logico-Philosophicus*, sec. 6·421.

CHAPTER 5 FOREFATHERS AND OTHER ANCESTRAL FIGURES

1. Peter Hylton, 'Hegel as Analytic Philosophy', in C.F. Beiser (ed.), *Cambridge Companion to Hegel* (Cambridge University Press, Cambridge, 1993), p. 477.
2. Thomas E. Willey, *Back to Kant: The Revival of Kantianism in German Social and Historical Thought 1860–1919* (Wayne State University Press, Detroit, 1978), p. 104.
3. Weber, *From Max Weber*, p. 129.
4. Allen W. Wood, 'Hegel and Marxism', in Beiser, *Cambridge Companion to Hegel*, p. 415.
5. Tom Rockmore, *Heidegger and French Philosophy* (Routledge, London, 1995), p. 29.
6. Quoted in S. Morris Engel, 'Schopenhauer's Impact on Wittgenstein', in Michael Fox (ed.), *Schopenhauer: His Philosophical Achievement* (Harvester Press, Sussex, 1980), p. 236.
7. Monk, *Ludwig Wittgenstein*, p. 144.
8. David Avraham Weiner, *Genius and Talent: Schopenhauer's Influence on Wittgenstein's Early Philosophy* (Associated University Presses, London and Toronto, 1992).
9. Wittgenstein, *Culture and Value*, p. 76.
10. Weiner, *Genius and Talent*, p. 15.
11. Ibid., p. 15.
12. Ibid., p. 10.
13. Ibid., p. 114.
14. Ibid., p. 79.
15. Ibid., p. 45.
16. Ibid., p. 41.
17. Engel, 'Schopenhauer's Impact', p. 238.
18. Ibid., p. 250.
19. Quoted in Buren, *Young Heidegger*, p. 371.
20. Ibid., p. 372.
21. Ibid., p. 371.
22. John Toews, 'Transformations of Hegelianism 1805–1846', in Beiser, *Cambridge Companion to Hegel*, p. 380.
23. Ibid., p. 381.
24. Dreyfus, *Being-in-the-World*, p. 299.
25. Ibid., p. 300.
26. Ibid.
27. Ibid., p. 299.
28. Ibid., p. 304.
29. Ibid., p. 311.
30. Ibid., p. 314.
31. Ibid., p. 322.
32. Ibid., p. 320.
33. Ibid.
34. Heidegger, *Being and Time*, p. 497.
35. Ibid., p. 494.
36. Dreyfus, *Being-in-the-World*, p. 336.

37. Ibid., p. 299.
38. Ibid.
39. Ibid., p. 333.
40. Ibid., p. 331.
41. See Gershon Weiler, *Mauthner's Critique of Language* (Cambridge University Press, Cambridge, 1970).
42. Janik, *Essays on Wittgenstein and Weininger*, p. 85.
43. Ibid., p. 84.
44. Jacques Le Rider, *Le Cas Otto Weininger* (Presses Universaires de France, Paris, 1982), p. 99.
45. Ibid., p. 107.
46. Harris, *Social Philosophy*, p. 50.
47. Kadarkay, *Georg Lukács*, p. 77.
48. Ernst Bloch, *Man on His Own, Essays in the Philosophy of Religion*, trans. E.B. Ashton (Herder and Herder, New York, 1970), p. 39.
49. Lukács, *'Tactics and Ethics', in Political Essays 1919–1929*, p. 18.
50. Harris, *Social Philosophy*, p. 40.
51. di Lalla, *Vita di Giovanni Gentile*, p. 89.
52 Ibid.
53. Harris, *Social Philosophy*, p. 40.
54. Quoted in Guido de Ruggiero, *Modern Philosophy*, p. 335.
55. Ibid., p. 334.
56. Herbert Marcuse, *Reason and Revolution, Hegel and the Rise of Social Theory* (Humanities Press, NY, 1954), p. 404.
57. See Jean Bollack and Heinz Wismann, 'Heidegger der Unumgängliche', in Pierre Bourdieu, *Die Politische Ontologie Martin Heideggers* (Syndikat, Frankfurt, 1976), pp. 115–21.
58. Zimmerman, *Eclipse of Self*, p. 16.
59. Löwith, *Nature, History and Existentialism*, p. 69.
60. Sheehan, *Heidegger*, p. 9.
61. Rockmore, *Heidegger and French Philosophy*, p. 119.
62. Monk, *Ludwig Wittgenstein*, p. 142.
63. Weiner, *Genius and Talent*, pp. 98–111.
64. Wittgenstein, *Tractatus*, sec. 6·421.
65. Zimmerman, *Eclipse of the Self*, p. 17.
66. Lukács, *History and Class Consciousness*, p. xiii.
67. Gentile, *La Religione*, p. 406.
68. Ibid., p. 340.
69. Harris, *Social Philosophy*, p. 182.
70. Ibid., p. 247.

CHAPTER 6 FRIENDS AND FOLLOWERS

1. Herbert Feigl, 'Wiener Kreis in America', in D. Fleming and G. Baylyn (eds.), *The Intellectual Migration* (Harvard University Press, Cambridge, Mass., 1969), p. 638.
2. Ibid.

3. Leszek Kolakowski, *Modernity on Endless Trial* (University of Chicago Press, Chicago, 1990), p. 108.
4. Giovanna Borradori (ed.), *Recording Metaphysics: The New Italian Philosophy* (Northwest University Press, Evanston, Ill. 1990), p. 202.
5. Löwith, *My Life in Germany before and after 1933*, pp. 28–9.
6. Ibid., p. 45.
7. Rockmore, *Heidegger and French Philosophy*, p. 1.
8. Quoted in Löwith, *Martin Heidegger and European Nihilism*, p. 12.
9. Harris, *Social Philosophy*, p. 14.
10. Merle E. Brown, *Neo-Idealist Aesthetics: Croce, Gentile, Collingwood* (Wayne State University Press, Detroit, 1966).
11. Paul Engelmann, *Letters from Ludwig Wittgenstein* (Basil Blackwell, Oxford, 1967), p. xiv.
12. Elizabeth Young-Bruehl, *Hanna Arendt, For Love of the World* (Yale University Press, New Haven, Conn., 1982), p. 307.
13. Neske and Kettering, *Martin Heidegger*, p. 134.
14. Young-Bruehl, *Hannan Arendt*, p. 442.
15. L. Kohler and H. Saner (eds.), *Arendt–Jaspers Correspondence 1926–1969* (Harcourt Brace Jovanovich, New York, 1992), p. 628.
16. Ibid., p. 634.
17. C. Wright Mills, *Sociology and Pragmatism: The Higher Learning in America* (Oxford, Oxford University Press, 1966).
18. Russell Jacoby, *The Last Intellectuals* (Basic Books, New York, 1987).
19. See Harry Redner, *The Ends of Science: An Essay in Scientific Authority* (Westview Press, Boulder, Col., 1987), ch. 5.
20. Creegan, *Wittgenstein and Kierkegaard*, p. 11.

Personal Names Index

Subject Index